[d i g i t a l]
TEXTURING
& PAINTING

BY OWEN DEMERS
CONTRIBUTING AUTHOR & EDITED BY CHRISTINE URSZENYI
SERIES EDITOR: GEORGE MAESTRI

New Riders

DIGITAL TEXTURING & PAINTING

International Standard Book Number: 0-7357-0918-1

Library of Congress Catalog Card Number: 00-100497

Printed in the United States of America

First Printing: August 2001

05   04   03   02   01   7   6   5   4   3   2   1

Interpretation of the printing code: The rightmost double-digit number is the year of the book's printing; the rightmost single-digit number is the number of the book's printing. For example, the printing code 01-1 shows that the first printing of the book occurred in 2001.

TRADEMARKS

WARNING AND DISCLAIMER

Publisher
David Dwyer

Associate Publisher
Al Valvano

Executive Editor
Steve Weiss

Project Director
Jennifer Eberhardt

Product Marketing Manager
Kathy Malmloff

Publicist
Susan Nixon

Managing Editor
Sarah Kearns

Development Editor
Linda Laflamme

Project Editor
Linda Seifert

Technical Editor
Brian Drucker

Cover Image
Owen Demers

Cover Design
Aren Howell

Interior Design
Kim Scott

Compositor
Suzanne Pettypiece

Proofreader
Bob LaRoche

Indexer
Lisa Stumpf

Media Development
Jay Payne

CONTENTS AT A GLANCE

TABLE OF CONTENTS

About the Author

Owen Demers has worked as an illustrator, graphic designer, 3D artist, and art director for a number of commercial and professional studios in both traditional and computer graphics. He has worked on many award-winning projects including the animated short *Bingo,* where he was the lead texturing and lighting TD. He currently works as a 3D artist and art director in New York. Owen's web site is www.tingun.com.

Contributing Author & Editor

Christine Urszenyi has worked as an architect, art director for film studios, and furniture designer for professional studios. She is currently based in Toronto, Canada, and is working on her own writing.

Dedication

To my parents, for your recognition and encouragement of my artistic talent, and to the rest of my family for your continuous support.

This is also dedicated to my very first painting teacher, Beth Nyaradi, whose love for painting, her generosity of spirit, and patience, lifted me over the hurdles of technique.

AUTHOR ACKNOWLEDGMENTS

Much love and thanks to Christine, the person who convinced me to write this book. These words cannot express my deepest gratitude for your steady concentration, detailed word-smithing and undying patience, support, and love throughout this roller coaster ride. This book is as much yours as it is mine.

To Frankie and Charlie for taking up the slack in the midnight hours.

Thanks to Steve Weiss and all the people at New Riders for their faith, patience and unfettered attention, and especially to Jennifer Eberhardt, Linda Laflamme, Suzanne Pettypiece, and Linda Seifert without whose humor and hard work this would have been a lot harder to do.

Thanks to George Maestri for getting me this "gig."

Thanks to Brian Drucker for his pep talks, unwavering support and advice, technical and otherwise.

To Gabor and Kati Urszenyi for their support and love for this and other projects of "ours."

I would like to extend my thanks and appreciation to Curious Pictures, especially Jesse Cromwell, Jeff Martin, Rich Shurtliff, Steve Oakes, Richard Winkler, Lewis Kofsky, Tony Tabtong, Joe DiLallo, Boo Wong, David Baas, Sarah Nahas, Adam Chao, Anthony Orkin, Kallan Kagan, Elliot M. Bour, and Saul Andrew Blinkoff.

I found that in this industry there is abundant knowledge and expertise of which I am extremely grateful. I found this wealth of knowledge easily shared by Kim Lee, Hal Siegel, Nikolai Stojanovic, David "Bones" Richardson, Steve "Og" Ogden, Andrew Pearce, and Lorna Saunders.

Thanks to Ignacio "Iggy" Ayesteran for his generous work modeling "Axle."

All the companies who came through with software:

> MetaCreations
> Alias | Wavefront
> Right Hemisphere Ltd.
> Discreet, a division of Autodesk
> Rick Barretto, WSI Multimedia

Especially IBM, without whom I could not have done the work.

Thanks to the generosity and magnanimity of the people at companies who gave permission to use the work I took part in creating for them:

> Lugz Shoes
> HBO—John Hoffman, Mary Healy
> Curious Pictures
> Alias | Wavefront

And to the people whose products, anywhere from a CD-ROM game still to antique veneer furniture on the streets of New York, grace the pages of this book:

Kenneth Bollella—Bollella Tile & Marble

Frank J. Tammaro, Atlantic Auction Gallery, Ltd.

Cyan

Mercedes Benz

Scott Einziger, thanks for the digi-camera.

To all my family and friends who understood my absence during this project.

Thanks to all the artists, galleries and museums who gave permission to use the beautiful works of art in this book.

Thanks to all the artists out there who inspire me with their beautiful work and push me forward in my own.

New Riders Acknowledgments

New Riders would especially like to thank Owen Demers and Christine Urszenyi for a beautiful and content-rich book. Your labor of love was no doubt worth the tremendous effort.

New Riders would also like to thank [digital] series editor George Maestri, for his continued support and enthusiasm for the [digital] series.

Last but not least, special thanks go out to Suzanne Pettypiece and Stacey Beheler, who spent countless hours on the phone and running to the fax machine to secure all the art permissions for this title; Mike LaBonne and Dennis Sheehan who did an amazing job processing all of the imagery; and Linda Seifert, who kept everything running smoothly on the back end.

A Message from New Riders

As the reader of this book, you are our most important critic and commentator. We value your opinion and want to know what we're doing right, what we could do better, in what areas you'd like to see us publish, and any other words of wisdom you're willing to pass our way.

As Executive Editor at New Riders, I welcome your comments. You can fax, email, or write me directly to let me know what you did or didn't like about this book—as well as what we can do to make our books better. When you write, please be sure to include this book's title, ISBN, and author, as well as your name and phone or fax number. I will carefully review your comments and share them with the authors and editors who worked on the book.

Please note that I cannot help you with technical problems related to the topic of this book, and that due to the high volume of email I receive, I might not be able to reply to every message. Thanks.

Email: steve.weiss@newriders.com

Mail: Steve Weiss
          Executive Editor
          New Riders Publishing
          201 West 103rd Street
          Indianapolis, IN 46290 USA

Visit Our Web Site: www.newriders.com

On our web site, you'll find information about our other books, the authors we partner with, book updates and file downloads, promotions, discussion boards for online interaction with other users and with technology experts, and a calendar of trade shows and other professional events with which we'll be involved. We hope to see you around.

Email Us from Our Web Site

Go to www.newriders.com and click on the Contact Us link if you

- Have comments or questions about this book.

- Want to report errors that you have found in this book.

- Have a book proposal or are interested in writing for New Riders.

- Would like us to send you one of our author kits.

- Are an expert in a computer topic or technology and are interested in being a reviewer or technical editor.

- Want to find a distributor for our titles in your area.

- Are an educator/instructor who wants to preview New Riders books for classroom use. In the body/comments area, include your name, school, department, address, phone number, office days/hours, text currently in use, and enrollment in your department, along with your request for either desk/examination copies or additional information.

Call Us or Fax Us

You can reach us toll-free at (800) 571-5840 + 0 (ask for New Riders). If outside the U.S., please call 1-317-581-3500 and ask for New Riders. If you prefer, you can fax us at 1-317-581-4663, Attention: New Riders.

TECHNICAL SUPPORT FOR THIS BOOK

Although we encourage entry-level users to get as much as they can out of our books, keep in mind that our books are written assuming a non-beginner level of user-knowledge of the technology. This assumption is reflected in the brevity and shorthand nature of some of the tutorials.

New Riders will continually work to create clearly written, thoroughly tested and reviewed technology books of the highest educational caliber and creative design. We value our customers more than any-thing—that's why we're in this business—but we cannot guarantee to each of the thousands of you who buy and use our books that we will be able to work individually with you through tutorials or content with which you may have questions. We urge readers who need help in working through exercises or other material in our books—and who need this assistance immediately—to use as many of the resources that our technology and technical communities can provide, especially the many online user groups and list servers available.

WHAT IS TEXTURE?

WHAT IS TEXTURE?

T EXTURE: WAY IN which the threads of a fabric or constituent elements of a substance are arranged and put together; sensation produced by this upon the sense of touch. —*The Universal Dictionary of the English Language, Wordsworth Editions Ltd., 1989.*

I.1 A HANDKERCHIEF IN BED CAN'T BE FOUND

> A coin, sleeve-button or a collar-button in a
> bedroom will hide itself and be hard to find.
> A handkerchief in bed can't be found.
> —*Mark Twain, notebook, 1935. (The International Thesaurus of Quotations, Harper and Row, 1970.)*

It is true that a linen handkerchief can't be found on a linen bed-spread—at first glance. So, if we were to re-create this scene in the computer, and if it is necessary for the scene to differentiate between the spread and the handkerchief, then we, as texture artists, would do so through our skills at looking, seeing, and painting. The differentiation will emerge when we discern the subtleties of shadow and light by determining their colors while carefully maintaining the material's integral texture and nature, linen in this case.

Essentially, how to differentiate between surfaces and how to execute the making of some of these materials and textures digitally for a project is what you will learn from this book.

Texture artists begin by asking questions such as, "What helps me differentiate between one particular texture and another?" "How can I articulate this texture or surface on the computer?" We, as texture artists, are given the wireframe models of a project and it is up to us to apply what we have learned through the questions we ask to make these wireframes live and breathe with detail and color.

I love textures. Not a day goes by that I do not stop and look at some rusted piece of metal laying on the road and try to figure out how to mimic it on the computer—or marvel at how humidity in the air creates such beautiful atmospheric depth and muted colors. This is why I do what I do in the CG field. I want to create vivid scenes and beautiful surfaces no matter how rusted and decrepit (see Figure I.1).

I.1   Beautiful rusted and painted metal.

I come to each digital project in the same way as a painter steps up to a blank canvas. As a painter, I approach the canvas—on an easel, or a computer screen; we still put brush to canvas even if it is digital—with an understanding of what needs to be done. As a painter poses a model in a luxurious costume, or sets up a still life to paint, I collect reference material—a practice I learned in art school. Reference material exists to assist you in illustrating a particular material or surface, whether the reference is a real piece of material or a photographic representation of the material. It assists you in the visualization of what the material you want to mimic looks like and how it changes under different conditions such as light, weather, or age (see Figures I.2 and I.3). With your reference material you need to create a library called a morgue (more on this in Chapter 2), so that you may have a variety of samples of materials and textures from which to draw information and inspiration.

I.2 Examples of how moisture, pollution, and other particles in the air affect detail and color.

I hope that you have come to this book because you have a fascination or a love of textures, painting, surfaces, or computers. Maybe, all of the above. Or maybe you have a curiosity about what a texture artist does— you want to see if it is for you.

Your digital textural design education starts with this book. You will begin with the discovery of your external world; looking, studying, and describing materials and their textures in the real world, collecting real or photographic samples, and going to the masters of painting to witness their technique and artistry around the subject of expressing texture and materials.

The whole concept of looking at real materials for reference, I mean really looking, is an age-old tradition in art. This is how Rembrandt (a 17th-century artist) and Michelangelo (a 16th-century artist) learned their skills, which allowed them to articulate textures and mood. It became second nature to these painters to be able to illustrate the differences between these materials by using different brushstrokes and thicknesses of paint. The expression of light on a metal goblet for instance, is the swipe of a brush along the lip with white paint (see Figure I.4).

They were taught basic concepts and rules and techniques in art from their mentors; people who, their whole lives, dedicated themselves to the pursuit of an artistic expression, and handed down these skills to the next generation. In turn, the next generation learned these skills and made them their own, creating their own expertise and then handed these skills, improved upon or revised perhaps, to the next generation.

1.3 The paint on the surface has been
     bleached out and wrinkled by the sun
     and illustrates the effect of light,
     weather, and age on a surface.

1.4 Closeup of metal goblet and spoon
     from Jean-Baptiste Simeon Chardin's
     "The Silver Beaker."

Réunion des Musées Nationaux/Art Resource, NY. Detail.

Included in this book are examples of paintings with my observations of the painter's color choice, how they achieved the expression of texture, and what we can learn from each example.

This book is an attempt to reconnect texture artists with this legacy. When learning to express your craft, you must simply remember that the seduction of technology and the ease with which you acquire it cannot take the place of the learned instruction from the masters. What you learn from them can help you deepen your understanding of what you do and how you do it.

Texture artists and what they create are vital components of any CG project. Textures and light create the mood of a piece, make the characters live, and depending on your style and the style you choose to express yourself in (this will be touched on later in Chapter 5), set your finished project apart from anybody else's.

In art there are no absolute right or wrong answers. As a texture artist, your responsibility is to achieve a vision that is a combination of yours and the project leader's vision. There are different art directors and art patrons (influencing the direction of art), who will challenge your talent and convictions, hopefully.

I.2 WHAT YOU CAN EXPECT FROM THIS BOOK

This book is written with the intention of giving you two things. The first is an understanding of how to decipher and describe what you are looking at. By exercising your eye—simply looking and getting into the practice of asking questions about what you are looking at—you will become more adept at translating what you are seeing into a satisfying and compelling digital re-creation of the surface you are trying to mimic.

The second focuses on how to create these textures. Using both digital methods, such as scanning in real items or photo references of the materials and methods using traditional mediums such as oil paints, I will take you through the process of creating basic textures and then lead you to the creation of more complicated textures.

I am not going to get into the math behind creating textures because the programs themselves do that well enough—you do not have to think about it. I would prefer that you use your eyes. Your eyes are much more finely tuned instruments than any dedicated computer program. So, to go beyond the math, using your eyes as sensors of distance, scale, and receptors for light allows you to create much richer and more satisfying textures. Simply looking at colors and asking questions such as: Is the color warm or cool? Do I need more black? More red? Less blue? What about yellow? Asking questions about surface quality: Is there a reflection? Is there refraction? Is it bumpy? Or questions about the light quality: Is the light absorbed? Brilliant or dull? Hot or cold? What is the color of the shadow? It is the combination of both light and shadow that helps you discern the essence of the texture of a particular surface. Observation and understanding the whole as well as the parts are significant when looking for such things as reflections, continuity, and color. Through this process, you will come away with a good base to begin your own discourse with your environment and everything in it.

1.3 WHAT YOU SHOULD KNOW

Of course before you begin, you must have a fundamental understanding of computers, computer graphics, painting software, and 3D software. I would like to show you how to achieve many different textural and artistic expressions by describing the techniques and steps I used to achieve the textures in the project section. I use all of my artistic training, from painting to graphic design, to using 3D software to achieve my goals. Any kind of artistic training that you may have had prior to this book will be an asset as well.

If you have time to take a traditional photography course or a painting class, or have the initiative to start painting at home, this will also greatly enhance your learning process.

In the computer world, we think in terms of color maps, bump maps, shaders, and so on. They are singled out in computer language to express these textural qualities in the computer which in turn enables us to understand what we are looking at in real life. The basics of looking can merge with our computer understanding by starting to describe shaders in terms of color, highlight, specularity, diffusion and so on, color maps in terms of color and pattern of the surface, and bump maps in terms of texture, light and shadow. An understanding of color theory and design through an introductory course or reading some of the many wonderful books on these subjects (many are listed in the reading list at the end of this book), will help you greatly in understanding these basics which I address.

What's most important for you to know is this: All you need in order to be a successful texture artist is the desire to create, the curiosity to learn, and the spirit of adventure. This is the impetus behind the successful execution of the texture artist's task—to interpret your environment and translate it into a digital style that is expressive and complete.

You, the artist, decide with the client, what is the best way to communicate the mood and artistry of the project. It is your vision and expertise that will guide the project to a successful conclusion. The computer is there to assist you. How much latitude you get from it and what breadth of expression the project has are totally up to you and your talent. The success of your project depends on how much you immerse yourself into your craft, and whether you understand the nature of the project and how to achieve it with the tools you have.

I.4   WHAT YOU WILL NEED

The tools are brushes, paints, solvents, and the computer and its software (see Figure I.5). It is not the type or style of brush, nor is it the cost of the paint or canvas that make a good painting. It is the understanding of what you are about to paint, and how to use these tools to express what it is you are trying to convey that makes it a good painting. Whether you are painting a muted still life or a brooding portrait, your talent and your craft, not the tools alone, will determine your ability to convey what is needed. It is not the type of computer nor the software that makes you a good texture artist, but drive and talent, and the intrinsic knowledge of the materials of what you are re-creating in the computer, and the diligence to go and find out what you need to know in order to re-create it.

I.5   Some tools of the trade.

Obviously, to get the greatest benefit from this book, you will need a computer and software that allow you to paint and manipulate images. You will also need to purchase a 3D software package in which you create shaders and lights to render your images.

You may also want to experiment with some tools most digital art books ignore:

- Oil paints

- Acrylics

- Watercolors

- Charcoals, pencils

When you get to the project portion in this book where I use these traditional mediums to create textures, roll up your sleeves and get your hands dirty along with me. You will see the benefits and happy accidents that can create a whole library of wacky and wonderful scribblings that can then be transformed to make useful and interesting textures.

As beginner digital painters, you should decide which software you want to use even if you have not purchased a computer as yet. Many 3D modeling and animation programs are available, such as:

- Maya or Power Animator (Alias | Wavefront)

- Softimage (Avid Technologies)

- 3ds max (Discreet, a division of Autodesk)

- Carrara (MetaCreations)

- STRATA 3D pro (Strata Software)

- Electric Image (Electric Image Inc.)

- LightWave (NewTek)

- Houdini (Side Effects Software)

All these programs have different ways to solve your rendering and lighting needs, and express these in varying degrees of mathematical accuracy. Because most of the textures you create are 2D, you will need to explore the different 2D paint and illustration programs available, such as:

- Photoshop (Adobe)

- Painter (Corel)

- Combustion (Discreet, a division of Autodesk)
- Illustrator (Adobe)

Ideally, you should get your hands on a few of these programs so you can explore what they have to offer. Try to get trial demos of software you are interested in or sign up for a beta program, if possible, and test the software before you invest in it. If your friends have a copy, then go to their house or studio and play with the software as much as you can.

3D paint packages allow you to paint a texture directly onto a 3D wireframe model. Some of these programs include:

- Painter 3D (Corel)
- Studio Paint (Alias | Wavefront)
- Amazon (Interactive Effects, Inc.)
- Deep Paint 3D (Right Hemisphere Ltd.)

The main programs that I will be using throughout this book are

- Maya 3.0 (Alias | Wavefront)
- Photoshop 5.5 (Adobe)
- Illustrator 9 (Adobe)
- Painter 6 (Corel)
- Painter 3D 1.0 (Corel)
- Deep Paint 3D (Right Hemisphere Ltd.)

The computer systems that I will use throughout this book are

- A Windows NT platform Pentium II (Intergraph TDZ2000 and an IBM Intellistation)
- 17 gigabytes of hard drive space
- High-end graphic cards
- 512MB RAM
- A 21-inch monitor
- A flatbed, or slide scanner
- A painting tablet

If you are like most of us, your budget is probably the main issue in your choice of software and hardware. You may have to start out with less complicated 3D software or own only one paint program and not the fastest machine. Don't let this discourage you. You can create anything and learn, as you must and will, to your benefit. Creative solutions come from us, the artists, and not the computer. Work with what you have. Never limit yourself by what you think you could have had.

If you can afford a little (or a lot) extra, then do so. Even though most of the work you will be doing is 2D in paint programs, some of these files can get rather large in size. In this case, RAM and processor speed should be taken advantage of and possibly 3D accelerator cards for tumbling around textured environments.

One important consideration when buying a computer is to know what software runs on what platform. This is especially true if you can only afford one computer. It is really handy to know the various programs that the box runs. This way you can switch from a 2D program to a 3D program without switching from one computer to another in order to start or finish some part of a project.

When I began my computer career, I started with a Macintosh LC computer. It came with a 12" monitor, a 40MB hard drive, and 8MB of RAM. I was able to produce many graphic design jobs on that little machine, most if not all of them using Adobe Photoshop to create some fairly large paintings. I eventually moved on to a Silicon Graphics (SGI) machine because my interests expanded into the higher-end 3D graphics field. At that time the SGI platform and other workstations such as SUN Microsystems were the only high-end platforms capable for such heavy computation. This is not the case today. Presently, I am working on a Windows NT-based system, like many others in this industry. This is not to say that NT is the choice of champions, although its ratio of cost to efficiency is low, therefore quite attractive when considering platforms for this type of work. Having said that, as you are most likely aware, every month there seems to be some new advancement of some kind or other in computers that can put your most recent purchase to shame, so it is up to you, the consumer, to know your choices. Talk to people who use these systems, read magazine articles on hardware and software, and so on. Know your options.

I.5 ABOUT THIS BOOK'S APPROACH TO SOFTWARE

Software developers come and go and software development is never in stasis, so to base this book on any one program and its features would be futile. The principles in this book are applicable to any of the platforms and software out there today. For the most part, this book will not dwell on some specialized plug-in or filter.

It is more important that you develop your intuitive artistic eye first, then choose which available tools to use. As you develop your talent of looking, the software will articulate and reflect your developed sensibilities in this area, and therefore your choices will be more lucid and reflective of your needs as an artist.

I like to think of this book as a tutor that will help you develop the software in your head. First, to help you develop the technique of "looking," and then to choose your software according to your needs.

This book will also address the differences between the functions as well as terminology. Software seems to be growing toward a homogenous feel and in most cases software companies borrow from one another. Whatever software you do own or decide to buy, it is imperative that you read the manuals thoroughly. Familiarize yourself with the concepts and capabilities, and work through the tutorials as well. They are very informative. It is to your benefit, as well as your checkbook's to do so. It will help you stay off the product help lines in the midst of some crazy project's deadline.

I.6 A FINAL WORD

With this book I hope to help you become first and foremost a better artist. I hope that you will no longer see just one way to create and paint textures for your projects and will realize just how much fun you can have furthering your exploration in the endless world of art—on and off the computer.

Simply by increasing your acuity, the world around you will never look the same.

THE ARTIST'S STUDIO, Johannes Vermeer "van Delft" (Delft 1632-1675 Delft), © 1665/66, Canvas: H 120 cm, W 100 cm, Inv. No. 9128

1

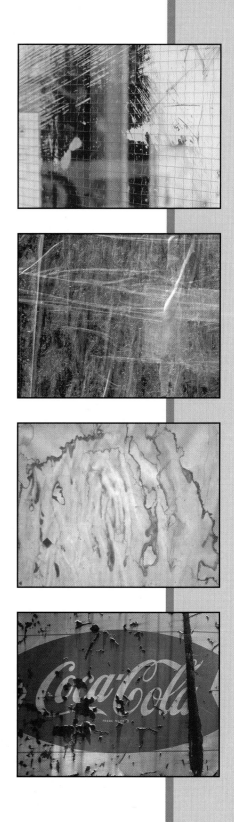

THE FINE ART OF SEEING AND DISSECTING

ART, TO ME, is all about looking, seeing, and recording. Whether you are creating art to tell a story, sell a product, or express your inner self, you must first start looking and become aware of what you see even if it only exists in your mind's eye. Because looking is the first step in creating, as artists we must spend a lot of time doing just that. There is no quick way around it. I liken this aspect of art to that of meditation. You do not become proficient at meditating or any other complex activity in a matter of hours. It takes many months, if not years, to grasp the notion of meditation, then understand it in reference to your life, and then apply it. To see what is *really* there and not what you *think* is there, you must "be in the moment," as you must for mediation. This chapter will help you in this pursuit by giving you exercises to test your intuitive sight as well as supplying you with questions to ask as you begin your practice of looking.

1.1 EXERCISING YOUR ARTISTIC EYE

To become proficient at any one thing you must start training for it. It is the same for your artistic career: You must exercise and develop your artistic eye. Exercising your artistic eye is much the same as exercising any muscle. If you constantly make the effort you will stay toned. If not, your ability will atrophy.

Your artistic eye is more keenly attuned to details of color, texture, and light because it works with your intuitive knowledge of these things. Your response and interpretation of these things will become more instantaneous when you exercise your eye. Even though you have been looking and seeing since your earliest recollection, I would venture to guess that you had not considered this artistic intent or focus, until just recently. Just as a doctor looks at the human body in skeletal and muscular Latin terminology, you look at your surrounding world in artistic terminology. And as doctors need to enhance their knowledge with real-life cases, exercises, so you must enhance your technical knowledge with your knowledge of the real world.

1.1.1 TAKE AN ART CLASS

So, how do you start training? One of the best ways to build artistic muscle is to start painting and drawing. If you have ever taken a painting class or any other art course, then you have already exercised your artistic eye somewhat. If you have never taken a course, I strongly urge you to take one—an evening still-life painting class, a drawing class, or even an art history class. A painting or drawing course, however, will more effectively introduce you to the process of looking at something intently for two hours or more at a time, so that you will start to notice details you need to re-create what is truly in front of you.

How do you go about doing this? As I said earlier, looking and meditation go hand in hand. For me, when I first started painting I soon realized that what I initially thought I saw, was not the truth of the subject matter I was trying to create. At first, I saw a myriad of confusing shapes, color, and form and tried to copy it. I did not realize that the fabric's highlight color was so rich or that the reflection in the wineglass was so complicated—or that it even existed.

After a lot of practice (sometimes spending days on a painting) something quite amazing happened. My brain stopped chattering, and I remained focused and in the moment. It seemed that there was an immediate connection between eye and hand, leaving my brain out of the process. I was seeing nothing more than pockets and patches of colors and shapes while understanding the overall composition of their integration. One of my favorite painting teachers at school would always tell us to "turn off our internal dialogue" while painting or looking, which to me meant, "shut your mind off and let it happen." You truly do become one with the painting experience.

Now when I paint, I am able to see the bits and the whole at the same time, and colors and shapes pop out at me more readily. For example, now, instead of seeing just an apple inside a bowl, I see an apple catching the reflection from the bowl and reciprocally the color of the apple transferring onto the ceramic surface of the bowl. The bowl must then have a reflective surface capturing other parts of the still life and its shadow on the white cloth below is not gray but is actually a bluish tinge with purple edges, and so forth. Even if I am having a particularly bad-painting-day (and it does happen and always will), I have certain methods that I use to help pull me back into the moment and provide me with answers I am looking for. Whether it is asking specific questions while I am painting or using other techniques to draw out something I need to know. This book is an exploration of these methods.

If you are unable to take an art course, then start at home. Create a schedule to paint or draw twice a week for a couple of hours or more in the evening. A good exercise would be for you to try to devote a full day on the weekend if you can manage it, and stick to that schedule. I love to paint. Even so, I find it hard to get motivated to do so when there's TV and a refrigerator around, so be diligent.

1.1.2 LOOK AROUND

Whether or not you are in a painting class, you can exercise your artistic eye by simply looking around and taking note of your surroundings. Every chance I get, I examine articles and environments around me and look at them as if I had to paint them. You, as a texture artist, must look at the world around you as your reference guide.

All the reference in the world will not be of service to you if you do not know how to look at it and interpret it from an artistic standpoint. Your task in this book is to familiarize yourself with various textures, looking at them and dissecting them. Then, when you sit down at the computer you will be able to articulate this knowledge.

Of course, you could always find real-world examples of textures and scan them into the computer, although this is not always a feasible option. Usually you do not have enough time during a project to walk around the city and find the right textures. Even if you do, you cannot pry a brick off a building or cut out an intriguing piece from the side-walk on 5th Street to bring back to the studio—not to mention what it would do to your scanner (see Figure 1.1). Ostensibly, you can photo-graph everything you need. You will make those decisions along the way.

1.1 Can't take this baby back to the studio.

When you do use photographs, as an artist, you must manipulate the scanned-in photography to fit seamlessly into your scene. You must use your artistic judgement and interpret scans to make them your own using the knowledge you gained by exercising your artistic eye. To paint your own textures, you must become more knowledgeable about surfaces through looking, seeing, and experimenting. Your confidence level as a texture artist will increase once you gain control of the process of creating the surfaces you will use in your work.

For instance let's look at the following simplified example. Let's say you need a weathered and abused glass texture that is transparent in some areas, but cloudy and dirty in others. You venture out with camera in hand and snap a picture of the perfect specimen on a beautiful sunny day. In the studio, you scan it, crop, and color correct it. Still, something is wrong. The project requires the glass texture to sit in a dimly lit factory. Because the surface of the glass is very reflective, your reference photo has the reflection of you and its sunny environment in it, making the texture stick out when placed as-is into the CG environment of the dimly lit factory (see Figure 1.2).

1.2 The reflection in the glass is of you and its home environment.

A better approach would be to study your reference and understand the basic ingredients of it. You can then reproduce the glass surface yourself digitally in your favorite paint package as a color layer, a scratched-up layer, a stained layer, a transparency layer, and a reflectivity layer. Finally, you can add your own reflection texture map of the factory environment to fuse the surface with the scene perfectly. This method has several benefits:

- You have the flexibility to modify any one of the layers if the director wants changes.

- The next time you need an abused glass texture you can modify the one you have or create a new one from scratch without even blinking an eye.

- You exercise your artistic eye while becoming more adept at creating texture and building your confidence.

- You do not become a slave to getting photographic reference for every change.

- It keeps the budget down in the real world of "time means money."

As you contemplate your subject over hours of just looking at it, its complex structure begins to become apparent to you, and you begin to understand how your eyes distinguish between one shape and another, one color and another, and one material and another. With this understanding, you can begin to achieve any style, whether it be simplified or hyper-real.

1.1.3 THE BENEFITS OF EXERCISE

At the end of each chapter, I will give you tasks that will encourage you to exercise your artistic eye, so that you develop and increase your sensibilities and sensitivity to textures and surfaces. You will begin to understand your world for its detail and depth. You will feel more competent at your craft, and your work will be more fulfilling and rewarding and will show it. Your audience will see something more whole, more pleasing, and integrated in your work and you will be more successful because of it.

1.2 MATERIALS AND TEXTURES DEFINED

To see, identify, describe, and then re-create a particular surface, you must first know what I mean by the two terms material and texture.

A *material* is the base substance of a surface. For example, *wood, metal,* and *glass* are examples of materials.

Texture is the adjective of the material, as in *rusty* steel, *brushed* aluminum, *soiled* cloth, *polished* marble, *red* fabric, or *frosted* glass. Texture has more to do with the look and feel of the material, the wear and tear of the material, and its design or pattern type. "Pine" wood is an example of this because "pine" is the pattern/adjective that gives the wood one of its unique features. As well, its shiny or dull quality, its bumpy or smooth quality, and its color are all ingredients of the material's texture. Figures 1.3 and 1.4 offer some examples. For a closer examination of materials and textures, as well as photographs of "pristine" and textured versions of the same materials, see Chapter 2.

1.3 Plywood.

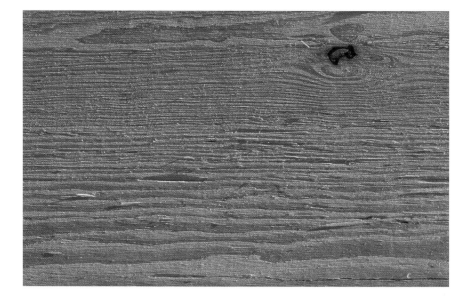

1.4 Rusted metal (*Photo courtesy of Brian Drucker*).

1.3 THE ART OF INTERVIEWING: WORKING FROM MACRO TO MICRO

Usually when looking for reference, you do not have the luxury of finding "virgin" materials in your environment. You seldom see materials without signs of aging and wear. Knowing the difference between materials and textures, you are ready to start identifying each of them. You can usually break materials with their textures into several different qualities or attributes, which will help you understand and re-create the surface at hand. I do this by "interviewing" the object or a surface itself.

Your own personal interpretation of what is happening to the surface, and what is commanding your attention, such as the reflection, is the definitive final word on how the texture will look. So, instead of using scientific or mathematical formulas to describe what you see, develop your creative eye and your intuitive knowledge. Learn to be a poet and a writer describing and interpreting your textures with your emotions and senses. Using smell, touch, and sound can add critical information to your visual experience, as do your emotions in regard to color. By bringing these to mind, no matter how absurd it may sound, your textures will be more personal and have greater visual depth.

As artists, you must be receptors to all the stimuli around you, take it all in, describe it, dissect it, and re-create it. The more adjectives you can come up with when describing a surface, the more informed you will be, and the more expressive your final product will be. With practice you will be able to separate, define, and differentiate between all these compressed elements. At the end of this book, you will be so proficient that surfaces will decompress as soon as you look at them. I want to take you step-by-step through the process of extracting all this visual information—of interviewing an object and its surface.

1.3.1   IDENTIFY THE OBJECT: WHAT ARE YOU?

Sometimes just identifying the object itself will help give way to a better understanding of the materials and textures you are dealing with. For instance, a fire hydrant straightaway tells you what shape it is, that it is made from thick steel, is exposed to the elements, and is painted, probably silver or red (see Figure 1.5). This could be enough for you to go on to make a convincing surface for the object in your scene.

1.3.2   IDENTIFY THE MOST IMPORTANT FEATURE: WHAT IS YOUR ESSENCE?

A good place to start is to identify the surface's most important feature. Sometimes "most important" might mean the feature that exemplifies what the surface truly is to you, or it might be what you notice first or like most. The key could be an attribute that exemplifies the style in which you want to express yourself or your project, or the attribute might reflect the preoccupations of your audience, or it could be both.

1.5   Fire hydrant in an Arizona suburb.

One way to start this discourse is to simply identify the object: a radiator, a vase, a fire hydrant. This may seem obvious, but as soon as you vocalize what the object is or picture it in your mind's eye, the object takes on a flavor, a quality. What I mean is, when you say, "it's a fire hydrant," the identification of the object comes with all sorts of imagery, preconceived ideas, and feelings you might associate with the object. For instance, if you were the kind of kid who played in the streets in the summertime, a fire hydrant might conjure up ideas of cool water, laughter, and sirens. Your life's experience affects your work in all sorts of ways. Once you become aware of this experience you can use it to begin to create a style uniquely you.

Looking at Figures 1.5 and 1.6, you will probably notice the color of the objects first and think this is their most important quality or feature, and it just might be. But the more you look, the more you practice your craft of "looking"; different things will start to jump out at you and stand out—make themselves known. For a radiator, the most important feature may be its rusty quality; for the object in Figure 1.6, its weathered-ness; and for the hydrant in Figure 1.5, it may be the new silver paint, reflecting the sun into your eyes.

By moving deeper and deeper into the surface's layers from most important feature to least, you are able to prioritize the steps needed to achieve a realistic, and then a stylized, representation of the object at hand. The process also helps to prioritize what is needed to convey the object's essence to your viewers. When you are faced with a tight deadline, you may have the time to paint the object's most important feature only, without thoroughly illustrating the object's other features. By identifying and then incorporating the most important feature of the object, you will have offered your audience the object's essence in the best possible light. You are also better equipped to stylize a texture for a simplistic style or graphic treatments that do not require the extra visual detail.

1.3.3   IDENTIFY THE MATERIAL: WHAT ARE YOU MADE OF?

Before you can peel away the many skins of a surface, you need to identify the material you are peeling them from. If you know the base material, the adjectives that describe it come more easily. For example, you are looking at an old metal sign (see Figure 1.7). You know that certain metals are susceptible to rust, so you look for traces of corrosion that has fused itself to the metal as a texture. If the sign's paint is old, then it most likely is chipping away or scraping off in areas. If the paint is new, then it may be shiny and somewhat reflective.

1.6   What is the most important feature you see?

1.7   An old rusted sign.

Consider another example: a box with wood as its base material (see Figure 1.8). If it is old, it is probably worn down, as wood is naturally soft. Wood also wears down in a distinctively different manner than steel or concrete. It may be varnished and shiny in some areas, and it may have nails in it that are rusted with some of that rust staining the wood. The wood material may have other textures added on top of it, such as scratches, nicks, or cigarette burns. As you can see, knowing what something is made of greatly increases your chances of successfully describing the surface: the material and all the qualities and attributes of the textures on top.

1.8   An old wooden box.

What happens when you cannot figure out what the base material is? Perhaps it is completely covered with texture leaving no traces of its underlying structure. You must make intuitive and informative guesses. Start by asking large picture questions. As you look at the abrasions and aberrations on the surface, ask yourself, "What kind of material would have these types of aberrations on it?" Your answers may spark ideas about the object's composition, so look for textural evidence that gives away the base material's identity. For instance, look for signs of wood grain that the paint may have seeped into or minute signs of corrosion that were painted over (see Figures 1.9 and 1.10). Perhaps traces of fabric weave underlie the whole texture. Take time to look at the object in Figure 1.11, and try to distinguish what the object's base material is.

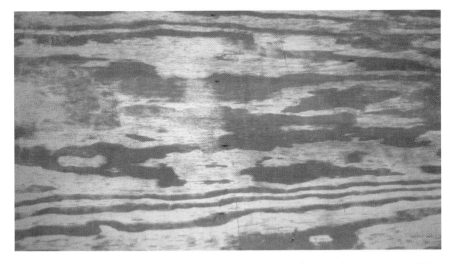

1.9 Base materials may be hard to find but they can't hide.

1.10 The rust gives away the material of this lightpost base.

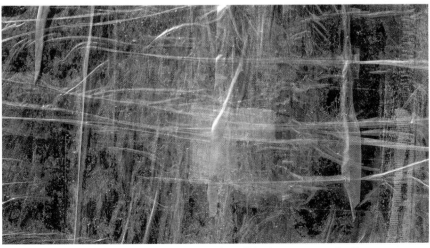

1.11 Can you tell what the material in this picture is?

Answer: Packing tape stuck on top of glass pane.

If no textural clues give away the base material, don't get discouraged or spend hours on the possible variations of the mystery material. In some cases, knowing the base material is not important and you can start by describing the texture you see instead.

If you are not ready to give up on figuring out what the material is, the following two techniques might help you in the investigation.

1.3.3.1 WHAT DO YOU SOUND LIKE?

It is also important to use your sense of touch combined with sound. If you are not sure what a material is, try tapping it with your fingernail or knuckle and listen to the sound it makes. Recently I was fooled by an artificial brass item. My eyes saw brass, but something told me that it didn't look right. I just couldn't figure out what it was. I tapped the item lightly and heard a light plastic sound, not the metallic brass sound I was expecting. You know what acrylic sounds like as opposed to glass, aluminum as opposed to steel, and plastic as opposed to brass. Ears are finely tuned instruments that pick up on slight variations that the eyes may not catch.

1.3.3.2 WHAT DO YOU SMELL LIKE?

At times, I use my sense of smell to find out what I am looking at. To me different metals have different smells. Bronze has a distinct odor different from iron or copper. Soft plastic has a distinctive smell as do vinyl, leather, and so on.

1.3.4 IDENTIFY THE LIGHT SOURCE: HOW CAN I SEE YOU?

Now that you have an idea of the materials you are working with, one of the first things to consider is the light source. The only reason why you see any surface at all is because of the light that is hitting it and reflecting back into your eyes. If the light source is warm (the sun, a flame, or an incandescent bulb), then the chances are good that the hotspot or highlight will be a warm color. The warm yellowish light bounces off and dances around the item you are viewing as well as its immediate environment; because of this, the environment and the object cohabitate. It takes a trained eye to recognize how this affects your interpretation, especially of the color of the surface as well as the texture.

A good exercise would be to take a reflective object and expose it to different light sources (see Figure 1.12).

When you sit in a room with a group of objects in front of you, a still life, and paint it on canvas, the environmental effects on each element in the still life are the same. Each element is exposed to the same conditions, is in the same environment, and is under the same light source. The still life has an integrated look. In the CG field, you seldom have an exact replica of the scene you are to create on the computer directly in front of you. Instead, you have the freedom to collect your reference from varied and interesting sources. Because of this freedom, it then becomes a challenge for you to merge accurately and stealthily the disparate elements into one scene.

Without having the real-life objects in front of you, training your artistic eye will help you decipher your reference materials, and interpret them so you may effectively modify and add them into your scene.

This collage approach can work, as long as you remember, either from notes you took while taking your own photos or from looking at your reference photos, what *time* of day or what *type* of day it was when each photo reference was taken. This is important because first and foremost you will be considering light (natural, indoor) and hue and saturation of color to begin your story of the surface. If it was a cloudy day, then colors will tend to be more muted and cool (see Figure 1.13) as opposed to a bright sunny day when colors are more saturated and have warmer hues (see Figure 1.14). Knowing where the reference was shot is a huge benefit to you. If it was shot in a humid climate, the hues will be softer and muted. Humidity softens light and shadow.

1.12 The photo on the left is reflecting the sky and daylight, while the one on the right is reflecting a room's interior lighting.

1.13 Color saturation, contrasts, and value range on a cloudy day.

1.14 Color saturation, contrasts, and value range on a sunny day.

1.3.5 IDENTIFY THE LOCATION: WHERE ARE YOU?

Is the item inside or outside? It may seem a simple, even obvious question, but a very important one nonetheless. If the object's habitat is outdoors, then it will be subjected to all the natural elements of that locale—sun, wind, rain, snow, sea salt, heat, cold, pollution, dogs, humans, —and all may affect the object (see Figure 1.15). Everything grows old. Just take something brand-new out of its package and notice how many hours it takes before the squeaky-clean look is diminished. If you are after realism, then knowing how to transform a perfect surface ("virgin" material) into one that has mood, texture, and atmosphere is your goal.

Dust, tarnish, scratches, nicks and ticks, dents, wax, varnish, solvents, moisture, and oils are a few of the everyday influences that add to the story of your subject.

I am interested in the effects on an object that speak of human intervention. This is another factor that you must take into consideration. How many times has the object been painted? Written on? Treated? Bumped into? Scraped? This is when things get exciting. I am curious about: the wearing away of paint on steps from continual use; scrapes made by a moving dolly along the baseboard of a wall; acrylic paint peeling away

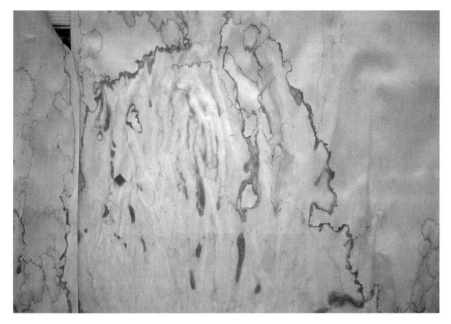

1.15 What liquid do you think caused these stains?

1.16 Notice how textures describe themselves on different surfaces.

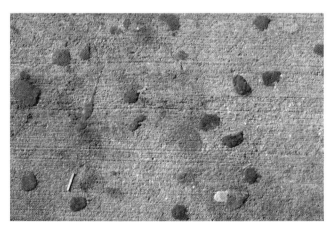

from a previous coat of an oil base paint; cigarette burns on tile or wood floors; chewing gum—the black spots on city sidewalks; lover's names and initials scratched onto park benches (see Figure 1.16). In other words, everyday wear and tear and it is everywhere for us to lovingly analyze, record, and re-create.

1.3.6 IDENTIFY THE APPEARANCE: WHAT DO YOU LOOK LIKE?

With a grasp of your object's base material, as well as its environmental and historical attributes, you're ready to pick away all the textural attributes of your object. Using all your senses and your art of description, you need to separate the textural information into layers or ingredients you can later combine in your 3D software to create the object's look. I am not going to get into the mechanics of the 3D software at this point. We will get into the nitty-gritty later during the project portion of the book. For now, I want you to be concerned with the art of looking and describing. If textures are the adjectives placed upon the material, then all you have to do is describe what you are looking at and make note of all the qualities you are describing.

1.3.6.1 WHAT IS THE COLOR TEXTURE?

Let's start with defining color texture. For simple surfaces, color texture can be minimal, such as the bright red of a brand-new billiard ball or the overall light-tan color of a piece of balsa wood. A texture artist's job is not so simplistic, and we are often confronted with much more complex color descriptions. Now, think of a plaid pattern on a blanket or an intricately defined wood grain of a piece of Bubinga, an exotic wood. The color texture of each of these includes much more than a single color. Even more complex color textures are possible, as Figure 1.17 illustrates.

One of the most important skills for a texture artist to master is that of color recognition. It is of paramount importance that you train your eyes and mind to be hypersensitive to all the millions of shades, tones, and hues that populate the world. The biggest drawback that you will face, if you have never painted before and work on the computer only, is not knowing how to identify and name the colors you are seeing.

I started painting when I was 13 years old. As a part of my education, I had to learn all the names of the oil-paint colors that I was using. Still to this day, I walk around looking at colors, distinguishing between different shades of reds and blues, yellows, and greens. I compare a blue sky to a light cerulean, or a deep blue to ultramarine blue with a touch of

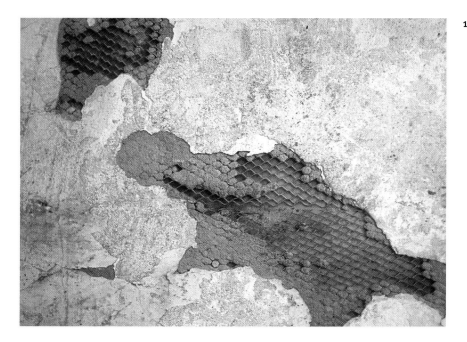

1.17 Look carefully and see how many colors make up this complex texture.

alizarin crimson; to me golds or amber-yellows typically are yellow-ochre with a touch of vermilion green. Because I am able to do this, it is easy for me to remember the color and apply it once I get back to the studio.

The color chart in Figure 1.18 should help you learn your colors, providing a better reference point than wondering where that color you saw on the street lies in the Photoshop palette window. The better you know your colors the more convincing your textural work will be. (Consult Chapter 3 for more detail about color theory.)

There is color in everything! There is actually very little pure white or black in our environment and the more you look at colors, the more you will realize this.

As an experiment, set up two still lifes. For one, use all white items: a white sheet, with some white paper on top, a white ceramic cup or vase, a white egg, and so on (see Figure 1.19). For the other, use only black items: black velvet, a black frying pan, a black cue ball, a black tar shingle, and so on (see Figure 1.20).

Study these two still lifes and you will begin to see that there are hundreds of subtle hues of different colors that are neither white nor black. Your light source has a great deal to do with the subtleties of color you are seeing. You may find that identifying the spectrum of colors in these two examples is at first a difficult task, so do not be discouraged. For you to gain the ability to see these subtleties takes hours of practice.

1.18   Common paint colors and their names.

Lemon Yellow Cadmium Yellow Light Cadmium Yellow Medium Naples Yellow Yellow Ochre

Cadmium Red Orange Vermillion Red Cadmium Red Deep Alizarin Crimson Cobalt Violet Deep

Cerulean Blue Cobalt Blue Phthalo Blue Ultramarine Blue Emerald Green

Green Earth Viridian Green Sap Green Burnt Sienna Raw Umber

1.19   Still life containing different white items.

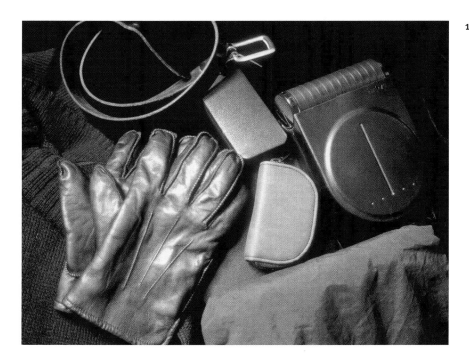

1.20 Still life containing different black items.

Try to paint the "all white" or "all black" still life. Painting the still life will demand that you take the time to really look at the colors you are seeing and then mix them on your palette. When I paint, I mainly mix my own colors from a palette of five colors: primary red (alizarin crimson), primary blue (ultramarine blue), primary yellow (cadmium yellow medium), black (ivory black), and white (titanium white), plus a few others that the main five cannot make, like the red of a geranium. Rather than relying on ready-made colors, I am able to get the color as close to what I am seeing to exemplify the color and its tone. It can be a reaffirming and invigorating experience to match the color exactly, knowing that your sense of color becomes more precise each time.

STARE

One method that is useful for color recognition is to practice staring at an object for a long time. Yes, you read it right! Looking at something for a long time without blinking. This brings us back to the part about exercising your artistic eye. Now you are not only looking at a surface with the intention to understand it—you are now using your eyes physically to alter your perception of what you are looking at. You may have stared at a pattern on a wall or the floor for a time and noticed that your eyes become unfocused and details begin to fall away. That is precisely the point. Simply stare at the part of the object or scene you wish to decipher. After a while, a color will just flash or pop out at you. It may take some time but it will happen.

Obviously, you don't need to practice this staring exercise for simple colors. Use it for more complex colors that live in the highlights or shadows, which are the areas that fool our eyes the most. The highlight can fool us because most of the time the color presents itself as an energy or a light, such as as a highlighted spot on metal does. As you know, it is difficult to look at bright light dead-on anytime, without trying to understand what color it is emitting. Our brain wants to give in and say "Oh, it's white," when really it isn't. Shadowed areas are the opposite. Our eyes see color and detail because of light so when light is diminished or absent, our eyes have to strain and work harder to pull out what color lives in these shadowy nooks and crannies. Believe me, there are colors that live there!

SQUINT

Another way to help find colors or patterns in textures is to squint or defocus your gaze when looking at the object. Sometimes there can be so much information coming at our eyes and brain that it helps to shut some of that information off in order to get at its true essence, simplifying it. I find this to be a great help to me when painting.

On a trip to the south of France, I spent every day of my three-month stay painting the countryside and still lifes. At the same time I was reading a book about strengthening your eyesight and it suggested that people who wear glasses should refrain from wearing them whenever possible. Because I wear glasses, I decided to give this a try while painting, and even when I did not squint, the blurriness I saw from my poor eyesight, helped me see more of what was there. So it worked, especially when on sunny days, I was able to see colors and patterns more easily and was not overly concerned with what objects those colors and patterns were associated with. It was also very helpful in creating depth of field. My paintings improved—as well as my eyesight—but my paintings did not lack coherence in any way. By painting this simplified, softened view, my compositions were much more accurate, and my textures closer to the truth. The end result was not a blurry representation at all. The paintings were stylized, yes, but still in the realm of representational picture making.

So, simply put, if you wear glasses, give your eyes some exercise and take your glasses off next time you are looking around, taking notes, or painting what you see. At first, it may be quite disconcerting. To see if my painting was making any visual sense even I needed to put my glasses back on from time to time. But soon I gained the confidence to continue in this way after seeing the results of my experiment and so will you.

If your eyesight is 20/20 or close to it, then all you really have to do is squint. I find that this is something most artists do without thinking, combined with head tilts to either side as they try to make out what they are seeing.

This is probably my favorite method for:

- Figuring out compositional strengths and weaknesses
- Simplifying color information and color recognition
- Simplifying complex patterns
- Determining level of detail in the foreground and background to create depth

LOOK FOR COLOR RELATIVITY

Color is a relative concept. This means that colors affect each other when they are in close proximity. Often times it is hard to distinguish what a complex color is, such as a muted gray or a very dark hue, if there are no other colors in the scene to compare it with. To understand this, cover Figure 1.22 and look at the colored square in Figure 1.21. Do you see any color at all or only gray? If you stare at the square long enough, does any color pop out at you? Keep trying!

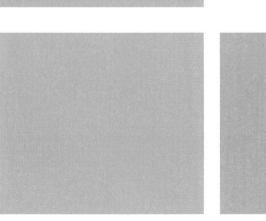

1.21 Square A.
Do you see any color in this gray square?

1.22 Squares A and B.
Can you now see what color tint is in Square A?

Now look at Figure 1.22. Square A in Figure 1.22 is the same color as square A in Figure 1.21, while square B is a different color. Can you now see what color tints Squares A and B have other than just gray? You should be able to see a slight green coloration to square A and a slight red tint in square B. The colors of the two squares are complements of each other. They give you clues as to what is really there because of their contrasting natures.

Looking for contrasts and complements as you stare at colors will help you identify them. So will asking yourself questions such as, "Is this color red? Green? Blue?" You will get answers. With a question such as, "Is this color warm or cold?" you will get other answers. Your artistic eye allows you to immediately answer, "That's not red or blue," and through this you will be much closer to understanding what you are seeing as the real color. If you say, "It doesn't feel warm," then you know it cannot be from the yellow family of colors because yellow is a warm color. You now can ask yourself if it is green? If it is, you will see it! If not, you can start again because maybe you missed something. So because color is relative, especially in those subtle difficult areas of high-light and shadow, you can place different colors against the color you're trying to identify to coax the color out into the open. Practice this with Figure 1.23.

1.23   What colors are in the shadows?

When painting a texture, either on canvas, paper, or the computer, I always start by putting colors on the canvas. For example, I may not be sure of the exact hue or tint of the surface in question, so I apply an approximate color to the canvas or computer screen and move my eyes back and forth from the real object to my painted object. I compare the two to see if I am close. From here, I make my revisions to the painted color.

1.24 These colors were mixed on a palette with a knife before being applied to the canvas.

1.25 As I paint, the colors in this quick color sketch are mixed right on the canvas.

You can also mix colors right on the palette before applying them to the canvas (see Figure 1.24). I like to put colors on the canvas next to colors I have already painted, however, because then I can compare each relationship of the colors on the canvas to the referenced still life or photograph (see Figure 1.25). If I am painting from a photograph, or from a picture in a magazine, I sometimes will put a dab of mixed color right on the reference to see how close I am to the color in the picture. This is used almost as a last resort when my eyes are not seeing what is there and my brain is talking too much, not letting the artistic intuitive recognition flow.

THE WHITE CARD TEST

Another way to discover the color of an object is to carry a white card (the size of a business card) around with you. This is especially useful when trying to distinguish between highlights and lighter colors, and the subtle differences in color that make them. Simply place the white card next to the color in question, and you will be able to determine what color it actually is (see Figure 1.26). The white card will train your eye to recognize that what you thought was white is actually a warm gold or cool blue, and so on.

For mid-tones and deep colors, you can use a neutral gray or a black card. The gray card is used for mid-tones that are in subtler shadow areas or middle-valued hues, and the black card for the deeper colors and dark shadows. These colors can be elusive because of the gradual and subtle changes from the true color into the shadows.

1.26 By placing the white card next to a surface, you can more easily decipher the highlight color.

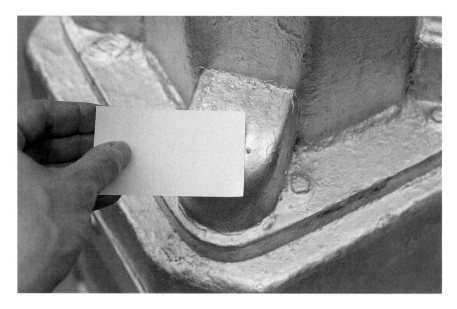

Carrying this card helps fine-tune your eye at looking, and as time goes by you may not need to carry any of these cards around with you. With practice, you will start to picture a pure white or black card in your mind's eye with which to compare and contrast the colors you are seeing around you.

THE EYEDROPPER TEST

Another way to coax colors out of hiding is to scan your reference and open the scanned image in Photoshop, and then use the Eyedropper tool to pick up the colors in doubt (see Figure 1.27).

The result can be surprising. The color that you thought you saw on the actual reference and the color you pick up with the Eyedropper may vary greatly. I suggest that the eyedropper test be your last resort in learning to see colors. It is more of a test of your perception rather than an exercise to build your perception. It is much better to rely on your eyes. Doing so will save you time and effort in the long run, and you can take your eyes anywhere at any time.

I cannot stress enough the importance to you, the artist, of training your eyes and mind to recognize colors. The high quality of your work depends on it.

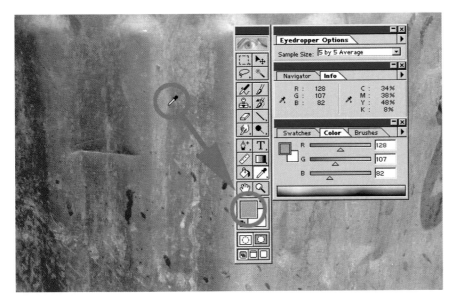

1.27 Using the Eyedropper tool in Photoshop you can get the exact color.

REFLECTIONS AND SHADOWS

Do not be fooled by surfaces that are shiny, glossy, polished, or reflective. In a reflective surface, the image that is reflected in the surface is not truly a part of that color texture. The picture on the left in Figure 1.28 is an example of a reflective surface that seems to have a bit of abstract complexity. Do you include all the information you see verbatim? If you look at the picture on the right in Figure 1.28, you will see that the colors and patterns are not part of the object's true surface but a reflection that must not be included as part of your color texture. The colors and patterns are transient and change with the placement of the object and its surroundings. Being on the lookout for these transient qualities helps you avoid including them in the color texture painting. You will add the reflected image to the surface when you render your scene.

When looking at a reflective object, as either a picture or real life, to use it for reference, many beginners forget to eliminate the reflected environment, and re-create verbatim on the computer what they are seeing. When they are done it looks like the reference material all right, but it does not relate to the environment they put it into. You must remember to add the new environment of the scene into the reflection, so the surfaced object can sit correctly within the scene.

1.28 The colors and shapes on the surface of the object look like they may be part of the object's surface (left). When you zoom out, you find that they are just reflections and should not be included in the color texture (right).

A cast shadow is another transient attribute resulting from something in the vicinity of your object. Be sure to note these shadow-casters while the object is in the original environment, because often when shooting the photo reference, the photo is cropped, close-up fashion, omitting the surroundings. When you get your slides back, you may not even notice the shadowed areas that are now part of the surface color texture but should not be included in the color texture painting. If you did not take notes of the surrounding elements in the environment when you took the photo, separating the cast shadow from the color texture will be difficult. These cast shadows can be from surrounding trees, signs, buildings, or from you.

Figure 1.29 (left), a close-up on the glass only, has a shadow cast from some other object in its vicinity. If you zoom out a bit to show more of the picture, you can better understand this shadow by identifying its source. Can you see a dark and light pattern that lies across all the materials in Figure 1.29 (right)? Over the wood framing, the ripped, tortured poster, and the glass? The cast shadow's source is a fence of some sort.

So, when scrutinizing reference, photographic or real, look for these patterns of light and dark that spill onto not only the object, but also the surrounding vicinity. Do not include this as part of your color texture, unless it suits your purposes.

1.29 A close-up shot of glass reference (left), and a full shot of glass reference revealing shadow pattern (right).

1.3.6.2 **IS THE OBJECT TRANSPARENT?**

Transparency is a fairly obvious quality to see on an object or surface. Materials, such as glass, are transparent because light rays pass directly through them, without scattering. Therefore, anything on a transparent surface that blocks the light's passage inhibits transparency. Examples of inhibitors are scratches, paint, dirt, and grease (see Figure 1.30).

Recognizing inhibitors will help you describe an object's transparent quality. Recording a detailed description of these inhibitors will later help you create a transparency map for your color texture to be applied at rendering time. I will show you how to create a transparency painting later during the project.

Not all transparent surfaces are 100-percent see-through. When possible, place a white card or your hand behind the object to establish what percentage is transparent (see Figure 1.31). Colored glass affects this percentage as do materials such as sandblasted glass or diffuse materials like vellum or molded glass (see Figure 1.32).

Transparent surfaces sometimes also contain refractive qualities. Refraction is caused when light rays bend, distorting the image that lies beyond or inside the transparent surface. A molded glass object, such as a bottle, does just that (see Figure 1.33).

1.30 Inhibitors such as paint, a posted notice, and the reinforced wire affect the transparency of this glass panel.

1.31 The colored glass affects the ability to see my hand behind it.

1.32 The texture of the glass alters its transparency.

In Figure 1.33, the trees outside are distorted due to refraction. It may be due to the thickness of the glass and the inconsistency of this thickness. Or, it could be from something in the container, like liquid, which bends light rays as they pass through. You can mimic this effect by creating a bump painting or bump map and applying it at render time. For now, simply make note of how much refraction is present and the pattern it is creating. Is it wavy or noisy? If it is refraction caused by the object's thickness or its contents, such as liquid, then you need to tell your 3D software to render with refractions through ray tracing.

1.33 Different thickness and color of clear glass alter the ability of light rays to travel in a straight line, which is what gives us different degrees of transparency and refraction.

1.3.6.3   IS THE OBJECT LUMINOUS?

Some other qualities that are characteristic of surfaces or materials that you must watch out for are those of luminousness. There are four sources of luminosity associated with surfaces, which are the emitting of light:

- With heat
- Without heat
- From an outside source
- From the object itself (other than a reflection)

An object could have one or two of these characteristics, and can be identified as being:

- Translucent
- Iridescent
- Opalescent
- Luminescent
- Fluorescent
- Incandescent

Translucency is defined as a material that allows light to pass through it yet it is not transparent. It receives light and can be luminous only from an outside source. A good example of this is a piece of paper. If you hold a sheet of paper in front of a light source, you can see that the light makes it glow, but you cannot see the light source through the paper because the paper scatters the light rays. Other items that have translucent qualities are wax, certain types of cloth, frosted glass, and petals and leaves, to name a few (see Figure 1.34).

Iridescence, which can be detected as a rainbow pattern on the surface of soap bubbles and gasoline spills, is an interesting phenomenon. It "…is caused by the interference of light waves resulting from multiple reflections of light off of surfaces of varying thickness. A soap bubble displays an iridescent pattern because light reflects off the top and bottom surfaces of the soap bubbles. As the thickness of the layer varies, the color seen will vary." (From *The Handy Physics Answer Book,* ed. P. Erik Gundersen.) Mother-of-pearl, a compact disc, the eye of a peacock feather, all share this quality. I have also noticed a similar quality on butterfly wings. Another type of iridescence is characteristic of the Morpho Butterfly through which the interference playing out allows a brilliant blue to emit while all other colors are absorbed.

Opalescence is similar to iridescence but is more closely associated to opal or quartz-like stones. Both iridescent and opalescent luminosity are created without heat and are the result of an outside source.

Luminescence is the quality of a surface that emits light without heat, and the object is essentially the source of light itself. The characteristic of a luminescent object is phosphorescence, as seen in the Firefly. It emits light without heat and is only seen in the dark.

Fluorescence is another quality of a surface that produces light without heat, and is characteristic of an object whose atoms are able to absorb a particular wavelength of light while simultaneously reflecting light of another wavelength. The verb to fluoresce describes what a particular substance does when ultraviolet (invisible) light hits it, and only in this way can we see the low energy light it emits.

Incandescent light is created by heat. Neon signs, stovetop coils, the lit end of a cigarette, an open flame are just some examples of incandescent light energy.

1.34 Translucent quality of a lit candle.

Why is it important to know all this? When creating an object with one of these characteristics, it is important to know that you may need to create a surface that has these light qualities. In Maya, for example, the software allows you to set translucency and incandescent attributes on a shader that is then applied to your object. Sometimes it is possible to create a painting/map that can fake these luminous characteristics as well.

1.3.7 IDENTIFY TACTILE QUALITY: WHAT DO YOU FEEL LIKE?

Another great way to understand what you are looking at is to touch the object and ask, "How does it feel?" From this question, you can find out many attributes. The tactile quality can inform you of the object's texture—not only if it is bumpy or smooth, but also if it is warm or cold, soft or hard. These tactile qualities are difficult to reproduce, and how you decide to interpret and apply them can change a texture from being everyday to very exciting.

1.3.7.1 TEMPERATURE

Is the object cool to the touch? If so, possibly the object is made of metal or it may be near a source that emits cold, perhaps a refrigerator or an air conditioner. What images come up for you when you think of cold metal? Do you think that if you touch it, you might feel cold yourself, or that your skin might even stick to it? If the object is cool

1.35 Condensation forming on a glass of water.

enough, it might have condensation forming on its surface. Perhaps, as in Figure 1.35, it is a hot summer day and condensation is forming on a glass surface, which is colder than room temperature. This instance illustrates how two elements of the environment, in this case the cold glass and hot atmosphere, can create a third element, condensation.

1.3.7.2 BUMPINESS

Another quality to watch out for when you are looking at a surface is its bumpy quality. If the surface has dents and nicks or scratches, then the light hitting this surface will create highlights and shadows from the surface imperfections. In Figure 1.36, both spheres' color maps are a solid red. You can see this clearly on the smooth sphere. The bumpy surface of the sphere creates a variety of red hues. This highlight and shadow information is not part of the color texture and you should not include this variety in your color map. You should save this bump information for a separate bump painting and let the computer do its work with light and shadow at rendering time. If the camera or lights are animated, then let the computer describe the bumpiness of the surface because the highlight and shaded areas will change in tandem with this movement. Although, it is less work for the computer if it does not have to figure out this bumpy quality, and your rendering times will be faster. Sometimes it is unavoidable and a separate bump texture painting will have to be created. There are times that you can include this attribute in the color texture. For example, when the camera and lights are locked off, meaning they are not going to move or animate in the shot.

1.3.7.3 ROUGHNESS

If the object has a rough quality when touched, then ask why. Is it rough because of rust and corrosion? Dents? Scratches or gouges? If so, you need to decide what part of this quality should be included in the color texture. Nonetheless, it must be included as one of the ingredients of the total surface, if you're striving for realism. In most cases, you will re-create the surface's rough or bumpy quality as a separate painting and render it as a combination with the color texture.

Rough, imperfect surfaces also affect the way light hits the surface and travels back to your eye. These types of surfaces tend to scatter the light across themselves and spot highlights are lessened or not visible at all. Unglazed pottery, wood, and paper products are good examples of non-specular highlighted, or diffuse surfaces.

1.36 The top rendered sphere is smooth and has no bumps, whereas the sphere on the bottom has a bumpy surface. Compare the differences in color texture.

Roughness can be sneaky. For example, unglazed pottery and paper have microscopic roughness that may not be detectable through touch. Keep your eyes open for such instances and compare the touch against its opposite. For example, when touching the surface of the object, pit it against something extremely smooth or extremely rough. Decide how important this attribute of the surface is and whether it needs to be included in the final reproduction. For a hyper-real genre, you may need to zoom in and see all of the bumpy roughness of a piece of ordinary white paper. Therefore, being able to detect the amount of roughness in the texture of a seemingly smooth surface is important.

1.3.7.4 SMOOTHNESS

If the surface is smooth to the touch, is it polished? Is it coated with varnish or paint? Is it metallic? If it is any or all of the above, then you must be on the lookout for spots of light, or *specular highlights*, on the surface, as well as for the highlight's colors. Once again, there are exceptions to this rule. Wax often feels very smooth, but it may have little or no highlight on the surface.

Another by-product of smooth surfaces is *reflection*. If the surface has a reflective quality, then by holding it you can most likely see evidence of your hand in the reflection. This is a good trick to enable you to see just how reflective and what parts of the surface are reflective. Often times we are tricked into thinking that if the surface is reflective, then it is 100 percent reflective like a mirror or a lake's surface. This is hardly the case.

1.37 This smooth white enamel diffuses the reflection.

1.38 My hand reflection is much more crisp and detailed than in Figure 1.37.

By holding the object, if you can, or at least putting your hand or finger near it, you can see the reflective quality. Is it a blurry, soft reflection? Is it the same color as your finger, or is it tinted with the surface color? Is it a crisp mirror-like reflection. Is the reflection broken up by a non-reflective affectation of the surface. If the reflection is broken up, you know the surface is not smooth, or that it has inhibitors on it, such as dirt, paint, rust, or scratches.

You could also try slowly moving your hand, or a white card, toward the object. At what point does your hand or the white card become visible in the reflection? Some surfaces, such as the white enamel cup shown in Figure 1.37, diffuse their reflections of their surroundings, softening any detail except for items very nearby. You can also figure out what percentage of reflection a surface has by holding the object or touching it. For instance, the percentage of reflection emitted from the white enamel coffee cup is much less than that of the silver espresso maker in Figure 1.38.

1.39 Reflective surfaces may not always be smooth.

Reflective surfaces may not always be smooth, however. Very rough or bumpy surfaces may be coated in a glossy paint or varnish (see Figure 1.39), which can be image reflective as well. These surfaces tend to break up the reflected image due to their inherent imperfections, much the same way a ripple in a lake's surface breaks up the image reflected in the lake. The reflected whole breaks up into smaller reflected parts. You can easily see how this occurs if the image reflected is something you can easily discern, such as your hand.

Other qualities detected by using your sense of touch are that of dirt, grease, oil, or chalkiness. Each gives clues to the surface's history. Many outside substances can affect the surface you are scrutinizing. By touching the surface, getting your hands dirty, you can better understand all the necessary parts that make up the whole.

1.3.8   IDENTIFY THE HISTORY: WHAT'S YOUR STORY?

Every surface in our world has a story. It has a reason to be where it is. It has an age, and a name. It lives in a neighborhood or your house and is affected by much of the same things we are. As texture painters, we must find out as much of the surface's history as possible by interviewing the surface.

1.3.8.1   STAIRWELL INTERVIEWED

Let's examine Figure 1.40, a photograph of a stairwell in New York City, so you can see how fun and easy it is to interview and record your findings. The lighting is fluorescent.

1.40   These stairs have a story to tell.

As you can see these stairs get quite a beating. Notice that there are several coats of paint that have worn away at different places, a record of how many people traversed these steps and how often. You immediately see the current color is grayish blue. Is that all we need to know? Is it important to know the base material of the steps? Is it concrete? Can you tell? How would knowing this inform the re-creation of your scene? What if it is concrete? Well, the stairs would weather the traffic over the years differently than if they were made of wood. Simply, a concrete step would not sag as a wood step would eventually over time, and paint would chip off more easily from wood. Illustrating these types of differences might assist the audience's psyche to accept your scene more readily because of its realism, whatever the style. So the habits of the climbers can be very informative and are worthwhile to note.

The steps are somewhat worn down on the sides from people walking up using the banister for support. They are not as worn on the top floors from people walking up because we tend to take the elevator for higher floors. But people use the stairs to go down more often and if they are anything like I am, tend to use the middle of the steps to reach the ground floor. Therefore, the steps are more worn down in the center. Knowing this, you can ascertain how busy a stairwell actually is. What does the wear look like? A person does not place a whole foot on a step, and, therefore, steps do not wear away evenly. Only the front edge of a step gets broken down. This may seem very obvious, but you would be surprised at how many people create a texture for a staircase that is evenly worn over the whole step. The New York stairs have elements such as scratches, dirt, cigarette burns, and gum, as well as paint droplets—elements brought in by a climber's shoes from outside. Now that you have identified and described the characteristics of the staircase, you can decide how many of these conditions to add to your re-creation.

It is interesting to note that the stairs from the main floor to the second are the most worn and the stairs get less and less abused the higher you climb. People are obviously very willing to walk a couple of flights rather than wait for the elevator, but not more than three flights. It is good to know things like this if you want to accurately catch the habits of people and the textures they create through their everyday activities. Remember, be aware and look around—ask yourself questions all the time.

If you wanted to or it was necessary for your project, you could simplify or stylize all this information. Just recognizing the pattern created by the act of walking on these steps is enough to get you started in creating a believable image.

1.3.8.2 BE THE MATERIAL

An interesting experiment to try is to pretend that you are the base material looking out into its surroundings. What do you see? If you speak from the material's viewpoint, you begin to see things from the inside out. For instance, pretend that you are the garbage container in Figure 1.41. A typical monologue of self-description might sound like what follows this.

1.41 Construction site garbage container.

"I am a garbage container made out of metal. Because I am on a construction site, I am very abused. I am painted red and initials are sprayed with white paint to identify who owns me. I've got scratches and abrasions that have ripped off my protective paint layer and now I am rusting in these areas. Splattered white plaster covers some of this, as well as dirt and dust. The red paint is sun beaten and has lost all of its enamel sheen, and if any of me is reflecting my surroundings, it is very minimal and probably isn't worthwhile reproducing. Some of the gouges in my structure, as well as the red paint lifting off of me by the plow-like effects of the scratches, can be felt by touch. The edges of my structure are rounded due to wear and tear, and all traces of paint are removed from these areas. Rust has worked its way underneath my body and is bubbling some of the paint off of my surface."

Learning to speak in the first person with materials helps you to free associate and improvise *attribute recognition*, as well as allowing you to create your own materials that do not exist or to add qualities of which you have no physical reference.

1.4   BECOME ATTUNED

All these exercises take time to practice and get good at. The art of looking and recording is not as simple as it sounds. One method may work better for you than the others; it is up to you to decide. Or, you may already have a method that works better than the ones I have described and if so I would love to hear about it.

In this chapter, I have described to you the process through which you can become more intimately knowledgeable about the surfaces you want to create. The success of the techniques relies on your ability to become more attuned with your surroundings. Through the techniques laid out in this book, you will become better acquainted with materials and surfaces so that your work will reflect this and come easier to you. In Chapter 2, "Reference Materials, Textures, and Practical Stuff," I will introduce you to some materials and textures, and put them into context. Chapter 2 is full of pictures, which is the best part of any book, but especially one about looking. Take your time with the chapter and have fun applying what I have just discussed.

1.5   EXERCISES

1. Start a sketchbook and begin drawing and making notes about materials and surfaces that interest you. Make sure to record all their characteristics.

2. Color mixing and matching for simple colors may not be so simple. A lemon is yellow, but what type of yellow? Is it an orange-yellow or pale yellow? Just because there is a tube of paint called "lemon yellow" does not mean it is the color of *your* lemon.

   Try it yourself. Take a lemon or any other item and, on canvas, paper, or the computer, start mixing colors. Compare your colors to the original by looking back and forth from one to the other.

   In your mind's eye compare the color with another color that you think is similar. Look closely at the color and observe if there are any subtle variances in hue.

3. Go around your neighborhood, observe and interview a few objects by asking each of them these questions:

   - What is the object or surface?
   - What is the most important feature that stands out for you?

- What is it made of, and does knowing this help you identify the surface or object, and what is it used for? What does it sound, smell, and feel like and does this help you find the information you need?

- How is the object or surface lit? Where is it? And how does this add to the textural quality of the object?

- Is it transparent, luminous, or refractive?

4. Take time to look at an object and try to discern what the object's material is. Be a detective and interview the object to understand its surroundings and its history.

5. Find a reflective object that you can carry with you. Expose it to different light sources and environments. Measure its reflectivity on a scale of 1 to 10. At what point does your hand or white card become visible in the reflection? What is its true color?

6. The color texture and surface quality of the piece will enhance or detract from your understanding of the whole, so it is necessary to be able to distinguish the layers of texture.

    See what happens to the complexity of the texture when you:

    - Look at it normally.

    - Squint at it.

    - Stare at it.

7. It is important to know how to recognize colors in highlights and shadows. Practice doing this with the help of your white, gray, and black cards.

8. Walk around your block and find an interesting object. Become that object and describe your features. Record yourself on tape or make notes of your monologue. Don't be afraid to go overboard. Have fun and don't edit yourself. Tell its story.

    For a bigger challenge, try recording a monologue for a material that does not exist, such as an imaginary material for a science fiction film.

2

[CHAPTER]

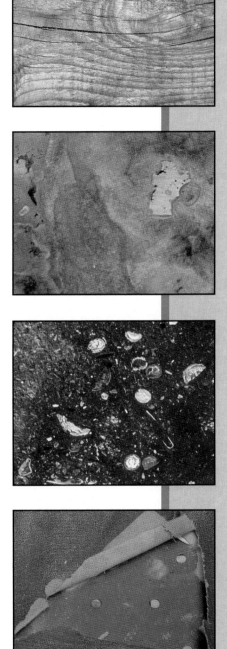

REFERENCE MATERIALS, TEXTURES, AND PRACTICAL STUFF

T HE PREVIOUS CHAPTER attempted to train your eyes and mind to take notice and ask questions by looking at real materials. This chapter prepares you to begin collecting reference materials in your mind and in your office. You begin by investigating materials and their textures in photographs and then see how you can use these photos to further your exploration of materials and textures. You will be asked to explore the different sources available to create a library of reference called a *morgue*. These sources include: magazines, the Internet, and real materials to name a few. Finally, at the end of this chapter, the "Photo Gallery" section contains several different photographs through which I discuss the effects of nature, and effects of other materials on surfaces, which all contribute to create textures. As you study these photographs, continue exercising your artistic eye and practice the art of looking and dissecting that began in Chapter 1.

Now it is time to fill your head with as much information about materials and textures as possible. What follows are some photographs that I took walking around Manhattan, a city very rich in texture. These photos are a very generalized and arbitrary overview of materials and textures that appealed to me. Please keep this book as a general reference guide by your desk. It will help you when you start on your own pictorial reference expedition.

2.1 BASIC MATERIALS

This first part of the picture reference section shows pictures of materials as close as possible to their *perfect* state. I found out during my collecting that it is difficult to find a perfect state in reality. I relied on material samples from stores and also thoroughly investigated surfaces in the real world during my exploration to find these basic materials.

What follows are some photographs of materials in their near-perfect state. Refer to them as you go through this book, and use them as a basic reference guide in your professional endeavors. It is important to know what materials look like in this state—raw and untainted like a newborn baby. Think of these materials as the first layer of your paint program. The "virgin" blank canvas on which every other detail falls.

Basic Materials

Metal: Brass

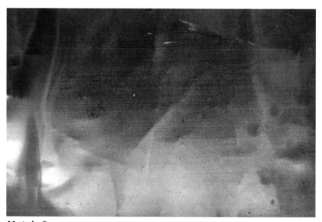

Metal: Copper

Metal: Galvanized Steel

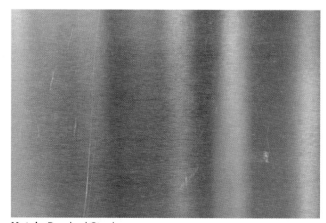

Metal: Brushed Steel

Metal Worn: Quilted Metal

Glass: Glass Block

Glass: Frosted Glass

Glass: Colored Glass

Wood: Plywood

Wood: Mahogany

Wood: Birdseye Maple

Wood: Purple Heart

Fabric: Blue Velvet

Fabric: Burlap

Fabric: Satin

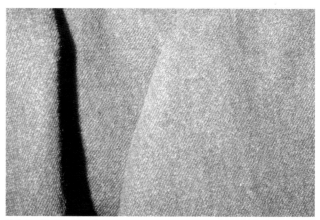

Fabric: Cotton Denim

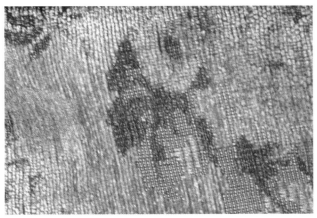

Fabric: Embroidered

Plastic: Black Stamped Vinyl

Plastic: Hard Acrylic Plastic

Stone: Brick Face

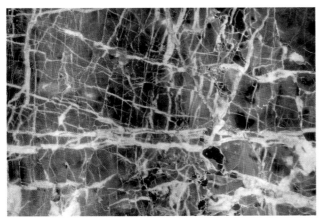

Stone: Marble

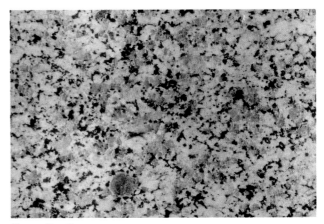

Stone: Granite

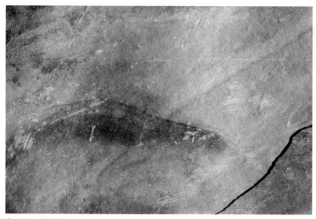

Stone: Slate

Stone: Agglomerated Stone

Concrete: Poured Concrete Sidewalk

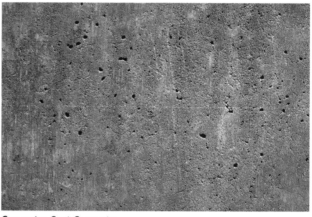

Concrete: Cast Concrete

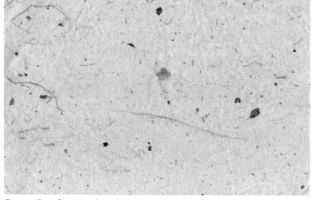

Paper Goods: Handmade Japanese Paper

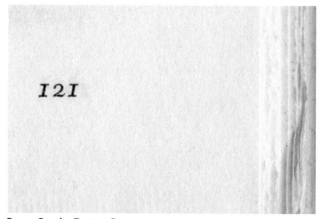

Paper Goods: Text on Paper

Paper Goods: Brown Paper

Misc. Materials: Asphalt

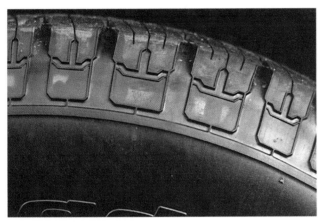

Misc. Materials: Rubber

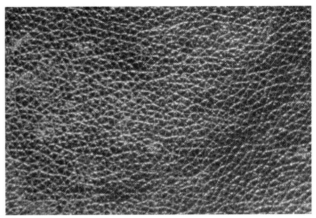

Misc. Materials: Leather

2.2 BASIC TEXTURES

Now consider the same materials with some basic textures added. I
could not always find an example of a material-versus-texture pairing.
Instead of a brass sheet material and brass sheet texture, for example, I
have found brass sheet material and brass doorknob texture. In other
instances I have a material and no matching texture—Japanese handmade paper material but no Japanese handmade abused paper. So, you
will have to use your imagination in such cases.

In order to achieve a believable representation of a texture in any art
style you must understand the subtle nuances that make up the texture;
what makes it tick?

Compare the textured versions with the "virgin" materials, exercising your artistic eye to identify the changes. Think of the textures as the layers on top of the base material in your paint package. Each layer has its own history and reason for being there, and in Chapter 1 you were given a number of categories you can consider to differentiate and separate the layers when encountering a surface.

Basic Textures

Metal Worn: Brass Plating

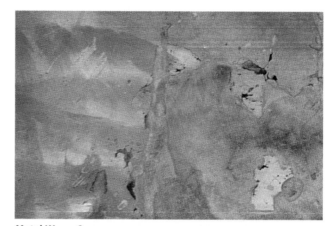

Metal Worn: Copper

Metal Worn: Galvanized Steel

Metal Worn: Brushed Steel

Metal Worn: Quilted Metal

Metal Worn: Rusted Iron

Metal Worn: Aluminum

Glass Worn: Scratched Faux-Frosted Glass

Glass Worn: Glass Block

Glass Worn: Reinforced Glass

Wood Worn: Plywood

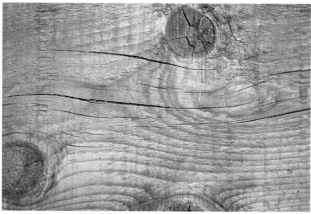

Wood Worn: Wood Plank

Worn Wood: Stained Oak Table

Worn Wood: Assorted Veneers

Fabric Worn: Blue Velvet Hat

Fabric Worn: Red Velvet Drape

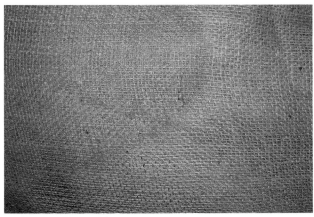

Fabric Worn: Burlap Sack

Fabric Worn: Satin Lining

Fabric Worn: Cotton Denim

Plastics Worn: Ripped Vinyl Chair Top

Plastics Worn: Pool Balls

Plastics Worn: Garbage Lid

Stone Worn: Brick Wall

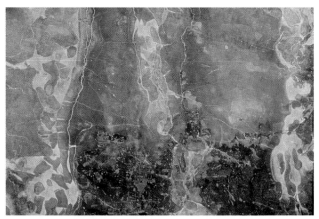

Stone Worn: Marble

Stone Worn: Granite

Stone Worn: Limestone

Stone Worn: Stone Road

Concrete Worn: Poured Concrete Sidewalk

Concrete Worn: Cast Concrete

Tile Worn: Glazed Ceramic Tiles

Paper Goods Worn: Cardboard Box

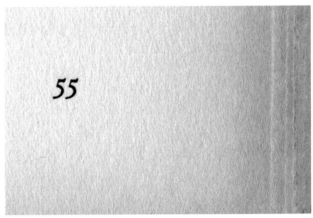

Paper Goods Worn: Text on Yellowed Paper

Misc. Textures: Dirt

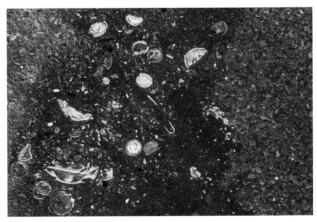

Misc. Textures: Asphalt

Misc. Textures: Rubber Tire

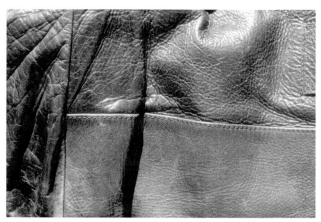

Misc. Textures: Leather

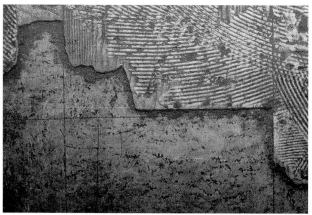

Misc. Textures: Linoleum Tile Under Wood

Misc. Textures: Auto Paint

The ability to differentiate between different types of surfaces and materials, as well as determining what makes up the surface and what gives the material its quality, is an important talent to develop. It allows you to make decisions quickly about the surfaces in your work as well as avails you with a new and exciting vocabulary through which to express it.

2.3 CREATING A MORGUE

An invaluable tool to start building right now is a *morgue*; a collection of images, photographs, samples and examples of colors and materials, and the like (see Figure 2.1). Your morgue should contain anything that visually inspires or affects you both in positive and in negative ways. It is a visual diary of sorts made from various sources, even your own work. It can contain real materials such as clothes, paper, rusty nails, washers—whatever you want to keep on record. For instance, I keep graphic design images to use for reference of type styles or current color usage.

2.1 Example of a morgue.

They all inspire me to create. Use your morgue not only as reference for reproducing textures for a project, but also to define your likes and dislikes—to see how they change over time. Morgues can be loose pages and items categorized into folders or pasted into sketchbooks or scrapbooks. This library-like collection is for you. Make it your own!

2.3.1 YOUR OWN PHOTOGRAPHS AS REFERENCE

I learned a great deal while taking photographs of textures and materials for this book. Like many of you, I am not a professional photographer, but I didn't let that stop me. They might not be the prettiest pictures, but they give me the information I need, the ideas I have been looking for, just as your own photography will do for you. The photographs you take do not need to be perfect in every way. Nothing ever needs to get in your way of finding reference, or creating it.

This book was a good exercise in encouraging me to rely on my own ability to capture what I needed from a photograph. I also learned a few lessons that may help you.

2.3.1.1 CAMERA CHOICE

Use a 35mm camera that has a reliable light meter either in the lens or handheld flash. If you have an automatic-everything camera, it is also helpful to set it to manual operation for focusing and bracketing purposes. In a pinch, you can shoot reference photos with an instant camera or a "party fun" camera, although these cameras lack the capability to capture the same level of detail as the professional types, because of the quality of their lenses.

A digital still camera can also be used to acquire reference materials. The one drawback is the resolution of the captured stills. Digital cameras vary in resolution. The two kinds I used for this book took pictures that ranged in size from 640×480 pixels (6.6×8.8 inches at 72 dpi) to 1536×1024 pixels (21.3×14.2 inches at 72 dpi). This means that if you need to enlarge these images for some reason, the detail falls apart because the pixels, which make up the image, start to become visible. Digital cameras are better for textures that remain small, for creating tileable textures, or just for reference shots. They are extremely easy to use and cost effective. There are high-end professional digital cameras that have much larger resolutions, but they have much larger price tags, ranging from $20,000 to $50,000 at the time of writing this book.

A digital video camera is another way to capture both imagery and sound, and is useful for recording audio and/or visual notes on the texture's natural environment. Like digital still cameras, digital video cameras are resolution-dependent, and the images cannot be enlarged without deterioration. The coolest feature about the digital video camera that I used was its capability to capture extreme close-ups. I had the lens about 1/16th of an inch away from my tabletop and the photo turned out beautifully crisp in detail.

2.3.1.2 FILM STOCK

Decide on the film stock to use based on when and where you are shooting. For this book I used Fujichrome Velvia 50 and 100 ASA for all of the outdoor shots and Fujichrome Tungsten 200 and 400 ASA for indoor pictures. Your choice is important, because colors will shift if you are not using the correct film speed. At all times I used transparency/slide film because of its color saturation and accuracy of detail. I prefer this to print film. If you are unfamiliar with the aspects of taking photographs such as: film speeds, grain, composition, lighting, indoor versus outdoor, and so on, then I suggest you look at books on the subject or take an introductory course in photography.

Make sure that you buy your film from a professional camera store. Film must be stored in a controlled cool environment and most corner stores do not have this facility. Keep this in mind at your end as well—carrying around your exposed film in your pocket for a month during the summer could also have an effect on the developed pictures.

2.3.1.3   ### BRACKETING YOUR PHOTOGRAPHS

An important procedure to execute when taking pictures is that of *bracketing*. It consists of taking three pictures: Take your first picture at the perfect light meter reading, take a second at an f-stop or half an f-stop below, and take a third at an f-stop or half an f-stop above the first setting. The results can be significantly different. A few of the pictures for this book were saved because of this technique. It may seem like a waste of film, but it is much more of a waste if you pay for developing bad pictures and have to retake them. Some photographers will bracket two or more pictures on either side of their first shot by 1/4 or 1/3 f-stop increments, but for your purposes, one on either side should suffice. You should be able to clean up and salvage one of the three pictures in a paint program, such as Photoshop.

2.3.1.4   ### RECORD INFORMATION

When you take a picture, be sure you record enough related information, such as the surroundings, f-stops, time of day, and the location. I must confess that it is a pain in the neck, and I did not do it for every shot in this book. If you can record the information, do it. It will help you get into the habit of looking around your surroundings. You will start to identify what may be affecting your photograph, such as cast shadows, the location of the sun, the amount of humidity, if any, and so on. All these things are good to know, especially a month or two after the fact. Instead of writing, try using a video camera or recording the information on audiotape. I walk around with a tiny tape recorder when I go out to get reference and "speak" my findings. Either way, I urge you to record somehow, and devise a system for cataloguing. This is information you do not want to lose.

2.3.1.5   ### SUNNY VERSUS CLOUDY

I took many pictures in both sun and clouds, and there are advantages and disadvantages to both. While bright sunny days offer you wonderful saturation and detail, the shadows cast from other objects onto the surface may confuse the textural information. Cloudy days, although they provide you with less saturated images, are void of harsh shadows and the lighting is more constant. In both cases, be sure you record enough supplementary information so that you can correct the photos, such as removing unwanted shadows or adding saturation, in a paint program later.

2.3.1.6 DEVELOPMENT PROCESS

You might take amazing photographs, but if you develop them at your neighborhood drugstore or supermarket you might not get the results you expect. The development of color film negatives or slides is a chemically intricate process. Fluctuation in temperature and time, or chemical impurity or staleness can create undesirable results. The same is true for the printing end of the process if you are shooting with print film. You will be much happier with your results if you spend the extra money and take the film to a professional photo lab. Find out where professional photographers send their film in your city and do the same.

2.3.1.7 SCANNING

Not all your reference (taken with a nondigital camera) needs to end up in a digital format, although there are times when it is really handy to have it at your digital fingertips. You never know when you might need to grab a texture off of one of your photographs to make it a tileable texture for your work or to send one of your photos as reference via email to the art director off-site. In these cases, you will have to scan in and touch up your photographs.

2.3.1.8 PHOTOCD

Most of the photographs I took for this book were immediately put on Kodak PhotoCDs. At first, I thought it was a bit expensive, but my time is also very valuable to me and I would much rather paint than sit at a scanner and scan in 400 slides. Besides saving you time, PhotoCDs give you a number of different resolutions, so you can choose which is best for your needs. Now I have a complete digital library of all my reference at the ready. Try to choose a shop that takes pride in what it does. This means that it first develops the film correctly and then makes sure there is little or no dust on the slide before it scans it (saving you time on the clean-up end). Also, if you pay a little bit extra you can get your CD back the next day. (Not all labs offer this, so ask first.)

2.3.2 MAGAZINES AS REFERENCE SOURCES

In addition to your own photographs, magazine clippings are a great way to beef up your reference library. There are multitudes of magazines published today from which you can obtain imagery and reference material. Here is a list of the types of magazines I use and what they offer:

- **Interior design or architecture magazines**   Building materials, paints and surfaces, environments, and color trends.

- **Fashion magazines**   Clothing, cloth, textiles, design, contemporary usage of colors, graphics, and fashion.

- **Industrial design magazines or annuals**   Contemporary surfaces, such as new synthetics, woods, and metals.

- **Graphic design magazines or annuals**   Typography, posters, packaging, color usage, and graphic trends.

- **Stock photography catalogs**   Moods, people and places, products, colors, use of light and textural qualities.

Whatever you are interested in is what drives you. It informs you as to where you will get your reference. This list is to get you started. Inspiration can come from any place. I collect reference constantly even if I do not have a specific project to work on.

Your own drawings or notes should be a part of this collection, as well. Lists of music and movies that inspire you should be too. Adding magazine clippings to your morgue makes sense. Doing so will save you time and money, and may completely do away with the need to take your own pictures as reference. Collecting on a consistent basis will make you ready for any project, and you are afforded more time when it counts. For instance, if you need to photograph something specific you can take the time to find it.

Having said that, I must provide a couple of points against using magazine cutouts verbatim as scanned-in textures.

The question of "reproduction rights" immediately comes to mind. The person who took the photo for the magazine, or the magazine itself more often than not, owns the rights on reproduction. This means that you must ask for permission or buy the rights to use their pictures in your project. The details and intricacies of this issue are far too complex and drawn out to get into here. This is just a friendly reminder that this concern exists, and you may be stealing someone's work if you use it without permission. So be mindful. This is not to say that you cannot use the photo as reference and paint it yourself, or your interpretation of it. Very rarely is there a texture that you pull from a magazine that form-fits your exact needs. No matter what the reference, it will always need adjustment here and there.

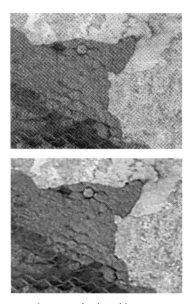

2.2 A scanned printed image comprised of cyan, yellow, magenta, and black dots may cause a moiré pattern (top). Using the "de-screen" function in your scanner's software will usually remove this from the scan (bottom).

The second point of concern is the structure of printed pictures themselves. If you look closely at a printed color photograph in a magazine, you can see the cyan, yellow, magenta, and black dots that make up the image. When scanning these pictures into the computer, this can create a moiré pattern (see top of Figure 2.2), and can be more trouble than its worth trying to remove it. Most scanners today have a *de-screen* function that in most cases gets rid of this moiré pattern (see bottom of Figure 2.2), and any evidence of the colored dots themselves. So if you are in the market to buy a scanner, be sure that it has this function in the software that comes with the scanner.

2.3.3 OTHER REFERENCE GOLD MINES

In addition to magazines for reference gathering, there are

- **Photography books**   You can glean textures, light and shadow, and color information.

- **Painting and art books**   Gold mines for learning how painters use brushstrokes to describe textures as well as color palettes. Art books also offer much of the same information as photography books do. Looking at the materials sculptures are made from such as stone, marble, and bronze can tell you about softness, brittleness, and pliability of the material.

- **Architectural and interior design suppliers**   They frequently have binders full of material and texture samples for real-world materials, such as tile, marble, wood, and cement.

- **The Internet**   Provides a wealth of information and reference. By entering keywords in any of the search engines available, you will most likely find a variety of pictures that can help you start your project.

Unlike many of the other specialties in this computer graphics business, a texture artist needs to accumulate an entire library of images, books, and materials from which to work to be good. It is up to you to know what something looks like and reproduce it; that is your job. It also helps your director or art director if you show images from your morgue to inspire initial ideas from which to start. Much work can be accomplished in this fashion concerning style, mood, and extent of detail. Then you may begin with a much clearer vision of the direction in which you want to take the project.

2.4 PHOTO GALLERY

So often we approach our projects with the attitude that the objects and surfaces we must texture are separate elements having no relationship with other things around them. We paint and texture the objects as if they stand alone when, in fact, these objects live together within an environment. They influence and affect each other as is evident in reflections and the wear and tear on an object or surface. This is the impetus of this section—to create a dialog between you and me and the photos that follow and put into practice exercising your artistic eye. I hope you did the exercises I set up in Chapter 1. Now let's take note of the interaction between real-world materials and items, and describe what's happening.

I took the photographs that follow while walking around New York and during other travels. In this exercise, all I'm doing is describing what I am seeing. See if you can spot what I am talking about.

2.4.1 NEW YORK BRICK BUNDLE

In Figure 2.3, look at how the pulley is constructed and what it is constructed of. The rope is not tied around the bricks because it would wear away and have to be replaced. As far as I can see, the rope is pulled through a hole drilled in the center of the bricks. I love the different colors of the three bricks and their condition.

If the bricks at this height indicate that the door of the garbage container is closed, then why are there scrapes higher up on the wall? Does the lid on the garbage sometimes fall into the container? Was there a different length of rope on an earlier version of the pulley? Why do the scrapes seem to get wider at the bottom? Is the paint on the wall being worn away or is the brick bundle leaving pieces of itself behind? Because the graffiti is being worn down I would guess that the wall and paint are being worn away.

Another interesting part of this picture is the branch-like pattern on the wall (top left). I didn't write this down when I took the picture so all I can do is guess. (See how important it is to write down supplementary details when you take the shot?) It looks as though the branches from the tree left their mark either from when the wall was wet, or from a very violent wind slapping them against the wall. (There are actual bits and pieces of the branches left on the wall.) Hmm. Would I have thought to put that in one of my pieces?

Does the graffiti just above the dumpster to the right bottom of the photo, look like it extends down the wall past the container? If so, then the container had to have been added later.

2.3 On Opposite Page
This photo was taken late in the day, around 4 P.M., on a shaded New York street.

2.4.2   SOUTH OF FRANCE WATER TROUGH

There are a number of things I would like to point out to you in Figure 2.4.

- Notice the different types of stone and their textural qualities. Both the top part of the wall and the bottom part are made from cut stone.

- Is the trough between the buildings stone tile? Because of how old the village is, I would guess that everything from the foundation of the house to its walls to the streets are all made from stone with very little concrete.

- Notice the cut indentation of the stone, the router edge. You would not need to model the indentation, the broken-off part near the bottom of the wall, and the three reddish-brown bricks (top-center); you could add these kinds of details to your wire-frames with your texture and bump paintings.

- It seems to me that to make the flowerbed, some sort of foundation of stone was laid and then a thin "paste" of concrete was laid on top. The stone layer beneath the poured concrete flowerbed can be created with one texture map; just remember to include the zone where the two materials meet and live next to one another.

- Notice the blue and black stenciled number and its over-spray onto the wall, as well as a remnant of an earlier painted arrow just above this. Beautifully subtle, but still evident.

- Take note of the crumbled away walls of the water drainage trough—no perfect CG edges here. I especially like the crack in the front corner of the flowerbed. Would you put one in your piece?

- Notice the dirt and dust that have settled on the wire gate horizontal framing. Also notice the subtle light reflection on the horizontal wires that cross the dark areas behind. How can you create the depth of this photograph?

- How would the dried-up, salt-stained part of the trough be expressed as compared to the wet part? What are the differences?

- Note the green algae-like color and the settled soot and sand in the water.

- Because of the overcast nature of the day, take note that there are no harsh shadows and that the saturation on the whole is low.

- Notice the lack of detail on the flowers and their leaves, but even so they are not just one shade of green or pink.

2.4   **On Opposite Page**
This photo was taken in the south of France in a little village called St. Clement. The light quality here seems to suggest a somewhat overcast day.

2.4.3 GREEN PAINTED DOOR

Several things draw me to Figure 2.5. The first is the rich green color of
the door and its beautiful bumpy textural quality. Look at all
the wonderful little details that are in this photograph.

- Notice the number of holes that have been drilled for different
  lock systems.

- The dust, which settled on the tiny boarded up window ledges and
  padlock apparatus, demands some attention.

- The ripped off plating made of some sort of mystery material is
  unprotected and rusting and creates a pattern with that ripped-off
  part and the glue left behind.

- Take note of the shininess of the paint, and the highlight color of
  its sheen.

- Notice the beautiful bashed up brass doorknob with paint rem-
  nants and the doorknob plate completely painted.

- Did you notice the pattern of the bumpiness on the door? What is
  it caused by—numerous paint applications, rust underneath, a thick
  paint roller? Notice the vein-like, high-lit edges from large dried
  and cracked portions being broken off, peeled off, and then
  repainted.

- Look at the different colors of rust, the painted over screws and
  spray paint graffiti.

- The color of the door is reflected in the metal objects on the door,
  the lock, and the doorknob.

2.5 On Opposite Page
A green-painted door in Soho,
New York.

2.4.4   UNIVERSITY AVENUE NEAR TWILIGHT

There are many things going on in Figure 2.6. Look at how the colors are affected by the moisture in the air. The saturation of colors of the buildings decreases whereas the saturation of the lights and the road itself increase greatly. Everything has taken on a slight bluish color. I love the color of the greenish lighting (how my film speed and aperture captured the fluorescent lighting) underneath the scaffolding on the left, and the golden-yellow light coming from one of the windows on the building just off to the right of center and up. Many of the windows are the same hue as the sky due to reflection.

If you cover up the sky and buildings in the distance, this could be a photograph taken at night. Hard to believe that there is that much light in the sky compared with the presence of light on the street. This is a product of contrasts. If you compare this sky to one of midday, this one would definitely be less brilliant. It seems much brighter though because everything else is comparatively darker.

Take note of the amazing depth of field, intrinsically a characteristic of twilight because of the angle of the light, now exaggerated by the moisture in the air. The buildings in the distance are just barely discernable. They are mostly flat, muted colors with light and dark boxes for their windows. As you move forward to the front of the photo, details start to become more apparent, but are downplayed much more than if this was midday because of the lack of sun. For example, you cannot discern every brick texture or even every brick on some of the buildings, and therefore, there is little "bump" information. There are still shadows on the ground under the cars. The sky and its ambient light are still powerful enough to cast shadows. How will these shadows change when the sun goes down completely?

Compare Figure 2.6 with Figure 2.7. What are the similarities and differences, and why?

2.6   **On Opposite Page**
This picture was taken on an autumn evening just as the sun was going down in New York City. It rained a fine mist earlier, which helped accentuate the effects of the twilight hours on the city.

2.7   **On Opposite Page**
This photo was taken in Venice around the same time of day as Figure 2.6.

2.4.5 AN OFFICE DOOR

Figure 2.8 is a good example of everyday wear and tear on a surface. By looking at this door I can imagine the stories it has to tell (at least how I perceive them). It is a steel door, which has been brushed to give it a shiny, wavy pattern. Notice how constant use has worn away this metallic, shiny finish. How does this happen? This door is fairly heavy because of how thick the steel is, so when people push through it they put their shoulders into it while others put one hand on the pushbar and the other where it is worn away. Also, when people open the door from the other side they often place their hands on this spot once the door is partially open to pull it open. I'm not sure why there are so many scratches in this area. Possibly from rivets, buttons on coats, and carried packages used to open the door. The same tool that created the brushed look probably caused the dark black-brown streaks in the worn away finish.

The pushbar reveals other textural affectations that apply to similar objects of the same shape. Notice how the edges of the bar have the finish worn off completely. Edges on objects like this are the first to feel the effects of human intervention, this is true for wood, plastic, glass, concrete, and so on. The fronts of these objects are less abused. This is an important point to remember to add to your textures for an added bit of realism.

I think my favorite part of this picture is the bolt in the middle of the pushbar. Look closely and you will see a radial scratch pattern on the bar itself. These are the kind of "human" intervention textures that I love to add (if I have the time) to my work. They add authenticity to my work. I can only image what or who made these marks, which is part of the story.

Notice how the doorframe meets the white wall and the slipping silver plate near the door latch. Take note that when things are constructed, they are far from being perfect. Something to consider.

2.8 On Opposite Page
This is a picture of the inside of the front door to an office in New York City. It was taken with a digital camera and flash.

2.4.6 ## RESTAURANT WALL

Notice how the paint on the fan's frame has been scraped and worn away, leaving the actual brushstrokes behind and revealing the warm wood material underneath (see Figure 2.9). Notice all the different hues and tones of blue.

- The random pattern of screws, some showing their heads, others filled in with dirt and grime hiding their details.

- Notice how all these surfaces butt up against one another or lay on top of each other. Each piece defines itself and its neighbor by trapping dirt and paint in the ledges, cracks, and meeting places of each material.

- The smudges and drips on the window panes—are they caused by a sloppy paint job?

- Look at how the reflection in the window panes is softly blurred. Why is this? Is the window greasy? dusty?

- Notice the pattern of the paint chipping off of the windows.

- Did you notice that the top-left window is cracked? How does that affect the reflection?

- Would you eat at this restaurant? (Just wondering.)

- The blue paint has a matte finish and therefore has no specularity or sheen to it.

The picture underneath (Figure 2.10) shows that the windows are not completely transparent, because they are dirty. There is also the contributing factor of the reflection, which hinders the clarity of the bottles and containers that lay behind.

- The bottom-two glass panes on the left are a molded, bumpy pattern that bends the light, which breaks up the articles behind them.

- The bottom-two panes on the right have some sort of wire mesh material behind them, which obscures the objects behind the glass. The long horizontal band of red in the top-left window panes—is it a reflection?

2.9 On Opposite Page
The photograph with the oily, dusty fan is texturally complex. This one is of a restaurant's kitchen window. It was taken around 2 P.M. on the shaded side of the street. I was particularly interested in the accumulation of grease and dust on the fan (as disgusting as it is), and all the different affectations of the glass frames and panes.

2.10 On Opposite Page
Another window section of the restaurant wall.

2.5 LOOK AND COLLECT

In this chapter, we expanded the idea of looking into one of collecting. Not only are you going around looking at many different examples of textures and surfaces, now you are collecting them into one place in a variety of different forms so they are at your fingertips when you need them.

I would like to round out your artistic knowledge with the theory of color. Color is one of the first things you notice about a surface, and I briefly wrote about recognition of color in shadows, and so on. The theory of color expands your knowledge from a visual aspect of art to a perceived aspect of art. When you encounter a color, in other words, it is not on a purely visual level; there are many other components attached to color that I would like to explore, and Chapter 3, "Color Theory," is about just that. There you will get acquainted or reacquaint yourself with colors and color theory.

2.6 EXERCISES

1. The ability to differentiate between different types of surfaces and materials, as well as determining what makes up the surface, and what gives the material its quality is an important talent to develop.

   Look at the photographs of materials and textures at the beginning of this chapter and see if you can start to distinguish the features that make up each surface.

   Identify what the common differences are between the virgin and textured samples.

   Look for patterns, lines, specks, and dots that describe the textures.

2. We have expanded the idea of developing an eye for looking to one of developing an eye for collecting. It is important to know what you need to collect and what to leave on the street or in the magazine. At first, it may be difficult to be selective. With experience and time, and management of your morgue, you will soon have a varied and impressive collection.

   Start setting up your own morgue by creating categories such as: types of materials, types of reference, colors, genre styles, preferences, likes and dislikes, and so on.

   Begin gathering photographic references from the sources I mention in the text.

Go to architectural suppliers, stores that cater to home improvement, furniture and bathroom stores, and so on, collecting as you go.

3. Start experimenting with picture taking. Get to know what it is you need to watch out for when collecting your own reference.

   Experiment with different types of film stock, lighting, and situations.

4. Like the pictures at the end of this chapter, rediscover your own photos and look at them in this new way.

   Scrutinize how materials meet or fit together.

   How perfect or imperfect is this joining?

   How would you re-create this in a painting or a 3D program?

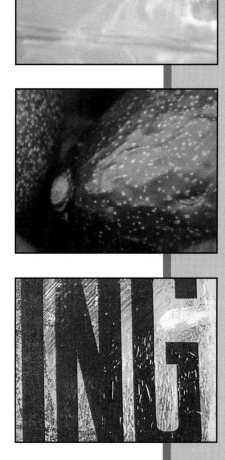

3

[CHAPTER]

COLOR THEORY

C OLOR IS ONE of an artist's most important tools. It assists the artist in expressing many facets of his personality; creates a signature. An artist can also create and manipulate a feeling or mood of a piece with her choice of color. To communicate visually and emotionally with your work, you need to be acquainted with the characteristics of color and its many variations. Even if you have already taken a course in color theory, this chapter will serve as a good refresher and may even give you some new perspectives.

3.1 ADDITIVE COLOR MIXTURES

Colors created by light in the natural world and recorded by your eyes and photography are known as *additive* colors. The term "additive" refers to the mixing of light. When equal intensities of the primary colors of light (red, green, and blue) are mixed, they produce white light. Newton discovered that white light diffracted through a prism produces a spectrum of colors: red, orange, yellow, green, blue, indigo, and violet. A good way to remember the order of these colors is to remember the name "ROY G. BIV." When there is no light, then all colors are absent and you see black; black is the absence, or absorption, of all light.

Look at Figure 3.1. The three primary spots of light and their mixtures produce very different results than what you would get by mixing pigments. As you can see, red light mixed with green light creates yellow as a secondary color; red and blue light produce magenta as a secondary; and cyan is the secondary color from a blue and green light mixture.

3.1 The three primary colors and their secondaries in additive color mixing.

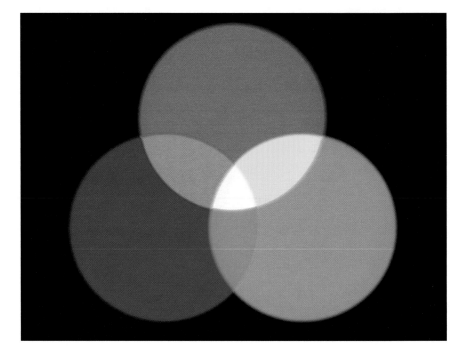

The center portion of Figure 3.1's chart is white because all three primaries are mixed together. In the additive color system, as more colors are added to each other they *add* to the purity of color or light, culminating in pure white. This method of mixing colors is opposite of the one you use for mixing pigments.

3.2 SUBTRACTIVE COLOR MIXTURES

The subtractive world of colors and color mixing is where most of us started as kids. It deals with the mixing of pigments such as inks, crayons, paints, and so on. Grade school art class taught you the three primary colors are red, yellow, and blue. You know that mixing red and yellow pigments gives you orange, mixing yellow and blue produces green, and combining red and blue gives you purple or violet. These color mixtures are called *secondaries*. The color wheel can be further divided to reveal tertiary colors, such as red-violet or yellow-orange, when neighboring colors are mixed together (see Figures 3.2 and 3.3).

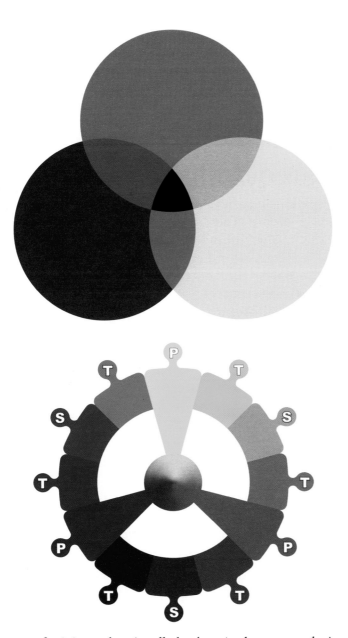

3.2 The three primary colors and their secondaries in subtractive color mixing.

3.3 The subtractive color wheel with its primaries (P), secondaries (S), and tertiary mixtures (T).

This system of mixing colors is called *subtractive*, because each time pigments are added to each other, the resultant color is less vivid or pure than the colors used to create it. Think of it this way: When light shines on an object, the light either passes through the object (as it does through glass), reflects back (as it does off metal), or is absorbed (as it is in a matte surface). Pigments absorb or subtract an amount of white light and reflect their unique color. "Hence, a combination of two such pigments is, by definition, the sum of their subtractions—or to put it in practical terms, a derivative color of diminished brilliance," wrote Charles LeClair in *Color in Contemporary Painting* (1991, Watson Guptill Publications/NY. p.47).

You should know both color-mixing paradigms because you will have to work in both. When you create with real paints (pigments), you create your textures primarily in the subtractive mode, and you might create your textures in the additive mode when mixing colors in your 3D program. You can work in either mode in Photoshop or Illustrator by selecting RGB (for additive) or CMYK (for subtractive) palettes.

3.3   COLOR QUALITIES

Whether mixed by an additive or a subtractive process, all colors share some common qualities. They are called *hue*, *saturation* or *intensity*, and *value* or *brightness*. Most 2D and 3D applications use these terms when dealing with color mixing and choosing. For instance, when you choose a color from a color "picker" or "wheel" in your paint program you can choose to use different modes for that color chooser. There is HSB (Hue, Saturation, and Brightness) mode or HSV (Hue, Saturation, and Value) mode. Defining these terms will make things easier when you begin to decipher colors, or look at photos and paintings together.

3.3.1   HUE

When you look at a color, the first thing you notice is its *hue*, its color: The vase looks *blue*, and the scarf looks *red*. Each color on the color wheel is a hue. A hue can also define similar or like colors; turquoise blue, ultramarine blue, and sky blue are all blue hues. The terms "hue" and "color," for the most part, will be used interchangeably throughout this book. Hue is the color you start with. Take a look at Figures 3.4 and 3.5.

3.4   Notice all the different hues present in this picture.

3.5   Now notice the shifted hues after changing the hue/saturation to (–65) left and (+65) right in Photoshop.

3.3.2 SATURATION/INTENSITY

Saturation is a measure of a color's purity or brilliance. Remember, in subtractive color mixing, the more colors you mix, the less pure the resulting color. Figure 3.6 shows two pure saturated colors and their less saturated, diluted mixtures. Saturation can also be thought of as *intensity*. How intense is the color you are looking at? In your 2D and 3D programs, saturation is adjusted by a slider that reduces or increases pigment or intensity. Color saturation can be taken completely out of a photograph, leaving a black-and-white version of the picture. Figure 3.7 shows how saturation can be decreased or increased in Photoshop.

3.6 The bar on the right shows the decrease of saturation from the pure hue on the left.

3.7 The picture on the left has had its saturation decreased. The one on the right, increased.

3.3.3 VALUE/BRIGHTNESS

Value or *brightness* is the light or dark quality of a color, or hue. Light or pale colors are regarded as high value, while dark colors are defined as low-value. Figure 3.8 shows value scales of purple and orange. The pure color lives in the middle, and by adding white successively to the color you lighten its value and create *tints*. By adding black successively to your pure color, you darken its value and create *shades* of the hue. In your 2D and 3D programs, value is controlled by a lightness or brightness slider that adds darkness or lightness to the present color, leading to complete black or white. Figure 3.9 illustrates this point with the flower picture.

3.8 The different values of purple and orange. The darker values are called shades, the lighter values are called tints.

3.9 The picture on the left has had its darkness increased. The one on the right, brightness or lightness increased.

Sometimes it is difficult to discern value as opposed to saturation. Both can affect each other. Areas of color in shadow may also look less saturated. In the twilight hours, the imminent night sky seems to suck out all the saturation from the world, adding its own blend of blue hues. In effect, both value and saturation are affected by the loss of light.

3.4 COLOR SCHEMES

The additive and subtractive processes describe the technical side of color mixing, but do not address the subjective or artistic side of bringing together a color scheme for an image. Nature composes and uses color successfully and effortlessly. I have never walked through a forest or open meadow and thought, "Wow, what an awful color; that doesn't fit here at all." Nature has been an artist for millions of years. Those of you newer to the craft need to work at your color choices when it comes to your compositions. The experience of other artists, however, can help provide a few guidelines. What follow are a few different color schemes, which you, as an artist, will use during your career as a texture artist.

3.4.1 COMPLEMENTARY COLORS AND COMPOSITIONS

Complementary colors are colors that enhance, strengthen, and brighten—in other words intensify each other. On a color wheel, complementary colors live directly opposite from one another (see Figure 3.10). The most basic or common complementary pairs are red and green, blue and orange, and yellow and violet. When complementary colors are mixed together, all the colors of the spectrum are present and they create middle gray as they cancel each other's chroma.

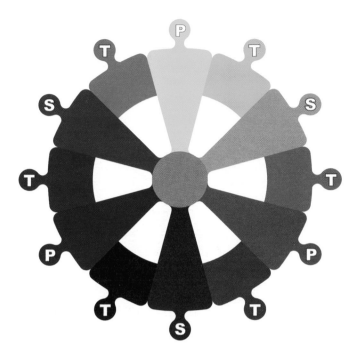

3.10 The basic complementary colors on the color wheel. When two complementaries are mixed they cancel each other's chroma and create what is known as middle gray.

These colors live in a harmony of vibration and contrast. The scientific definition of complementary colors is stated as, "a primary color opposite the secondary color produced by the other two primaries." (*Dictionary of Art Terms*, Thames and Hudson Ltd., 1984.)

For example, take a look at the red/green complementary pair. Red, a primary, is complementary to green, which is a mixture of the other two primaries, yellow and blue. Complementary colors are not limited only to the pairs mentioned previously. Other combinations can be found on the color wheel. For instance, yellow-orange, a tertiary color made from a mixture of orange (a secondary color), and yellow (a primary color) is a complement with blue-violet another tertiary hue made from blue (a primary) and violet (a secondary).

Van Gogh, Monet, Matisse, and the Fauves are just a few of the painters that use a complementary palette to express energy and vitality in their work (see Figure 3.11). This is not to say that they always did this, but they knew if they wanted to evoke a higher energy, a complementary palette was one way in which to achieve it. This energy is created by the dynamic opposites of the complementary hues; dynamic because of the constant vibration between them. Could this be why advertising designers adopted the scheme for themselves?

The painting by van Gogh shown in Figure 3.11 demonstrates a beautiful use of complementary colors. Because these colors are more complex complements, they retain a high-energy, but sit down enough to welcome the viewer in. In other words, your eyes do not feel attacked by the large amount of yellow and the colors do not feel overly acidic or loud.

3.11 The dramatic use of complementary colors in this painting, *L'Arlesienne*, by Vincent van Gogh belies the subdued nature of the sitter.

The Metropolitan Museum of Art, Bequest of Sam A. Lewisohn, 1951. (51.112.3) Photograph ©1979 The Metropolitan Museum of Art

As mentioned previously, designers and advertisers also take advantage of these complementary palettes as seen in supermarkets, magazines, and on TV.

Take a look around the next time you go to a store and see how many variations of these complementary harmonies speak to you from the shelves (see Figure 3.12). Purple type on a yellow background or a picture of oranges set against a dark blue background—all vibrating and vying for your attention. A classic example is the many combinations of the colors red and green stores decorate themselves with to evoke the spirit of Christmas.

3.12 Complementary colors used in advertising to get your attention.

Aside from looking at artists and designers for clues on how to use color, you can look at nature. As mentioned previously, I have never seen nature go wrong when it comes to color. Take a look at a wild field on a sunny day, and it seems that there are always clusters of purple flowers with clusters of yellow flowers. Red poppies always stand out when there is a field of green around them in the French countryside (see Figure 3.13). It is fascinating to witness. I suggest a field trip for anyone who is interested.

3.13 In real life, these poppies, with their velvety red against its perfect complementary color, lush green, brings life to this grassy field.

3.4.1.1 SPLIT COMPLEMENTARY COLORS AND COMPOSITIONS

Split complementary colors are found on the color wheel by choosing the first color, finding its complementary color opposite it, and then choosing the colors that live on either side of the complementary color.

For example, see Figure 3.14. The first color is green, its complement is red, but instead of choosing red, pick the orange-red and the red-violet. The feeling of these split complements in compositions is a little more harmonious than straight complementaries, yet, they retain a high energy. They are a little less obvious choice for your palette and add a bit more complexity in your composition.

3.14 An example of split complementary colors.

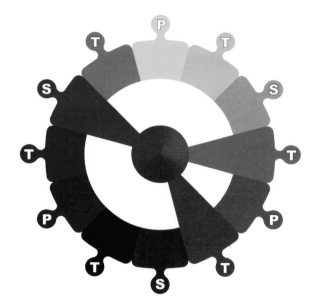

DOUBLE-SPLIT COMPLEMENTARY COLORS AND COMPOSITIONS

Double-split complementary colors are similar to split complementary. This time, the colors that live next to the complementary ones in both cases, are used. In Figure 3.15, when you pick orange and blue as your complements, it follows that you use green-blue and blue-violet with yellow-orange and orange-red as the colors for your palette. Once again, this color scheme is another step forward in harmony, a little more complexity but still very high in energy and vibration.

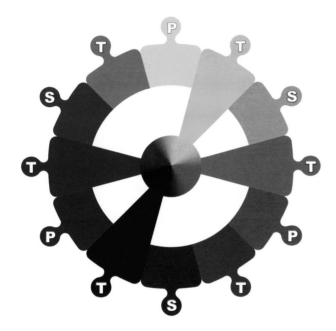

3.15 An example of double-split complementary colors.

TRIADIC PALETTES AND COMPOSITIONS

Still another high-energy color combination can be found by using a triadic color selection. Triadic colors are found on the color wheel by choosing three colors that are equidistant from each other. The primaries (red, yellow, and blue) are triadic colors, as is yellow-orange, red-violet, and blue-green (see Figure 3.16).

3.16 An example of choosing triadic
colors.

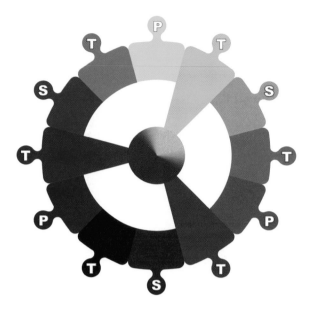

3.4.3 ANALOGOUS PALETTES AND COMPOSITIONS

Another palette that is used in compositions consists of analogous colors.
Analogous colors are neighbors of each other on the color wheel (see
Figure 3.17). These colors tend to live more harmoniously and peaceful-
ly with one another because they are relatives of each other. They can be
less vivid or saturated, less bright, more subtle and muted, although not
always. They have less contrast and vibrational energy than complementary colors. Think of the purple, blue, and magenta colors in a twilight
sky or the yellows, golds, and oranges in an Arizona desert. A pine forest
has light greens to blues and purples deep within its depths.

3.17 Analogous colors are neighbors of
each other on the color wheel.

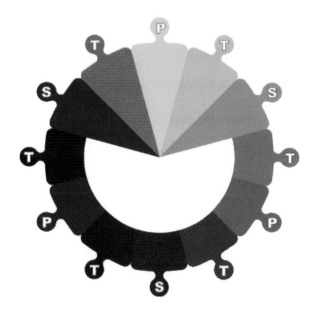

The painting in Figure 3.18 and the photograph in Figure 3.19 have analogous colors in their compositions.

Tom Thomson, Autumn's Garland ©1916, oil on canvas, 122.5 × 132.2 cm, purchased 1918 National Gallery of Canada, Ottawa

3.18 In this painting, Tom Thomson uses a wide range of analogous colors from the color wheel.

3.19 This photograph shows a more muted range of analogous colors.

3.4.4 MONOCHROMATIC PALETTES AND COMPOSITIONS

Another color scheme that artists and designers use in their compositions is monochromatic color. Monochrome colors are created by picking a color on the wheel, adding black or a darker color incrementally to create *shades* of that hue, and adding white incrementally to the original color, or by diluting it, creating *tints* of that hue. Figure 3.20 shows the color wheel with shades and tints created. Their energies are more subdued and peaceful due to the lack of color contrasts. Monochromatic compositions are very harmonious, (see Figure 3.21).

3.20 This color wheel illustrates each color and its monochromatic values.

3.21 This photo, taken at St. Stephens Cathedral in Budapest, dramatically demonstrates the effects of light spilling through the opening in the cathedral ceiling creating tints and shades of the stone's color in a monochromatic composition.

3.5 WARM AND COOL COLORS

The "cool blue" ocean or the "red hot" fire are some of the adjectives we use to describe things in our world. We relate to our environment in several ways, one of which is kinesthetically (an imagined or subjective sense of feeling), and describe our world to others as if we could touch, even untouchable items. Not only can the ocean be cool to the touch, but also the color blue itself represents coolness. Even though the whitish-blue part of a flame is hotter than the orange-red part, we still do not relate blue to warm things. The same is true for warm colors. If the ocean turned red one day, would you walk toward it with great trepidation? Fearing that if you walked into it you would be consumed like a moth by a flame?

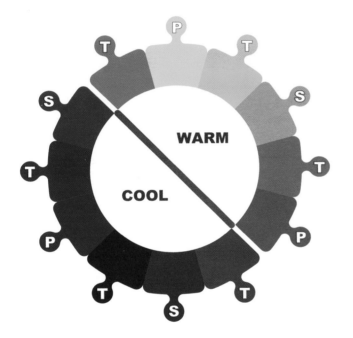

3.22 I have divided this color wheel in half to show you the division of warm and cool colors.

As a painter, you need to learn about the warmth or coolness of colors because the energies given off by such colors deserve their respective places in your compositions. Cool colors tend to recede from us, and warm colors tend to advance toward us. This is valuable information, because you need to understand how to give focus to certain elements in your scenes (see Figure 3.22). If some element needs to take a background plane, you can give it a cool overtone or cool lighting. If something needs to pop out, then you can give it more warmth. Green, blue, and purple are cool colors, while red, yellow, and orange are warm ones. There are many other combinations of warm and cool colors though. For instance, you can cool a red down by adding blue to it or warm a green up by adding yellow.

3.23 Notice the beautiful hues of blue in the trucks in contrast with the warm orange-red bricks of the buildings. Which color pops out at you the most?

Shadows are, for the most part, cool in color, which helps them sit down on the surface and anchor the object that casts them. This is not an absolute. Some painters can get away with surprisingly warm shadows, and I would suggest that you try this as an exercise when you are painting. Try to find some paintings that exemplify warm and cool compositions. Figure 3.23 shows warm and cool colors occurring naturally in New York.

3.6 COLORS—PSYCHOLOGY AND PHYSIOLOGY

Beyond suggesting warmth or coolness, colors can have a psychological and physiological effect on all of us. As an artist, a user and manipulator of color, you need to be aware of some of these effects. This section on color psychology and physiology is a combination of personal observation and the ideas and observations of two major authors and their books on the subject: *The Power of Color* by Dr. Morton Walker, and *Color Psychology and Color Therapy* by Faber Birren. These two authors, and the experts they cite, delve much more finely and deeply into this vast area of color theory than there is room for in this book. I have taken the highlights, as it were, from these sources just to give you an idea of what it is you are dealing with when considering color. If you are interested in furthering your knowledge here I suggest you give them a read.

From this research, it seems that the jury is still out on the definitive psychological effects of color on living things. Yet, certain professionals, such as chromotherapists (therapists who use color for medical purposes), believe color affects us so powerfully that subjecting patients to different colored lights has curative qualities for their various ailments. This is not a New Age idea. Dr. Morton Walker, in his book, *The Power of Color*, p. 32, states that,

> "…The ancient Egyptians, for example, built temples for the sick that were bedecked with color and light. They set aside special colored rooms as sanctuaries where the sick could be bathed in lights of deep blue, violet, and pink. Native American Indians also used color for healing…to fight chronic illness and to heal injuries sustained during buffalo hunts and intertribal warfare."

According to William G. Cooper, president of the Cooper Foundation, (a nonprofit educational organization offering natural methods of healing to the public), in *The Power of Color*, p. xiii;

> "…Light is a nutrient and, like food, is necessary for optimum health. Research demonstrates that the full spectrum of daylight is needed to stimulate our endocrine systems properly."

I give you these two examples to show you that the use of color is not reserved simply for pretty picture making. It is a subject taken quite seriously by other professionals aside from artists. Many books have been written on color and color psychology, and I suggest that you consult the reference section of this book to find some extracurricular reading that supplements the highlights I cover in the following sections. By looking into the psychology of color more deeply, you can better influence and illustrate the message, mood, and flavor of your projects.

So, how do we feel about one color over another? We all have personal color likes and dislikes based on our own lives and experiences. Whether you love red, and hate orange based on some wonderful or tragic event in your life, there seems to be underlying similarities with color and living things, not only humans. In this light, take a look at the colors of the spectrum.

3.24 Not exactly sport cars, but red seems to be the color of choice in Budapest, Hungary in 1989.

3.6.1 RED

Red is the most arrogant, attention-grabbing, and energetic color of the spectrum. In terms of temperature, it is the warmest color. Emotionally, we relate red to love and passion. Red is the color associated with our hearts, roses are red, and so are boxes filled with chocolates on Valentine's Day. It is the color that excites us most and makes us take notice—the color of stop signs, fire engines, and alarms. Red is an in-your-face color that demands your attention, and not a color that sits idly by waiting for you to take notice. Because red excites us, it is not the choice of color in psychiatric wards, prisons, or hospitals. Excessive subjection to red can lead to agitation, anger, and even violence. "It stimulates appetite, increases breathing, and elevates blood pressure." (*The Power of Color*, p.51)

Advertisers and designers who understand this can easily manipulate our attention with it. Sale items in stores display red tags. Fast sports cars, and now, even *not-so-fast* cars are often painted red (see Figure 3.24).

3.25 The color of autumn, orange, is clearly apparent in this photo from the city of, what was once called, West Berlin.

3.6.2 ORANGE

Orange is a warm color because it is the marriage of red and yellow, and is considered a happy and lively color. It represents Halloween and Thanksgiving and is the color of autumnal landscapes and fire's flame (see Figure 3.25). Not as energetic as red, it is known to "…stimulate creativity and ambition along with energetic activity." (*The Power of Color*, p. 15) It has a luminous, glowing quality that captures our attention. Orange is the color used for construction signs on roads and highways. It is a popular color in sports as seen on many jerseys (oftentimes coupled with blue, its complementary). It is not considered as an elegant color.

3.26 This no-parking sticker hopes to get your attention. Does it?

3.6.3 YELLOW

A warm, bright, and vibrant color that represents many things to us, yellow is the color of the sun, gold, spirituality, and inspiration. On one hand, we relate yellow to goodness and joy, on the other, cowardice and caution. Would the "happy face" be so happy if it were red instead of yellow? Yellow is the color chosen for yield signs and warning labels (see Figure 3.26). The color of graphic lightning bolts, it suggests energy and electricity. Used in interior design, it brightens up the room that is otherwise dull. Yellow roses are a symbol of friendship, less passionate or threatening than red ones.

3.27 The freshness of these avocados is heightened by their vivid green coloring.

3.6.4 GREEN

The color of the vegetal world, green represents freshness and nature (see Figure 3.27). Its cool quality soothes, calms, and has great healing powers. Surgeons dress in green, "complementing" red blood. Green represents life, hope, and growth. We can be green with envy, green at our job, or have a green thumb. Where it doesn't belong, green has negative connotations—on a person's face it suggests sickness, and on non-green food is the color of decay.

3.28 This picture taken in Arizona, can only begin to tell the story of how truly refreshingly cool the blue water is.

3.6.5 BLUE

A cool color and the hue of the daytime sky, blue is the most sedate of all colors (see Figure 3.28). Blue can "…slow the pulse rate, lower body temperature, and reduce appetite." (The *Power of Color*, p. 52) Designers use blue to describe ice and minty freshness. It symbolizes the heavens and divinity. It is a fairly serious color depending on its variations. Blue is the color of choice in the business world when it comes to logos and suits. Overexposure to blue can create depression, as in, "I'm feeling blue," or "I've got the blues."

3.29 The purple irises help to calm the sunny courtyard of this hospital where Van Gogh once stayed.

3.6.6 VIOLET/PURPLE

Violet, the most exotic color, has long represented royalty. Back in the middle ages, because of how it was acquired and made; the color crimson is made from the mucous glands of snails. It takes a thousand snails to yield 1 gram of crimson making it was very expensive and only royalty could afford it. Therefore, subliminally it can represent wealth, both monetarily and spiritually (see Figure 3.29). It is the color of the twilight sky, exotic bird's plumage, and butterflies. In spiritual terms, it represents transition, as evidenced by Lent and Advent colorings. It is a deep, mysterious hue. It is mystical and meditative.

3.30 Pure? As the driven snow.

3.6.7 WHITE

When all colors are present in perfect balance, we see white. White in all its perfection is known to symbolize purity, truth, and goodness (see Figure 3.30). "Pure as the driven snow," or "a white lie," are a couple of the many statements to describe this quality of white. In old western films, the good guys always wore white. White suggests antiseptic cleanliness. In religious paintings, white is the color reserved for the presence of the Holy Spirit, God's robe, and glowing angels.

3.31 The mysterious beauty of black.

3.6.8 BLACK

In light terminology, black is the absence of white light, and therefore the absence of all colors. Black can represent the antithesis of white and is known to symbolize white's opposites, the "bad guys," and deceit. It is the color of funerals, death, and mourning. The "Black Market" and "Black Monday" are examples of the negative representation this color has on us. However, it is better to be "in the black" than "in the red." It can bring us feelings of despair and loneliness. It is also mysterious, the color of night, and the place and habitat of shadowed detail (see Figure 3.31).

3.6.9　THE PRACTICAL SIDE

So what does all this color psychology have to do with you and me? Knowing how colors affect you emotionally and what you link symbolically to colors will allow you to better place colors to get desired effects in your work. For instance, if you have to texture a circus and capture all its energy, you will probably want to stay away from less energetic colors, such as blues and greens, and go straight for the more energetic reds and yellows for most of your palette. Conversely, if you are texturing a hospital for the criminally insane, you will probably want to steer clear of bright yellows and reds and head straight for the calmer, cooler colors and even muted values of these.

It is beneficial, for you in the working world of deadlines, to narrow down and focus on the range of possibilities. Using these guidelines and hints can help you develop the right set of ingredients at the start of any project. Reinventing the color wheel and its psychological impact may be a great thesis, but you will probably only receive glazed-over looks from your director. This is not to say limits can't be pushed, just do not try it on a tight deadline. With that said, remember that these are only guidelines and the loose and isolated color categories of blue, red, black, etc., can't begin to define the possibilities in their many tints and intensities, and their relationships with other colors.

3.7　STUDY PAINTINGS IN MUSEUMS

Color is, more often than not, an expression of the times. There is much to be learned from the masters of painting of the past and the present, regarding the use of color. During the Renaissance, for instance, artists used color to express what they saw in front of them (adding their own flavor, of course), and contemporary painters use color to evoke the mood and essence of the subject. One of the best ways to study color and color usage is to become familiar with a few artists' work.

What is so rewarding about studying painters is that they have already done much of the work for you. They have sweated over their craft to provide a playground of paint by numbers for the rest of us, illustrating textures as they saw them. All we have to do is look and take note.

Sometimes in the real world, it is difficult to see all aspects of a surface, its color and texture. The light on the subject may be too hot or it may be in an awkward place to get close to it. Studying paintings is the simplest way to see the aspects of a subject such as colors and their highlights and shadows that may allude you in reality.

In the masters' paintings lies a plethora of ideas and answers to everything I have raised in this book thus far. I myself refer to them time and time again. I urge you to treat yourself to a tour through an art gallery, and make it a habit that will last you throughout your professional career.

Short of that, Chapter 4, "Paintings," is a walk through an art gallery I've created for you, filled with some pieces of art I like best. Here, I attempt to apply all the principles I have written about: the art of seeing and looking, identifying materials, surfaces, and textures, and the art and psychology of color. Walk with me now and see what there is to learn from paintings.

3.8 EXERCISES

1. Scan in one of your photographs and start playing around in Photoshop (or your favorite paint package) to become more familiar with hue, saturation, and value, brightness and contrast, etc.

   Take that same photo and manipulate it to change the time of day or the light-source. For example, if the photo was taken on a sunny day, change it to a cloudy day, or change it to night. Make it look like an old 1900s photo, and so on.

2. In high school, my English teacher gave the class an exercise to practice writing styles. He would pick an author's book and choose a paragraph. Then we were asked to mimic the style by putting nouns where there were nouns, commas, verbs, adjectives, and so on. Doing this allowed us to see the style unfold.

   Looking at a painting, maybe one from this book, study and mimic the schemes complementary, split complementary, analogous, etc.

   Get your hands dirty and paint the painting, mimicking the brush-strokes and style.

3. The psychology of color:

   Create a painting of a calm environment with energetic colors or vice versa. What do you have to do to make those colors behave? Do you have to mute them? Make them less saturated as from red to pink?

   Take a tour around your city, your town. Go to hospitals, municipal buildings, churches, dance clubs, sports arenas, cafes, restaurants, diners, different shops, law and doctor offices, etc., and walk through them, noticing the color scheme. Notice how you feel.

Try to determine what a room or area is used for. See how effective the colors are in providing the environment it set out to. For instance, in the waiting room of a doctor's office do you feel calm? Do the colors help or hinder your mood?

4. Get acquainted with your own color preferences and the emotional or physical reactions you have to them.

Paint an abstract color painting with the sole purpose to explore colors. Do not feel the pressure to make "Art."

How do the colors affect one another when mixed together?

Which colors do you keep reaching for?

Which ones do you use the least?

What mixtures do you like? Dislike?

Do any colors make you feel physically ill?

Lucian Freud, English, b. Germany, 1922, Two Japanese Wrestlers by a Sink, oil on canvas, 1983-87, 50.8 × 78.7 cm, Restricted gift of Mrs. Frederic G. Pick; through prior gift of Mr. and Mrs. Carter H. Harrison, 1987.275
Photograph courtesy of The Art Institute of Chicago.

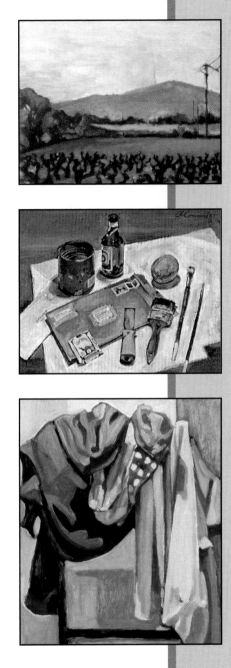

4

[CHAPTER]

PAINTINGS

I HAVE TALKED A GREAT DEAL about *how* to look and *what* to look for. Now it is time to put theory into practice by looking at some paintings. Each of the twelve paintings in this chapter illustrates and elucidates key points from the previous chapters, and using my artistic eye, I describe what I perceive to be the valuable lessons I have learned from each one of them. Follow along with your own developed artistic eye, and see if you agree with the observations. This exercise demonstrates the value of looking at the work of others to further your understanding of materials, textures, and surfaces, as well as, to cultivate an appreciation of what it takes to express these through your craft.

4.1 EVOLUTION OF A STYLE

Looking at paintings, especially, emphasizes that there are many different ways in which to express the same things. These different expressions are what begin to create "style." It is important to look at these works first with an eye of emulation, while working toward an understanding that you will eventually define your own style through this type of exploration.

One way you will begin to define your own style is through your use of color. Every one of the painting masters—Rembrandt, Michelangelo, David, and the others—developed a "signature" color palette during the course of their careers. They knew their colors, and became attached to certain ones which "spoke" to them, and their art. Their expression became inextricably linked with the colors that they chose to use. Their works are described with the same hues and tints of color, which became part of their "trademark."

You, like them, will be able to explore what color means to you, whether you wish to over-saturate or de-saturate it, mix it up or keep it pure. With practice, you will develop your own personal palette. Once you know how to see colors in the natural world, you will be free to do what you want with them. Look at paintings, become aware of what you see and begin to identify this individuation.

Another way that artists define their style is through the application and use of their chosen medium. When I first began oil painting, I had a lot of trouble just handling the paint itself. It was either too thick or too thin, the colors were mixing to mud, or I was using altogether the wrong brushes. It is the same with anyone learning to use a new tool—it takes time. With the help of my painting teacher, I was able to get past all these barriers and start to create more acceptable paintings. The more I painted, the more I became selective about the type of paint and brushes I used and what mediums I mixed the paint with, how to roll the brush as I painted to keep a thin line, as well as how to keep a steady stroke. All of this adds to defining a personal style. Willem de Kooning, p.132, for instance, paints with the strangest looking brushes. The bristles are over four inches long, giving his paintings that fluid, calligraphic look. These brushes and the amount of paint he uses, along with his arm movement further define his style.

Just as your handwriting is an inextricable part of your own expression (unconscious or conscious), so too eventually your style will become a part of you. It already exists in you. You just have to draw it out. So, whether you have a fluid arm movement or a jittery, short-stroked one is neither good nor bad, it is just simply you!

Artists throughout the ages have defined their style in many ways. While it seems that before the 1800s, most painters "hid" their brushstrokes, expressing their paintings in the *trompe-l'oeil* (fool the eye) genre, it is true that the thickness of the paint was played and experimented with by classical to contemporary painters alike. The crusty thick paint on the face of a sitter for Rembrandt is there to show volume and realism as much as it is of the face of a sitter for Freud.

4.2　SUBJECTS THAT INSPIRE

Subject matter is another part of what makes art a personal experience and again defines an artist's interest, along with color, stroke, and style. Ultimately, though, it is left up to interpretation by the on-looker, what each individual experiences when looking at a particular painting. Gerhardt Richter, p.136 paints landscapes, portraits, and still lifes in a realistic style. Of his paintings he says, "I am not trying to imitate a photograph; I am trying to make one. I'm not producing paintings that remind you of a photograph but producing photographs." Edward Hopper, p.124, paints the isolation of American urban and natural landscapes. Lucian Freud, p.144 is primarily concerned with painting the human form and recognizes its temporality as well as the heaviness of existence.

During your career, you will be able to paint many different subjects or styles, and you will eventually discover which of them interest you and which do not, sticking with the ones that really inspire you to keep painting. So get to know what you like to do. In the CG field I am interested in the challenge of making CG look non-computer generated. What I mean is that I am much more interested in the dirt and scratches of a surface, which express its history. Surfaces that have aged a bit and show it are, to me, more interesting than surfaces that are crisp, clean, and "perfect." Because I know my preferences, I make sure I take every opportunity to get involved in a project that calls for my kind of texturing. You, eventually, will gravitate toward the types of projects that best suit you, and use your talents to the utmost. Your preferences are what make you, you. And, frankly, what make you marketable. So do what inspires you.

Art is a passionate profession and I do not want to be a jack-of-all-trades. Rather, I would like to become an expert at what I love to do. Anything less than that is a compromise. The artists that we will look at would certainly agree. It is also a reality that even the best artists must do things they do not want to. It is up to you to find out what you can live with doing, and to ensure that you never lose your artistic eye. For example, even when Michelangelo was painting the Sistine Chapel, he was sculpting the "slave" series at his studio. He was a sculptor at heart.

If you are just starting out on the road of art, then I recommend experiencing all sorts of art, styles, and subject matter. It is not natural, as an artist, to narrow your focus too soon. I have learned a lot from working on projects that I did not want to work on at first.

Edward Hopper, Morning Sun. Columbus Museum of Art, Ohio: Museum Purchase, Howald Fund

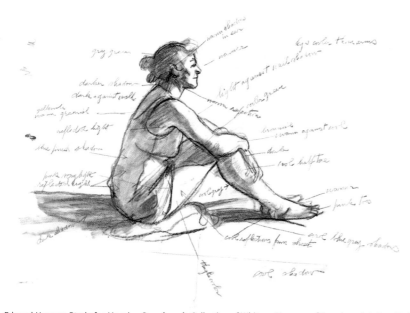

Edward Hopper, <u>Study for Morning Sun</u>, (1952), Collection of Whitney Museum of American Art, New York, Josephine N. Hopper Bequest

4.3 THE PAINTINGS

We all see things differently, and we are drawn to different things at different times in our lives. What inspires me in the paintings of the "masters" that follow, may not inspire you. As I explain what about them helps me understand my role as a texture artist, I invite you to express your own observations and appreciation of these paintings. Above all, really look at them.

4.3.1 MORNING SUN
EDWARD HOPPER (1952)

The first thing that draws me to Hopper's work is his color usage. He is very meticulous about painting the colors he sees. Look at the sketch and color notations he made for this painting.

Look at the beautiful purple in the shadows on the white sheet, as well as many other subtle hues—blues, greens, ochre from the reflected wall color, the color of the shaded wall versus the lit part. Hopper effectively shows us how the sunlit part of the wall—a relatively warm color, can be cooled-down just enough to sit back and not interfere with the figure's place up front. Note the greenish colors in the skin's shadows against its sunlit pale creamy hues. Look at the green behind her ear!

Texturally, his paintings are wonderfully simplified. The sketch-like depiction of architecture by his use of sparsely applied, scrubbed on pigment, gives the paintings an energy of colored undulation that is fresh and not overworked. He saves his thicker application of paint to describe the figure. He is less concerned with the actual surface quality, such as the bumpiness of some surface, and more concerned with the color-texture information. For instance, the sky outside the window is painted in much the same way as the interior wall, and parts of the woman's skin are painted similarly to the sheet. He is more interested in capturing the essence of light interacting with form. This is not to say that each item in this painting looks like every other, not at all; the white sheet is soft and warm from the sun, the wall is hard and mottled, the flesh, milky and soft, and the window frame suggests wood covered with green patchy paint. Hopper lets his brushwork subtly describe the textural information for his surfaces. This is where his true genius lies. I see all he is trying to say and all that he feels with an economy all of us CG artists definitely need to learn from.

On Opposite Page:

Edward Hopper is one of my favorite painters. His color and his brushstrokes fill in the blanks on several levels. Look closely at the sketch and compare the color notes to what he actually painted, i.e. under her calf reads "cool gray." Is it?

Charles Bird King
Poor Artist's Cupboard, c. 1815
oil on canvas
In the collection of The Corcoran Gallery of Art,
Washington, DC
Museum Purchase, Gallery Fund, and Exchange

Hopper's concern for color and his lack of detail is the extreme opposite expression than say de Heem's *Sumptuous Feast* (p. 130). Where de Heem entices you to appreciate the painting on a salacious level, almost shallow and lecherous, Hopper speaks of a deeper feeling of sensual longing or visceral melancholy. The hot, bright sun, the bed, and the way the women stares out the window all evoke a reflective mood that speaks of the morning after. There is no mistaking the mood in any of Hopper's pieces.

4.3.2 *POOR ARTIST'S CUPBOARD* CHARLES BIRD KING (1815)

I am drawn to this painting because of the artist's sensibility and sensitivity toward the subject matter—paper and books. I can feel the texture of each different type of paper just by looking at it. I can hear how they would sound if I were to touch it.

King understands the many important qualities of simple things—as simple as a piece of paper. He creates that delicate balance of depicting the edge of a page without actually *painting* an edge. He creates the translucent quality of paper, conveys what pages look like bound, and captures the subtle coloration of aged paper. His brushstrokes are fairly loose and he lets the quality of these brushstrokes define the subtle texture of the cloth-bound books and the pages themselves. The piece of bread on the plate suggests very successfully its fluffy freshness without having to paint each and every yeast-producing air pocket. He achieves all this realism without being overly concerned with fooling you into believing that this is a photograph.

 The water-worn, crinkled pages of the book *Advantages of Poverty*, the pattern of the light thrown by the water glass against the pages, and the colors that live in the shadow are all painted beautifully. I love the way he uses the brilliant red for the folder in the foreground to draw your eye back down and through the painting, and the subtle transparency of the "Sheriff's Sale" note in the upper-left corner. I love the softened edges of the *Pleasures of Hope* pages and the worn away binding on the book just behind it.

Overall, colorwise, this is a very warm painting and it is nicely balanced by the smatterings of blue hues—particularly the roll of paper, the plate, the reflection on the knife, and the tiny blue bookmark in the *Lives of the Painters* book.

On Opposite Page:

I find it interesting that with all the white paper in this painting there is little pure white pigment anywhere to be found. Don't you?

The Old Cupboard Door by William Michael Harnett (1848-92) Sheffield Galleries and Museums Trust, UK/Bridgeman Art Library,
New York

4.3.3 *THE OLD CUPBOARD DOOR*
WILLIAM MICHAEL HARNETT (1889)

I just had to include this painting because of what is represented in it. I love broken and abused things. This piece is successful in three ways.

First, all the surfaces express their true qualities to me. The old tambourine is excellently depicted. Harnett captures what is probably waxed animal skin expertly. The cloudy depth of the paper underneath it is beautiful as well. (The corner is just about touching the animal skin surface. Can you see it?) There are stains on the thinly painted wood from the rusty hinges. Look at the heads of the nails and screws on these hinges—some rusted, some not, one missing, one broken off. The abused and cracked wood from nails being yanked out and the torn, dog-eared papers add to the rest of the elements, which speak of a time gone by—memories and reminiscences. These are the things that you could miss out on if you are not mindful. Because it is possible to make perfect surfaces and duplicate them, we forget that sometimes things get banged up, parts break and go missing, all signs of age. These are the qualities and the characteristics of a piece that can start speaking to an audience.

I love the cracked and chipped plaster wall, as well as the worn-away edges on the frame of the cupboard, because they are not overdone. All of these, along with the pewter candlestick holder, the bronze statuette, and the crackled tiny ceramic vase are wonderful examples of this artist's love for these items and his undeniable ability to capture surfaces, materials, and textures. Even the string demands our attention. His level of detail seems quite consistent and not overworked allowing our eyes to wander over the painting's surface, seeing it as a whole. And so it is with remembrances. A brochure, a ticket, a dried rose equally hold our attention while we remember an event.

The second way this painting is successful is that the items also evoke some feelings for me. They cause me to reflect on my own life, and what has meaning for me. The artist must have had this kind of attachment to the objects he painted. What do you think?

The third way this painting is successful is in terms of color harmony. The palette lives together effortlessly. The rust, the violin, the papers, the metals, and so on, are all the more believable due to the accuracy of color and the harmonic blending of the whole.

Which depiction of paper do you like more? Harnett's or Charles Bird King's?

On Opposite Page:

What do you suppose the green splotches on the key are? Would you have thought to break one of the hinges off exposing the unpainted wood underneath?

Jan Davidsz. de Heem, Sumptuous Still Life with Parrot 115.5 × 170 cm courtesy of Gemäldegalerie der Akademie der bildenden Künste in Wien

4.3.4 *SUMPTUOUS STILL LIFE WITH PARROT*
JAN DAVIDSZ DE HEEM (1660)

This painting is almost a complete encyclopedia of materials and textures. It is an amazing piece of reference for realism.

The somber, muted background wall, the faded, serene landscape, along with the dark blue-black velvet cloth on the table in the foreground all provide an unencumbered backdrop against which to paint the rich saturated colors of the still life's items. These items are then juxtaposed, enhancing one another and creating excitement and interest by contrasting their different qualities. One reflection is contrasted with another, one textural quality with another, one color against another. The parrot is a study in contrasts itself. There is the play with spatial relationships: The curve of the parrot's body mimics the curve of the plate, and the hardness and edge of the metal piece contrast with the amorphous soft quality of the parrot.

Looking closer, I begin to see a play with groupings: The parrot, the plate, the meat, and the basket make one specific grouping which forms a center, creating movement and contrast. This particular arrangement helps your eyes sweep from item to item in an almost swirling motion. An attempt, perhaps, to make you dizzy and even nauseous, which overwhelms the senses. What a party!

Looking at each individual item, I am drawn in particular to the wonderful depictions of the metals—silvers and brass, the golden platter, and the silver and gold tassels of the fabric. He has captured with perfection the dusty dull and polished aspect of grapes, as well as their mouth-watering volume and translucency. Take note of the colors of the highlights on the fruit, glass, and metals. Are the colors what you would have expected? Notice how he lets details fall away to depict distance and shadow. The reflections in the silver sweet tray on its side (bottom-left corner) are wonderfully detailed and more crisp than the reflections in the brass item (lower right). The glass items seem to have the more crisp reflections on their surfaces, which at first almost seem false, if you forget that the objects are most likely crystal and not just plain glass.

While admiring the painting's strengths, I also take note of its weaknesses. For instance, some of the items have materials that are dubious to me. I am not sure what the black fabric is that is hanging above the parrot. The silver-capped jug-like container in the bottom-right corner could be glazed pottery or some sort of metal, but I am not exactly sure. Is this just because I have never seen anything like it, or did de Heem just not "nail it on the head?" The highlights in both of these mystery materials give me no clues as to what the materials really are.

On Opposite Page:

As the title suggests, this truly is Sumptuous. But how does de Heem do it? He creates this sumptuous quality by exciting contrasts.

de KOONING, Willem.
Woman, I. (1950-52)
Oil on canvas, 6' 3 7/8" × 58" (192.7 × 147.3 cm).
The Museum of Modern Art, New York. Purchase. Photograph © 2000 The Museum of Modern Art, New York.

4.3.5 *WOMAN 1*
WILLEM DE KOONING (1950–52)

I chose this painting to illustrate the extremes in paint texture and palette choices. De Kooning is an abstract expressionist and his use of color and vigorous mark-making illustrates his passion and energy for his work. There are many things going on in this painting, yet it manages to come together as a whole. How does de Kooning achieve this?

First, he achieves a successful balance by his use of color. At first glance, if you are not familiar with de Kooning's work, you may think that he made very few color choices for his palette. True, there are many hues present in this painting, and it is the amount and the placement of these colors that balance the work. This is not an easy task. When you are working in the abstract realm, it is a difficult thing to know what the work needs to be complete, as opposed to looking at a model sitting in front of you and painting in a realistic style. If you look at other paintings by de Kooning, you will see that he indeed has his own unique palette. Notice how he uses green to provide a cool background for the warm reds, yellows, and whites of the figure.

Secondly, like the other painters' styles in this chapter, de Kooning's style, or mark-making, is another unifying factor in this chaotic figurative landscape. The energy and vitality of each stroke are his own. There are no concerns with minute textures, no real representation of believable skin or cloth. Just the essence of the body entangled in a forest of thick gestural paint; gestures that are completely de Kooning. How does he use the paint texture to draw your eye in and around this piece?

If you can, try to paint a purely abstract work in oil, water color, or acrylic. Don't worry about what it will look like in the end, do not try to create a work of "art." It is more important for you to learn about paint for paint's sake. Start moving it around, let it mix together, explore mark-making, shape creation, color composition, and best of all, texture making. How many different types of textures can you make using one brush? You can learn a lot from this type of *playing*!

On Opposite Page:

What is it about you and your painting style that is, like de Kooning, completely you? Explore your color preferences, composition of shapes, and brushstroke styles, by painting an abstract work.

The Metropolitan Museum of Art, Marquand Collection, Gift of Henry G. Marquand, 1889. (89.15.21)
Photograph © 1993 The Metropolitan Museum of Art

4.3.6 *YOUNG WOMAN WITH A WATER JUG*
JOHANNES VERMEER (1660–67)

In this painting, the textures look stylized in a paint-by-numbers way. Art historians suggest that Vermeer used a tool called a *camera obscura* to trace his compositions. It is a camera-like apparatus that projects an image onto a piece of paper or glass plate. A somewhat blurred and highlight-dotted image is sometimes the result due to deficient lenses. If you look closely at Vermeer's work, you can see these tiny pockets and soft patches of color coming together to describe the whole. Whether this is due to the camera obscura, to me, is not as important as Vermeer's decision to keep these details in his work, recognizing the wonderful quality of depth and detail it gives.

For instance, the richly painted thick and heavy tapestry that covers the table looks as though each and every thread has been painted. However, upon further scrutiny, this is not the case. The same applies for the map, an article that appears in many of Vermeer's works. It suggests that each of the streets along with their names are included, showing this artist mastering his craft and painting only what is needed and nothing more, to get across these textural qualities to express realism.

One of my favorite parts of this painting is the wall texture. Much care and observation went into painting it. Take a good look—notice the many subtle nuances. As well, when I first saw this painting I was overwhelmed by the stark white head-cloth that the servant is wearing. Look at all the multitude of colors that exist in this one piece. Notice the wide range of tones from pure white to gray, with the blue of her frock showing through expressing its slight transparent quality. Compare the color of the highlights on the gold water jug to the whites on this headpiece. Which one is pure white? This painting, like so many of his others, is elaborately rich in color. The ochre in the map, the alizarin and cadmium red of the tapestry, the deep indigo frock complementing with the butter-like color of her vest and the wall, all superbly combined in this piece. Can you see that there is an overall golden sunlit quality to the painting? Each color carries the color of the sun in order to unify the painting as a whole. See how the reflections in the jug and basin are depicted, and how they describe the surfaces they rest on.

A great lesson to be learned from this work is the quality of the edges. Some are hard and some soft. This creates the convincing presence of sunlight, creates depth, and lets objects live in harmony with each other.

On Opposite Page:

Do you like the glass-pane window? What is in the box?

RICHTER, Gerhard.
<u>Wiesental</u>. 1985.
Oil on canvas, 35 5/8 × 37 1/2" (90.5 × 94.9 cm).
The Museum of Modern Art, New York. Blanchette Rockefeller, Betsy
Babcock, and Mrs. Elizabeth Bliss Parkinson Funds. Digital Image © 2000
The Museum of Modern Art, New York.

4.3.7 *WIESENTAL — GRASSY VALLEY* GERHARD RICHTER (1985)

Bet you thought this was a photograph! I did. Gerhard Richter is a very interesting artist. His painting style is at once quite simplified and graphic, achieving a photo-realistic quality that defies the brushstroke.

So, how does Mr. Richter do it? How does he, with very little detail make us think we are standing right where he stood? I attribute this realism to the level of detail. From this painting, if we look hard enough, we can see that even in the distant muted pasture, which looks as if it is one flat tone, it actually has very subtle color and textural information going on. This stops the painting from becoming flat. Our eyes pick up on this subtle information and move back and forth across all these patches and flecks of tonality. This is so important to remember. Often, times we think a wall is one color so we paint it with that one color. Even the most soft or subtle variation in color or tone will help a texture seem just that much more believable. Painting with oils or acrylics can allow this to happen quite naturally because of the nature of the pigments mixing and blending into one another—not so with computers. We need to make this happen consciously if we are to imbue our own paintings with vitality.

This painting illustrates the beauty of atmospheric depth and how colors become muted and less saturated, and details diminish with its presence. Notice how the sky color seems to seep over the distant vista. Compare this painting to the pictures in Figure I.2, in the Introduction. It teaches us that this softness in detail does not lessen its realistic quality. In fact, the softness exemplifies realism; it *is* realism. Even in the foreground where we would see the most detail in crisp focus we allow the painting this camera-like characteristic of choosing our focal point for us—the hill just behind the first clump of trees. Remember this trick for one of your projects when you want to control the focus!

On Opposite Page:

Can you smell the grass? Can you hear the traffic off in the distance?

The Metropolitan Museum of Art, Robert Lehman Collection, 1975. (1975.1.186) Photograph © 1998 The Metropolitan Museum of Art

4.3.8 *PRINCESSE DE BROGLIE*
JEAN-AUGUSTE-DOMINIQUE INGRES (1853)

If you ever want to know how to paint fabric just look at Ingres' work. Other than the semistylized face and skin, I am convinced of every surface's authenticity in this painting. The satin dress, the silk fabric on the chair, the transparency of the lace shawl about her shoulders, the silky gloves, the gold molding on the wall behind her, the metals and pearls of her jewelry. All these elements are wonderful references, showing us how to reproduce these things for ourselves.

Notice how different fabrics fold. Compare the crinkles and folds of the blue satin with those of the lace and the soft white cotton throw over the chair. What is the range of tonal value in these fabrics? What is the deepest color in the blue satin dress? In the white cotton? Once again look at all the sizes and colors of the highlights, and notice the sheen of each different material. Remember that highlight size and color are very important qualities to capture accurately when describing a surface. The slightest discrepancy can completely alter its truth. For example, you can easily make a metal surface that you are trying to produce look more like hard shiny plastic by simply changing the highlight color to white. So beware of using white when expressing fabric or metallic highlights.

Take note also that as realistic as this work is, Ingres has not painted every last detail of every thread in these fabrics, so we need not do the same if we desire a similar look.

Look at how little detail there is in the skin. Do you see any signs of brushwork? Ingres' color palette in this painting is very stunning. The elegant cerulean blue dress next to the golden-green chair, the tiny traces of red in her jewelry and coat of arms on the wall, all expertly balanced. The muted tones of the background wall and the fabric covered bench complement and force into the foreground the delicate tones of the porcelain skin.

One thing Ingres has done successfully, and has made look easy in fact, is to sit the diaphanous lace shawl atop the woman's skin. The color chosen for that overlay could have so easily ruined the painting. His expert eye in color recognition is responsible for this success.

On Opposite Page

What color are the shadows in her skin? How does he keep the coat of arms in the background with all its little details? Jean-Auguste-Dominiqie Ingres (1780-1867).

Nicolaes Ruts. Copyright The Frick Collection, New York.

4.3.9 NICOLAES RUTS
REMBRANDT HARMENSZ VAN RIJN (1631)

Rembrandt's works must be seen in person. Photography cannot capture Rembrandt's technique of expressing skin, which upon close examination, is comprised of many layers of thick paint and glazes that blend into the most luminous flesh I have ever seen. Rembrandt mastered the technique of applying a glaze of dark tones overtop the dried *impasto* parts, then, wiped away the glaze leaving it only in the recessed areas, producing a beautiful 3D effect. Painters from this time began their paintings with a thin coat of dark burnt-umber or reddish-brown stain on the canvas on top of which the thicker lighter hues were added. If a dark tone was needed sometimes, this canvas ground was left showing through as seen in this painting on the shoulder, parts of the fur, and parts of the dark-shadowed skin. It is an interesting technique to try when creating textures for the computer. Start from dark and work to light.

Notice how he successfully depicts the fur collar and hat. It is definitely soft. Even the silhouette suggests softness. The frailty of the white lacey semi-transparent collar is also wonderfully painted. I especially like the sheen from the dark-black leather on the sleeve compared to the rougher leather of the coat. I can feel the weight of this man's clothing and how hot he must have been posing for this painting.

Compositionally, Rembrandt moves our eye in and around this painting in a circular fashion by using colors, their values, and tones. The head surrounded by the white collar is first and foremost the main attraction, then the white note and the hand that holds it. These are the two most important elements to see in a portrait of this era. The face, of course, is self-evident, and the note is probably of some significance of the person he is or what he does. Moving further on down to the hand resting on the red leather chair, finally rising up to the warm orange fur on the shoulder. The elegant and subtle hues and values on the wall with the darkness falling from the top of the picture exaggerate this motion and help our focus remain on Mr. Ruts.

See how he lets details fall away as they retire into the darkness of the picture. Rembrandt, as well as Carravagio and George La Tour, was a master at using *chiaroscuro*, "…the technique of modeling form by almost imperceptible gradations of light and dark" (*Dictionary of Art Terms* p. 48), to create beautiful depth in atmosphere and mood. This is where you need to take note as a CG artist. Don't be afraid to let parts of your composition fall away into the shadows. Not everything in life is perfectly lit like it is in product photography for magazines and TV.

On Opposite Page:

What kind of brush and brushstroke do you think Rembrandt used to paint the soft fur of the man's outfit?

© Bildarchiv Preussischer Kulturbesitz, Berlin, "Bouquet of Garden
Flowers in a Pitcher," Johann Wilhelm Preyer (1831).

4.3.10 *BOUQUET OF GARDEN FLOWERS IN A PITCHER*
JOHANN WILHELM PREYER (1831)

Organic items, such as flowers, are quite difficult to reproduce success-fully on the computer. Although with this painting as reference, we can begin to recognize the textural qualities that help us distinguish them from things like plaster walls and marble surfaces. With reference like this, we can get closer to their true essence. What is that essence? This painting shows many of the attributes of flowers—delicacy, frailty, healthiness, and fragrance. The textures themselves are delicately painted, and not expressed with a heavy hand. The smooth blend of colors illus-trates their softness.

There are no harsh shadows on the undersides and the volumetric quali-ty of the flowers and bountiful depth of this bouquet, are not lost. Notice the different highlight colors and qualities on the large green leaves. The lower ones are not as shiny as the top ones which gives us the sensation that the top leaves are waxier (reflective) and in direct sun-light. Johann Wilhelm Preyer knows what to do to create depth. His trained eye tells him to paint in great detail what extends out toward him from where he stands, which is what lends authenticity to the reali-ty of the viewer. He most likely scrutinized the front flowers because their textures are exaggerated enough to shrink the perceived distance between you and the flowers—a dynamic experience. Your eye perceives distance as lack of detail, and the flowers in the back express just that. To paint them with detail would have made the painting over-textured and difficult to look at. CG painters must keep this in mind. Just because you can texture everything does not mean that you should or that it is even necessary.

My favorite part of this painting is the large ox-blood red and yellow flower. He has faultlessly captured its pattern and its partially dusty sur-face quality. The pitcher that the bouquet sits in is also very scrump-tiously textured. The speckled, slightly bumpy surface is no doubt ceramic because of its white highlight glaze.

Look at how much variation and interest he can get from using basic monotone hues for the leaves and most of the small delicate flowers. Each of these seems to be painted with nothing more than subtle varia-tions in value of the main hue. I love the usage of the orange flowers in the center of the bunch. It creates just enough interest in the piece and our eye returns there almost imperceptibly and then carries on through the piece. Without this, it would be a very different painting.

On Opposite Page:

Do you like the marble slab texture? Does your nose get itchy when you look at the hanging yellow flowers? What is the ring made of?

Blond Girl, Night Portrait (1980-85) by Lucian Freud, Private Collection for Bridgeman Art Library, New York.

4.3.11 *BLOND GIRL, NIGHT PORTRAIT*, LUCIAN FREUD (1980/85)

Lucian Freud analyzes through paint what his grandfather Sigmund Freud analyzed through psychiatry. But, unlike his grandfather, he actually looks at his subjects—intently. (Freudian psychology seats the therapist behind the "subject.") The human condition of the subject and physical presence is more clearly realized than if we were actually in the room with the model. His mastery of color and brushstroke as well as his accuracy in depicting form, for me, are unsurpassed. Even though we are keenly aware of his skillful thick application of oils, the first thing that pops out is the dimensionality of his subjects and props. Each stroke defines the form like a sculptor defines form with clay. Much like Rembrandt's painted skin or van Gogh's thick painterly style, the subsequent blending of these strokes is a natural happenstance of his style of painting. The brushstrokes define the movement of the figure and then the curvature of the couch. The carefully chosen hues, which sit next to one another, give the illusion that they have been blended together with a soft brush.

His flesh-tones are gorgeous and not at all exaggerated. Look carefully at your own skin and you too will see the light violets, pale yellows, ochre, gray blues, gray greens, warm and cool creams, and vermilion reddish browns that Freud has in his works. Then, at the same time, the depiction of the skin is almost hyper-real because the quality of the skin is modeled by the colors he uses, suggesting that he looked closely at its color. The coloring of the legs and the arm of the couch allow them to sit in the foreground, but not without the white sheet. In this way, he creates depth. The face takes on a darker pallor for the same reason. Freud creates visual balance, so the only disturbing part about this painting is the circumstance it portrays.

Freud captures the personality of the beat-up old couch on which the model slouches. Is he really trying to comment on the model's state of mind? Heavy, bulky, tired, and worn. Freud lovingly paints them both— as if they were one. Yet the couch seems to have more vitality than the model. Is this where Freud starts to play with contrasts? He sees contrast not in color—his palette is analogous and subdued, but in the "presence" of different elements, such as physical and mental presence. For instance, the model has the foreground, yet is she truly present? And the couch is in the background yet, it insinuates itself into the foreground. Is it alive? The fabric painted by the same painter in the same manner as the model, however, is not made of flesh or is even fleshy. It is cloth stuffed with cotton and not muscle. It does not have the same luminous quality or complexity as the model's skin and therefore there is no confusion as to the different surfaces in this painting.

On Opposite Page:

His mastery of color and brushstroke as well as his accuracy in defining form, for me, are unsurpassed.

There is an excellent give and take, or contrast, also, in the level of detail. The wooden floor is void of any textural information besides the actual brushstrokes, and even the couch at its most detailed is not as defined as the model, giving the main focus to the figure.

4.4 STUDY AND QUESTION

I could show you hundreds, if not thousands, of my favorite paintings and discuss the multitude of things to be learned from them, but I won't. I will stop here and leave the rest to you. Do some looking for yourself at a museum or gallery, and develop your own repertoire of paintings that speak to you. It doesn't matter if the gallery shows old or new works of art, only photography, or only sculptures. There is much to be learned from all the forms of art.

4.5 EXERCISES

Visit a museum or gallery and bring along your sketchbook. While looking at works that inspire you:

Make sketches.

Take color notes.

Keep in mind these questions:

- What is the mood of the piece?
- What is the style of the work?
- How much atmosphere, depth of field is present?
- How does the piece make you feel?
- What is the quality of light?
- What is the color palette?
- Are the colors saturated or muted?
- Is there a good balance of warm and cool colors?
- What are the contrasts? Severe? Soft?
- How much detail is there?
- Can you see the brushstrokes?
- How do the brushstrokes and paint define form and texture?

- How are the materials and textures represented or treated? Realistic? Stylized?

- What is the focal point?

- How does the composition enhance the work?

- How does your eye travel through the piece?

- If you're studying sculpture: How does the light play off of the surface?

5

MAKING DECISIONS

WHEN BEGINNING A PROJECT, there are a few things which you can do to help it move along smoothly—considering all the details and available information.

When you gather information, make sure you

- Ask the right questions before you start.
- Take advantage of pre-production materials, such as story-boards.
- Know your media, audience, and style.
- Consider factors while texturing the project, such as special effects, mood of the piece, and so on.

Throughout this chapter, you will learn more about these issues from a general point of view and then you can begin to apply them to your own projects specifically.

5.1 ASK THE RIGHT QUESTIONS

When I was in art school, studying illustration and design, one of my instructors drove home the point that as designers we must do a lot of research in order to get a feeling for the direction of our designs. Every class project, we would spend anywhere from two days to a week—a third of the allotted time—collecting reference materials, watching movies, looking through books and magazines, filling our heads with the concrete examples of our vision for the styles and looks of our pieces.

As you research, you automatically start to put together all the puzzle pieces of your finds, synthesizing all the information you have gathered to make a whole from disparate fragments. Eventually, you can express your thoughts through these reference fragments in a way you would not have conceived of perhaps before you began. The results will inspire you and help you overcome those creative blocks all artists find themselves in from time to time, and help you take the project in new directions. The same applies in the CG world. It doesn't matter whether you are working on a TV show for preschoolers or a full length multi-million dollar movie, someone is paying you to find a creative solution, and this solution is found by exposing yourself to a multitude of reference materials that inspire you.

As visual artists, it is your responsibility to give clients the look they want, and how successful you are at this rests on your ability to ask the right questions.

Recently I was talking to the director about the main character of a project I was art-directing. He explained that he saw it living in lichen-infested walls. With this little information, I could have walked away to begin painting what I thought he meant by "lichen-infested" and my own ideas of it. I was curious, though, to know what he was really thinking when he said that, what he meant by the term "lichen-infested." So I asked, "Is the room made of rock or concrete?" I thought he would answer rock, but to my surprise, he said concrete. This may seem elementary, yet it opened up a dialogue that involved his visual ideas and mine, which was very satisfying. He started to have fun with it and continued to describe the environment. He saw dripping water, and dimly lit stairs with darkness falling into the corners. He thought the project's character had lived there for quite some time, and that the room was musty and dark. I suggested a few things to round out the visual. He agreed and I went away and created the final piece in a matter of hours, which he approved the first time around.

By taking the time to ask a few simple yet direct questions, you can save many hours of wasted creative energy and by asking questions, you walk away much more confident to start the job. The questions can be the same ones you asked yourself during your visualization exercises earlier in this book, creating stories for each material you use in any given project.

5.1.1 THE QUESTIONS

Before you can make decisions on what you need to texture and how, you must learn as much as you can about the project. Start asking questions of the clients or review the information they have provided for the project. The following questions are ones that I ask for each and every project I am involved with.

- **What pre-production materials are available?** For example, a storyboard, board-a-matic, bible, or pre-vis movie?

- **What do the storyboards tell you?** For example, ask about the length of the shot, the setting of the piece, the time of day, and the mood of the shot. What does the dialogue track offer? Are there any close-ups? What is the depth of field? Is the camera moving and is there any motion blur? Are there any special effects?

- **What is the style of the piece?** For example, is it realistic, hyper-real, stylized, simplified, graphic, or fantastic? What are the client's impressions?

- **Who is your target audience?** Find out what demographic the piece should be aimed at, as well as the targeted group's likes and what they believe in.

- **What medium is the final piece in?** Is it for television, film, the Web, print, or for a CD-ROM or Playstation game?

Depending on the project, the specific order in which these questions are asked can vary, but in one way or another they all provide critical information to your job of creating textures.

5.1.2 THE PROJECT

The DuneBugs project that I will be using as an example for creating textures is a real project that I worked on with Curious Pictures. Because it is a "real-world" example of a project that was modeled, animated, rendered, and composited, and it contains a good variety of materials and textures to paint ranging in styles, I thought it would be a great example to learn from. Because it was a proof-of-concept rendering, the project was quick and dirty. It took eight days for me to do my part.

The DuneBugs_firstPass movie on the CD is the first final rendered test that was put to tape and shown to prospective networks. This initial project shows you what can be done in such a short time. When given even a longer deadline, you can produce some impressive results. For this book, I reworked most of the textures, and as you work through the book's exercises, you'll see what a little more time can give you.

> **NOTE**
>
> Decisions are made at each and every stage of a project. Constructs can change midstream due to some unforeseen hurdle or because of the client's wishes, so do not hold on to any particular set of decisions. Projects are living and breathing organisms, and have minds of their own. We are really only project-tamers keeping the wild beasts in line.

ON THE CD

Take a look at the "DuneBugs_firstPass.mov" or "DuneBugs_firstPass.avi."

As I stated earlier, the order in which I ask the questions, and the order in which I list them here is arbitrary. Usually all these questions are answered virtually at the same time, so the order doesn't matter. What matters is that you understand that one depends on the other.

With that in mind, you're ready to examine more closely the key questions themselves.

5.2 WHAT PRE-PRODUCTION MATERIALS ARE AVAILABLE?

As texture artists, you decide (with the client) what details are necessary, how large you are to paint the texture maps, and what needs to be lit. Invaluable tools in this process are *storyboards, board-a-matics, bibles, and pre-vis movies.*

5.2.1 BIBLES

A *bible* is a little booklet prepared by the creators of an artistic property such as a movie or an episodic television program. It contains information, both written and drawn, about each of the main characters, the main settings, and moods. It also may contain a full script of one episode and one-page descriptions of other ideas for the remaining episodes. See Figure 5.1 for an example of a bible.

5.1 A spread from a typical bible showing a cartoon drawing and descriptions of a couple of the characters.

"Cro-Magnon" at the bar

Main Characters

Mr. Sensitive

Mr Sensitive is a product of our times. He is a good looking, single 35-year-old who has never been married and dreams about finding that special someone. He has been taught to be sensitive to women's issues and has trained himself so well at doing this he has lost touch with his own masculinity. He has carefully contrived his self-image to be a rennaissance man of taste, education, manners and spirituality. He feels that he knows what women need... someone to listen to them.

Cro-Magnon

Cro-Magnon is Mr. S's nemesis/alter ego. He is a mouth-breather that the ladies have a hankering for. Dressed in fur skins, complete with wooden club, he peruses bars, restaurants and nightclubs looking for dinner, if you know what I mean. He appears in every episode, playing kind of a "Where's Waldo" with Mr. S. Every time Mr. S is close to striking out with one of his dates, you can hear the grunting of Cro-Magnon getting closer. It seems that Cro-magnon never needs a reservation anywhere, unlike Mr. S.

copyright Ceremony Chagall Inc. 2000

This piece of information is invaluable material to the texture artist. It tells you right from the start what the creators have in mind for their show. It gives you clues into what the client is looking for in terms of style/genre, level of detail expected, and the basic scope of everything you will paint textures for. Once you get into the actual work of creating the project, the bible hopefully is flexible enough that needed changes can be made. The bible serves as a great starting place for discussion and lets you know how flexible the creators are with their vision.

5.2.2 PRE-VIS MOVIES

The next valuable piece of information that the client may supply you with is a *pre-vis* movie, short for *pre-visualization*. In my experience, this is usually done in house after you acquire the job. A pre-vis movie is a basic blocking out, shot by shot, of the actual animation and camera work, produced on the computer-usually with lo-res models and environments that will then be given to the animators to finesse to completion. This is where you as the texture painter, acquire more information as to the questions and the factors which need to be considered before you begin. It is a good idea to be involved at certain stages of this pre-vis stage. A good pre-vis director will be savvy to some of your texturing concerns and invite you to participate in the development and the completion of the piece.

> **ON THE CD**
>
> Open the "DBS_previs.mov" or "DBS_previs.avi" on the accompanying CD to see a typical pre-vis movie.

5.2.3 STORYBOARDS AND WHAT TO ASK FROM THEM

The storyboard is the most invaluable piece of information you can have for a project. If it is done well, it tells you exactly what you need to know about a project. Shown in Figure 5.2, a storyboard is a sequence of rough sketches of the project's key scenes. Through them you see the story quickly; you see what camera angles have been decided on, and what potential camera moves there are. Without storyboarding, the details of the project are literally left to chance on the day of the shoot, or in your case, you are left to make last minute decisions as you create the project on the computer. Some clients may arrive at your studio with storyboards or some sketches for you to work from. If not, it is important that you have storyboards created before you begin.

Not using storyboards will leave you in the dark and you may overcompensate when painting details. This leads to creating very large file sizes "just in case." So help yourself by knowing the extent of the textural detail by consulting storyboards first.

5.2 A storyboard from a commercial that was done at Curious Pictures for a Mercedes-Benz commercial.

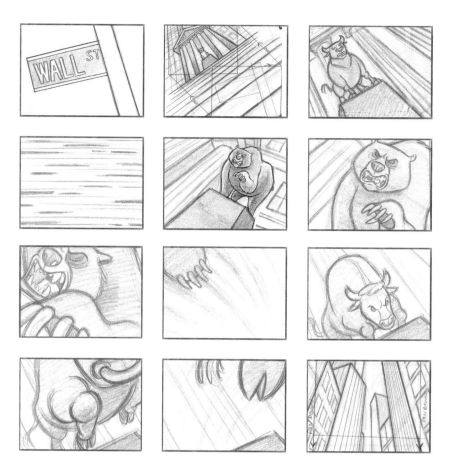

The sections that follow outline a few questions that you might ask yourself while consulting the storyboards (or board-a-matics) to help you determine the level of detail that is right for your project.

5.2.3.1 How Long Is the Shot?

For film and TV work, an important element to glean from the storyboard or board-a-matic is timing. How long does the camera stay on a particular shot? The more time the camera spends on a shot, the more time the viewer has to look around the surroundings and notice detail. Is the camera moving the whole shot? CG elements in live-action films are typically quite short, usually less than 10 seconds (they are, however, getting longer). When a CG sequence flashes or blurs by, this is an opportunity to overlook certain things, not putting so much time and effort into the microscopic details. The same thing can be said for TV, especially commercials. If you are working on a 15-second breakfast cereal commercial, chances are it will have many cuts to achieve greater variety and impact. In the entire 15-second spot, you may texture a shot that is only visible for 3 seconds or less. It is important to know where to put emphasis when you have only 3 seconds. Do you spend most of your time on the main character's face or on his shoelace? If you ask the right questions of the client and director, you will acquire a very good understanding of when to accent and articulate your detail, and when to hint or fudge it.

Sometimes we need only to hint at detail in a scene. Our brains fill in the rest of the pieces if we have a few really good pieces to start with. So, it is vital that you know where to put your efforts as you proceed through your project. Major motion pictures, especially horror flicks and those made before the dawn of CG, know how to do this, and we can benefit from their lessons. Watch any of the earlier films such as *Alien*, that have quick fright scenes in them and consider just how much detail you thought you saw compared to what was actually there.

ON THE CD

Open the "bmatic.mov" or "bmatic.avi" on the accompanying CD to see the storyboard above as a board-a-matic. (Also, the complete storyboard panels are on the CD.)

5.2.3.2 WHAT IS THE SETTING?

The setting where the action takes place in a shot is a simple, yet vital part of the information you will need before you proceed to paint. Setting can be defined as a doctor's office, a country, a planet, or an undefined location such as a netherworld filled with abstract color washes and shadow, or a simple white background with the character running about (see Figure 5.3). All these, however, are settings nonetheless and you must do your research accordingly.

5.3 Examples of possible settings: An interior; left, exterior Venice, middle; and way-exterior, outer-space, right.

Let's say that you are working on a 15-second commercial which takes place in a kitchen; this is all you are provided with concerning setting. You need to expand the perception of this setting by asking questions like: What country, city, is this kitchen in? You may not always be creating work for the country or city in which you live. If the target market has been decided, then, what neighborhood? What is the income of the family that lives there? What is their design taste? What is their culture? Knowing answers to these questions helps you narrow your focus of gathering reference for certain kitchens and designs.

The characters in The DuneBugs Project live and play in a desert. Is this desert in Saudi Arabia? Utah? Arizona? Each of these deserts has its own look and feel. I wanted to represent a desert in the locale of California and Arizona and chose references that, to me, exemplify this environment.

The correlation of location and texturing are quite obvious. Because our characters live in the desert and they drive around all day in this desert, the textural adjectives that come to mind are heat, sand, dirt, mirages, sunburn, and isolation. The list goes on. The scene could become beautifully rich because of the elements, which affect the environment simply because of the location, such as:

- Paint blistering off the dune buggy.
- Caked and baked mud on everything including the characters' faces.
- Bleached out colors from the sun.
- Hot specular highlights coming off the chrome exhaust pipes, etc.

Other locales would provide other adjectives. If it were a netherworld, would there be sunlight? Dust? Weathering? Are the lights from practical sources such as lamps or flashlights, or is it studio-lit as if shot on a soundstage somewhere?

5.2.3.3 WHAT IS THE TIME OF DAY?

The time of day is another factor that can give you some interesting ideas about texture. Take a look at the differences in light and texture qualities in Figure 5.4. Most of the time you will texture something as if it were perfectly lit by the sun leaving the CG lighting itself to describe the time of day. For example, just because the shot you are texturing takes place at night, it is not a good idea to paint it in dark blue hues with little detail. If there were to be a change from the director (and there usually are many) and she wanted to have the main character turn on a light, you would have to repaint your texture to compensate for this.

5.4 Look at the differences in light and texture qualities from noon (left), twilight (middle), and nighttime (right). Which one has the least contrast?

What is more important with regards to the time of day is thinking how you can enhance it with the colors in which you choose to paint your textures. We can add beautiful complements and contrasts by being observant of small details like this. For example, let's say the shot you are texturing is an urban night scene with a street lamp overhead shining down on a poster-filled wall. Your rendered scene will contain a lot of blue and black hues where the light drops off. This is where you can make better color choices for items such as the posters and wall by picking hues that go well with blue and black, such as warm oranges and golds. This will provide beautiful contrasts in the lit section of your scene giving the light source even more presence and giving balance to the scene as a whole. Picture in your mind's eye how this would look if you chose only blue and green hues for these items.

If you want to paint in the time of day, one way would be to create your perfectly sunlit texture first. Then take it into your paint program and change its hue and saturation there to reflect the lighting that would occur for the shot, saving both versions so that you can easily go back and have the perfect one if needed.

The DuneBugs Project takes place in the blazing sun of midday so everything will be out in the open and textured as such.

5.2.3.4 WHAT IS THE MOOD OF THE SHOT?

Mood is not only defined by lighting; color and the level of detail define mood also. If the mood were somber, then you would not create textures with bright yellows and lime greens in them. The detail is not crisp; it is softer with muted tones. If the mood is upbeat and sunny, then details may be more defined and colors brighter and more saturated. Take a look at the different moods created by the different lighting conditions in Figure 5.5.

5.5 Moods created by different lighting conditions and their effects on color saturation and details.

If mood is set largely by lighting and that lighting changes during the piece, then you must texture according to the reality of the environment. For example, if the lighting changes from a street lamp outside to the lights being turned on inside in a realistic scene, you must texture that space as if the lights were on and let the lighting change its mood, and not the textures.

If the lighting is going to be soft, then you may not notice on-screen if the material has a bumpy quality or not, and the highlights may not be as strong. In this scenario, it might not be necessary to create bump maps.

If the lighting is severe and there are harsh shadows, then you can have a lot more fun by creating bump maps to take advantage of that style of lighting.

5.2.3.5 WHAT DOES THE DIALOGUE TRACK OFFER?

It is necessary to read the script or listen to the dialogue track in order to glean textural references made by the characters in the animation. An example of this is one character may say to another, "Nice green tie, Charlie." Obviously, if you read that in the script or on the storyboard, you will know that Charlie should be wearing a green tie. However, along with reading the words you have to consider context and inflection as well. If there is a recorded dialogue track, then listen to how the actor says that line. Is it sarcastic? If so then do you paint the tie in a hideous green color or pattern? If it is a truthful statement, then do you paint a really fashionable green tie? What if the character is being mean? Which tie do you paint? All these questions can be answered if you read the script and storyboard as well as ask questions of the director.

The DuneBugs Project has no dialogue as such; it is just an animation "look and feel" test.

5.2.3.6 ARE THERE ANY CLOSE-UPS?

Close-ups demand larger file texture resolutions because the audience will need to see more detail, and so will the renderer. The closer the camera gets to your texture, the larger you will have to paint it.

While creating textures for *Bingo*—a short animation to show off Alias|Wavefront's Maya 1.0—I learned a lot about making large texture files. The project has a circus stage and the flooring needed to be quite large because it covers a huge expanse in the scene and is the most

ON THE CD

Take a look at the Bingo.mov.

5.6 Here is the original shot of the peanut butter tin. From this distance the lo-res color texture file (884×446 pixels) provides enough clarity.

5.7 This severe close-up shows the deterioration of the same small color texture file in Figure 5.6 and is unsuitable for the shot. Notice the blurry and pixelated/aliased artifacts.

prevalent and constant texture in the piece. I needed to make it crisp, clean, legible, and have photographic quality. This can only be achieved by giving the file a high resolution through a large number of pixels so it became a texture file size of 2K (2048×2048).

The rendered images, Figures 5.6 through 5.8 show an example of this. Figure 5.6 shows the peanut butter tin from a wide shot. From this vantage point the color texture map size (884×446 pixels) is sufficient. Zooming in to an extreme close-up as shown in Figure 5.7, you see that this texture map size starts to fall apart. You can see the aliasing or stair-casing that is now evident; the actual pixels that make up the painted map. To fix this I used a much larger color texture map size of 4716×2378 pixels. Quite an increase in file size, but necessary for this type of shot. The aliasing is much less apparent and the blurry quality seen in Figure 5.7 is now much more crisp in Figure 5.8.

In most instances, it is wise to start painting a little larger than you need to compensate for future changes to camera angles, print, and close-ups. Creating larger canvases allows you to scale a texture map and still be able to retain beautiful quality.

5.8 The color texture map has been changed to a larger file size (4716×2378 pixels) and now has much more clarity and less aliasing than Figure 5.7.

For The Project, the car body and the character's face have nice full-frame shots so I painted them at 1k. I reworked these for this book and increased them to 2K or larger and painted most of the other textures at 1k. I need them at this resolution because certain pictures from this animation are printed in the book and they need to have this clarity (see the section on Print Medium in this chapter). Another way to do this is to have several size/resolution versions of the same texture. That way for far off shots, you can use the lo-res versions and for close-up shots, you can use hi-res ones.

Because there are close-ups, other concerns need to be addressed such as: Will there be reflections in the close-up? Should I use bump maps or displacement maps? Is there enough time to do everything I want to do? If there is not enough time, a savvy director will change the shot to make it more doable or opt out of shooting it all together. Compromising quality of the piece is not an option. As a prepared and knowledgeable texture artist, you will be able to assist the director in making these decisions, and in some cases, if you are lucky, these decisions may be entirely yours to make.

5.2.3.7 WILL YOU USE DEPTH OF FIELD?

The storyboard can also give you clues as to whether you need or want to consider using depth of field. Depth of field mimics the falloff of detail with distance.

For texturing purposes this means that if you are to implement depth of field, then the farther away things are in your shot, the less detail you may need to include in your texture file and you may be able to use smaller file sizes. Take a look at Figures 5.9 and 5.10. Here it is a wise thing to do some tests to see just how the depth of field affects your work to make an educated decision on how to proceed. Another thing to consider is that rendering times may increase (depending on the 3D software you are using) because of the somewhat heavy computational overhead.

In The Project, the desert is a vast, somewhat flat landscape, and I wanted to see some sort of depth of field. The textures in the vast distance are small in size, 256×256 pixels or 512×512 pixels.

5.9 This figure has been rendered without depth of field.

5.10 This figure has been rendered with a significant amount of depth of field. Notice how details in the foreground also fall away in this example.

5.2.3.8 IS THE CAMERA MOVING?

If the camera is moving, then possibly you do not need to have as much detail in the background, the midground, or the foreground. It depends on the shot. With fast camera moves, you may get away with creating smaller texture file sizes. For example, in a pan-shot with the camera mounted on a car, the midground or background elements are on screen for a matter of two or three frames and may be completely blurred (see Figure 5.11). When speeding in a car down the highway, both depth of field and motion blur are at play. When you look out the side window, the foreground—things that are close to you—blur, and as the scenery moves further away from you they slow down, and details are affected by distance. Therefore, there may be no need for microscopic detailing. Similarly, for a camera zoom illustrated in Figure 5.12, the sidewalk texture has blurred out most of the texture information.

5.11 An example of a moving camera pan and its resultant blur on the scene in its field of view.

5.12 An example of camera zoom and how it affects textural details.

ON THE CD

Look at the two camera zoom animations on the CD. One is without camera blur called "zoomCam_noBlur.mov" and "zoomCam_noBlur.avi." The other has motion blur on the camera called "zoomCam.mov" and "zoomCam.avi." See if you can spot the difference between the motion blur and non motion blur.

For The Project, the camera is moving only from time to time and it has no real effect on the detailing and texturing I have provided for the main character. He, except for the opening shot, is the main focus and the background is expansive and far away.

5.2.3.9 WILL YOU USE MOTION BLUR?

In the same way as depth of field, motion blur calculates and simulates the effect of moving objects when they are in your field of vision. Your eyes cannot take in all the detail of an object as it zips past you and so detail and recognition of objects are limited. This obviously affects how the textures that you paint get rendered. Be careful to consider whether you need to include such things as bump maps, scratches, and reflectivity, if you know your subject matter is going to be always on the move. Render a few frames with motion blur turned on to see how your textures hold with the movement of the character. This will give you a good idea of how much effort to extend when creating the final texture (see Figure 5.13). It also may help the director decide how much blur to use if any at all. Check your board-a-matics for timing issues and talk to the director to get his input as to what his vision is for the work.

5.13 The blurred ball on the right shows very little of the same level of detail as the one on the left. If you are using motion blur and if your character never sits still, then you may not need to worry about how much detail you paint for him.

For The Project, we definitely want to implement motion blur. This animation is about speed. The 3D motion blur in the test render affected a few things, such as the texture on the cactus. It was fairly detailed, but was so blurred that all that was left was a green smudge on the rendered frames. Revealing that the cactus doesn't need so much texture. The motion blur also affected the ground passing by. This helped to enhance the movement of the hot rod; it gave it speed and an edginess that would be lacking without motion blur.

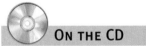

ON THE CD

Also check out the movies "noBlur.mov or .avi" and "Blur.mov or .avi" on the CD. Which one looks more realistic and natural to you?

5.2.3.10 ARE THERE ANY SPECIAL EFFECTS?

Special effects can range anywhere from exploding bombs to simple glows. If there are any effects in the animation, then we need to know if we are responsible for contributing to them texturally. For instance, the effects person (if it's not you), may need you to paint a glow texture map and you will need to discuss what resolution and how much detail you need to provide for it. Conversely so, an *effect* may completely obliterate your texture in the background, so time may be better spent on something else other than the texturing if this is the case.

ON THE CD

Open "dustFx.mov or .avi." This is an animation of a very obvious dust cloud that appears when the ball hits the road. It was created with simple geometry and an animated texture.

ON THE CD

If you want, take a look at the movie "DBS_previs.mov" or "DBS_previs.avi" again.

A related question is: Are any textures morphing or animating? Several texture files may need to be generated for the morphing or animating sequence if there is one, or they may need to be created procedurally which I will discuss later during the making of The Project.

For The Project, there are some special effects such as plumes of dust. I would also like to see fire from the exhaust pipes, glows from the engine manifold, and bulging gas hoses. Time, as always, will dictate what I can actually get done.

5.2.4 WHAT PRE-PRO MATERIALS DO I HAVE TO WORK WITH?

So to recap, for The DuneBugs Project, the animation director, along with an animator, created the pre-vis movie on-the-fly. There were no storyboards for this piece so they created a short little narrative that had high energy, and good close-ups to show off the quality of detail we wanted to put into this project. This, besides a creative bible, was what I had to work with while creating textures for the work. From this little movie, I could tell what we were up against in regards to painting the landscape, close-ups for the main character's face, the detail of the car, and the duration of each camera shot.

5.3 WHICH STYLE IS APPROPRIATE?

You can illustrate an idea or story in many *styles* or *genres*. Style is the expression with which a piece is created, and is the overall look and feel of a painting, movie, and so on. Genre is the categorization of any form of expression according to its style. Art historians categorize similar flavors, themes, or techniques of artists into genres in an effort to organize the vast timeline of art.

While looking at the storyboards and speaking with your client, you will eventually intuit the style of the piece even before it is named. There can be a number of reasons why a certain style is chosen over another. The client could be primarily concerned with the target audience's taste and choose accordingly, or could choose based on her personal preference. Whatever the case, there are a number of aspects concerning style to consider when one is finally chosen.

As art evolves, the number of genres that are created for it increases. Each of the following styles has its own characteristics, which makes it tick. And they each affect our painting specifications greatly.

For the DuneBugs Project, styles intermingle texturally. There are parts, which are realistic, hyper-real, graphic, and so on. It takes place in the natural world, yet DuneBugs does not really exist, so you can have some fun with fantasy and expression.

5.3.1 REALISTIC

For the purposes of this book, a *realistic* style is one that imitates the real world as a photograph does, see the painting by Ralph Goings in Figure 5.14. There are some important things to consider when creating this style: Your drawing ability and color palette must be precise, and, in order to create accurate depth of field you must let details fall away with distance.

5.14 In this painting by Ralph Goings, there is the requisite depth of field and softness, which lend themselves to a reality we can recognize.

Ralph Goings "Sugar" 1995 oil on canvas 44.5 × 64 in. O.K. Harris Works of Art, New York, NY.

Figure 5.15 is a realistic rendering of a leaf. Take a look at how much detail there actually is. Is everything in crisp focus? Can you see every cell? Not really. Still, it is represented in such a way as to mimic how our eyes see it in real life. If you were to paint the leaf in this style, you need to be aware of things like bumps, reflections, and specular highlights. The realistic leaf will need to have these attributes present to lend authenticity to the work. Not only do they need to be present, they need to be realistic in their amounts.

> **NOTE**
>
> Just as painters begin painting their surroundings realistically, so too, must you look at and describe your reality in the same way, before moving away from it. Abstraction takes us away from the obvious, and goes beyond the surface or the "facts" of the reality, and speculates as to what is beyond it. Still, its origins at one point are taken from reality itself.

5.15 A rendering of a leaf from an ivy plant. What makes this realistic?

For The Project, the most realistic elements, in my opinion, are the steel braided hoses. I took a photograph of hoses that were the type I wanted to create. There is little or no expressive interpretation of these cables in Figure 5.16. They look very close to the real thing.

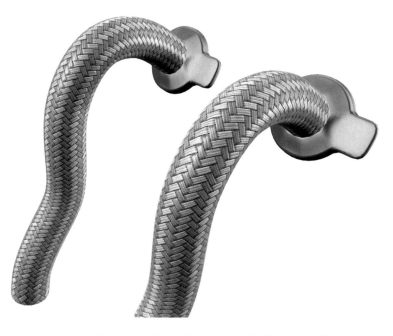

5.16 The hose seen here is realistic because it shows just enough detail without being overly descriptive.

Realistic artists to check out are John Baeder and Charles Bell, to name a few.

5.3.2 HYPER-REAL

Look at the painting in Figure 5.17 by Chuck Close, and see how crisp and clean the face seems to be. There is much more detail than you would expect to see in a photograph from the same distance.

This style can be more arduous than others to paint. The time it takes, depends on how exaggerated you want your painting to be. The more hyper-real, the more time.

NOTE

Some basic considerations for the realistic style are

- Match your CG depth of field to the camera's depth of field.
- Detail the textures, perhaps using a softer version of the texture to allow it to "sit" in the scene.
- Allow details to fall away with distance.
- When working with live action, match the lighting to the live action lighting.

John, 1971-72
acrylic on canvas, 100 × 90"
Photograph by Ellen Page Wilson, courtesy of Pace Wildenstein
The Robert B. Mayer Family Collection on loan to The Art Institute of Chicago.
©1972 Chuck Close

5.17   Hyper-real artists go deeper than reality. They have the ability to uncover and express the realistic world much in the same way as a microscope does, and deepen our experience of our world.

Hyper-real artists seem to have the ability to see down to the cellular level of the things they create. Take a look at the rendering in Figure 5.18 of the leaf and witness its transformation as an example of the hyper-real style. What has changed? There is more attention paid to providing clarity where there was none in the original realistic image. The flesh of the leaf is accentuated and emphasized and ends up looking like bumpy pillow pockets.

5.18 The leaf as rendered in a hyper-real style. Notice the differences in level of detail from the realistic render (see Figure 5.15).

NOTE

Creating a hyper-real CG texture requires a different set of constructs that allow you to exaggerate, amplify, and enhance.

Change attributes by magnifying, enhancing, and exaggerating bumps, reflections, and color texture. This style requires the artist to use imagination, intuition, good reference, and research capabilities to take the viewer into a new reality.

Our main character "Axle" in the project is the hyper-real part of the texturing. I wanted to accentuate and hyper-realize his dry, scaly skin. This, as well as his coloring, contrast well with his vibrant red dune buggy that helps him stand out. I think it is successful (see Figure 5.19).

5.19 The main character needs some hyper-real details to give him the added attention and visual punch so that he stands out in the animation.

Other hyper-real artists to look out for are Richard Estes and Evan Penny.

5.3.3 STYLIZED

A personal interpretative journey, the stylized genre involves a personal signature and is either loved or hated because of this interpretation. Look at the painting in Figure 5.20. Freud gives us an expression of this scene you would not be able to get from a straightforward photo. Creating a stylistic piece can be the most rewarding for personal expression. The only advice I have for you in this regard is to stay consistent in your expression. When you apply a certain set of rules to one thing make sure you apply it to everything else in a scene if it is to live harmoniously. And if there are no rules, then keep it that way.

5.20 This kind of expression deals more with a heartfelt passionate approach to painting as opposed to the more analytical approach used by the realistic or hyper-realistic genres.

Lucian Freud, English, b. Germany, 1922, Two Japanese Wrestlers by a Sink, oil on canvas, 1983-87, 50.8 ×78.7 cm, Restricted gift of Mrs. Frederic G. Pick; through prior gift of Mr. and Mrs. Carter H. Harrison, 1987.275 Photograph courtesy of The Art Institute of Chicago.

The leaf has now taken on this stylized genre (see Figure 5.21). It is more expressive in brushstroke and color and is less concerned with details and more concerned with its vitality and energy; however, it is still recognizable as a leaf.

Creating an expressive stylization on the computer can be a very difficult task. Looking at our examples of the leaf and Freud's sink (see Figures 5.20 and 5.21), how could we create these on the computer? It is possible if we use things like transparency maps and layered shaders to overlay CG paint strokes on top of each other and bump and displacement maps to make geometry less perfect. The stylized genre may seem easier to paint—and harder to implement.

5.21 The leaf seen from a stylized point of view. How would you paint and stylize this leaf?

For DuneBugs, the mud texture on the buggy is one of the more stylized parts of the piece (see Figure 5.22). It became its own kind of mud. The bump map I used for it gave it this really thick look which stands out well for the close-up shots, and adds a certain cartoon-i-ness to the dune buggy, balancing the other realistic aspects of the animation.

5.22 The mud on the exhaust pipes is not realistic or hyper-real, it is more stylized. Thick and full.

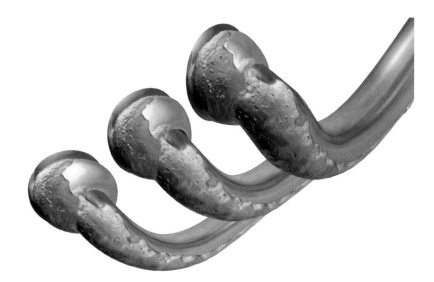

Other artists to look at are Thomas Hart Benton, Max Beckmann, and Chaim Soutine.

5.3.4 SIMPLIFIED

Simplified is a further abstraction from reality and more than any other style, begs the question, "What are the most important features to get across each element?" Figure 5.23 is from the TV show, *A Little Curious* (the "Series"), a Home Box Office (HBO) production, which I worked on. The target audience was preschoolers. I used key features and nothing more when creating textures. For instance, the important features for wood, I decided, were the color and woodgrain pattern.

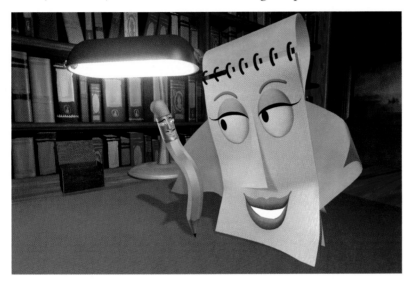

5.23 The simplified style creates conundrums around the amount of detail needed to get across the complexity of the scene.

Consider how I painted the leaf texture in Figure 5.24—by identifying what the most important features are for me. Here, there are no bump, specular, or diffusion maps. It is leaf-green, has veins, and a cell-like pattern. It is quite *simply* a leaf!

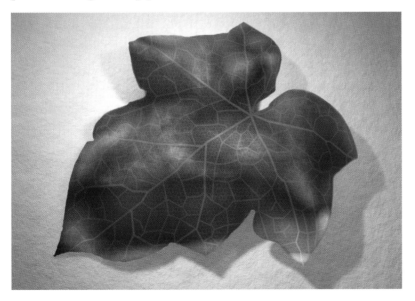

5.24 Our leaf has now been simplified. How is it different from stylized?

The Project also has some simplified textures in it. The background world does not have every rock or stone painted into it. It is sandy in color, and is sandy in texture, not much else. The cactus in the scene also have simple textures. Because of how fast "Axle" is travelling, the cacti are completely blurred out and no detail except for the color green was really needed for the animation. Take a look at Figure 5.25.

5.25 For the purposes of this animation, the desert world was treated in a simplified way. The main focus was not the sand, so we did not spend too much of our efforts in that area.

The simplified style brings to mind artists such as Edward Hopper, Georgia O'Keefe, and Eric Fischl.

5.3.5 GRAPHIC

The graphic style is largely 2D in nature, although it is more than an expression of 2D objects or shapes. It sometimes can allude to being a 3D flat world.

The graphic style achieves a bold, stark quality usually void of shadow. At times, it can evoke volume, a 3D look, and is associated to the simplistic style in certain cases. Looking at Stuart Davis's painting, Figure 5.26, we can see that there is little or no concern for the truth of materials. Instead, his concern is more about color and style, almost cartoon-like definition such as in his depiction of clouds or trees.

In Figure 5.27, the leaf shape retains its leafy essence but has moved away from color variation and a slight bumpy surface to a much simpler representation. The drawing of the leaf is graphic because it does not include all the little imperfections of the leaf's edge, nor does it include

The Metropolitan Museum of Art, Edith and Milton Lowenthal Collection, Bequest of Edith Abrahamson Lowenthal, 1991. (1991.24.1) Photograph ©1990 The Metropolitan Museum of Art

5.26 Stuart Davis expresses little or no detail at all. There is no blending of edges from one color to the next or one object to another. Each is defined by a hard, paper cutout-like, painted edge.

the subtler nuances of its color variations. It has three shades of green for the body and a light green for the veins. That is all. Quite a difference from even the simplified version.

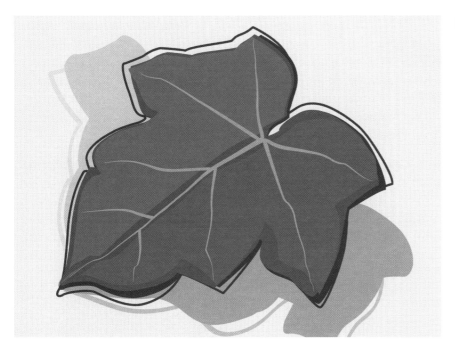

5.27 Can we simplify this anymore? Is a line drawing the next step?

For DuneBugs, the bug pattern on the dune buggy started out as a graphic treatment and then evolved into a more distressed and realistic texture (see Figure 5.28).

5.28 My love for graphic design wanted some sort of graphic texture for this animation. I chose to show this style in the flame/bug markings on the dune buggy.

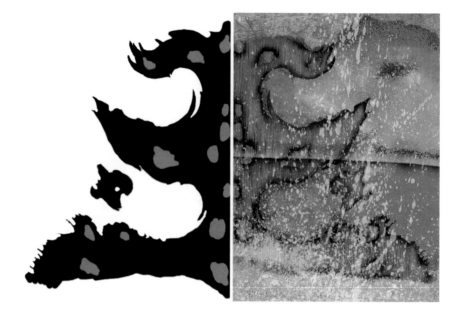

NOTE

You can see many graphic examples on the Web. Artists are creating very graphic-looking animations using Flash, which prefers vector- or Illustrator-based artwork. Some major studios are employing "toon-type" shaders that are applied in 3D scenes and rendered which mimic this 2D graphic cel animated look.

Artists such as Andy Warhol, Roy Lichtenstein, Fernand Leger, and James Rosenquist also employed this graphic look in their work.

5.3.6 FANTASTIC

The fantastic style evokes images found in *Dungeons and Dragons, The Hobbit, Brazil, Blade Runner, Star Wars, Matrix,* and *City of Lost Children.* All narratives of things otherworldly. With this style, you can be more expressive when you create places unforeseen either on this planet, or perhaps any other planet or a different plane. This expression of the subconscious is the starting place for any "what if" premise of an idea. See Figure 5.29 by Meret Oppenheim.

Still, more often than not, you must take your ideas for texturing from your own existence and experience from the stuff that surrounds you. Consider our leaf (see Figure 5.30). See how it has now transformed into the fantastic style. I wanted to paint the leaf as a metaphor to the human body. The leaf veins became human veins and the cells and leaf matter/body became capillaries and flesh. I also wanted this fantastic leaf to be rendered fairly realistically for more visual impact bordering on creepiness.

OPPENHEIM, Meret.
<u>Object</u> {Le Déjeuner en fourrure}. (1936).
Fur-covered cup, saucer and spoon; cup, 4 3/8" (10.9 cm) diameter;
saucer, 9 3/8" (23.7 cm) diameter; spoon, 8" (20.2 cm) long; overallheight 2 7/8" (7.3 cm).
The Museum of Modern Art, New York. Purchase. Photograph ©2001 The Museum of Modern Art, New York.

5.29 As seen in this work by Meret Oppenheim, the fantastic style is allowed to diverge from reality. Here you dream up and express things in such a way to diverge from what you know as reality and create something new.

5.30 The leaf veins have become human veins and the cells and leaf matter/body are made of capillaries and flesh. Kind of creepy! What would your fantastic leaf be made of?

For DuneBugs, the whole premise is quite fantastic. These little guys do not really exist, but for this show they exist on our planet, in the desert. Look at Figure 5.31. It is a rendering of Axle's *fantastic* goggles. Axle's goggles *are* his bug eyes. He shouldn't leave home without them.

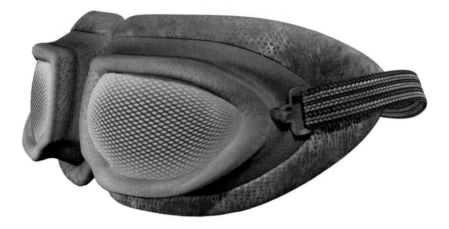

5.31 These goggles have bug-eye lenses instead of flat glass lenses. If you were a bug wouldn't you use these?

Surrealists such as Salvador Dali, De Chirico, and Yves Tanguy painted detailed works inspired by the subconscious and dream imagery.

5.3.7 GET THE CLIENT'S IMPRESSIONS

Familiarize yourself with as many art styles as possible; they will give you a place to start as you translate your client's written or spoken word into a visual experience. You need to ask your clients how and where they visualize starting and what their expectations are for the final product. If your clients are unfamiliar with these art styles, show them some examples of different styles from your morgue. Have the clients pick from these images what best represents their vision. Doing this can save you a lot of time. Not everyone shares the same verbal understanding of what something looks like, so it is important to get to the visualizing as soon as possible.

5.4 WHO IS THE TARGET AUDIENCE?

When deciding how the piece will be painted as mentioned previously, the target audience must be considered. So before you begin creating, find out who you are creating for.

There is a lot to consider once you know your audience; it is not enough to know that they are three- to four-year-olds, or 25- to 40-year-olds. It is essential to know what that target market likes and

believes in. It is also good to know where the project is playing, if it is
a commercial, during what time slot, or if it is a movie, what rating, and
so on. If you are working with an advertising agency or marketing
department, it will have this kind of information.

I worked on several commercials for the running shoe company, Lugz
Shoes. These commercials were fast-paced, in-your-face ads. The setting
was urban and the target audience was for the young and hip at heart
(see Figure 5.32).

5.32 Lugz Shoes' target audience is obviously very different from the
preschoolers'. The ad appeals to
hip urban dwellers. Take a look at
both examples (Figures 5.23 and
5.32), and try and list the differences and similarities. Do you think
this particular ad can appeal to
preschoolers?

ON THE CD

Open the file "Lugz_spot1.mov"
or "Lugz_spot1.avi."

At Curious Pictures we worked on an episodic show for preschoolers,
(see Figure 5.23 earlier in this chapter). By doing my research and asking
the director questions, I discovered that there would have to be few
camera cuts because young children get confused if there are too many.
Textures, I decided needed to be simple yet still have a compelling look
that was complex enough to maintain the preschoolers' interest without
overdoing it and scaring them away.

I achieved this effect through my use of color and lighting. By keeping
colors rich, fairly complex, and saturated, and not limiting the palette to
only primary colors, I offered the kids a variety of vibrant colors to look
at. Lighting also lends itself to creating depth and mood, even when the
textures are simple. The lighting, along with the colors, added more visual complexity while maintaining the simplicity of the style.

At the other end of the project spectrum are such movies as *Matrix*,
Fight Club, *Brazil*, and *Blade Runner*, which share a target audience of

18- to 45-year-olds. These projects have quicker cuts, which may mean lingering on close-ups with great details will be minimal. What does this mean in regards to the style of the piece? There is a higher sophistication in texture quality, because of the scrutinizing nature of this target market. A high level of detail is feasible because the budgets tend to be larger for this type of creative endeavor.

In all these cases, the target audience considerations I describe help to define and identify a project's style. As you will learn in the exercises, a project's style influences how you handle detailing, as well as the budgeting of your time.

5.5 WHAT IS THE INTENDED MEDIUM?

When a job comes into a studio, one of the questions that you need to ask is about the medium. Will the audience see the final piece on TV, the Web, or film? Each of these different mediums requires you to create artwork that is suitable and compatible with it. Each has its own standards and confines that you must know about before running to your desk to begin painting.

As I stated earlier on, we made DuneBugs for broadcast television. Some still images were also needed, however, for the print medium for this book.

5.5.1 TV

Creating textures for use in television has some important considerations and limitations. Let's look at them.

5.5.1.1 TELEVISION COLOR SPACE

Television color space is limited to a certain palette of colors. This means that the millions of colors that you see and paint with on the computer are not all reproducible when converted to TV, and some of the ones that are reproducible are not allowed. These forbidden colors are called "illegal" or "hot."

These colors can be detected by using a color scope that is attached to an NTSC (National Television System Committee) color monitor. Figure 5.33 shows how these colors are too hot and must be made less saturated or luminous to be broadcast legal (see Figure 5.34). This legalizing can be accomplished in digital paint programs by reducing the color's saturation or luminance; in 3D packages by reducing color or light intensities; or in compositing packages that use filters to find the offending colors and let you decide how to make them legal.

If you work in television for an extended time, it is a good idea to have a scope and NTSC color monitor connected directly to your computer. Use Adobe's calibration kit that comes with Photoshop to get it to mimic as close as possible the NTSC monitor.

Keep the rgb_NTSC_legal.tif color palette handy to pick hues from it when you are creating and painting textures for TV. Lights in the scene can intensify these colors making them illegal, as well. You will run into this intensification problem far less with an NTSC-safe palette than if you start from a full RGB palette.

ON THE CD

Open the "images rgb_computer.tif" and "rgb_NTSC_legal.tif" from the book's CD-ROM and compare them. See how the brightness and saturation of the center colors have been diminished. This gives you an idea of which colors are illegal or hot.

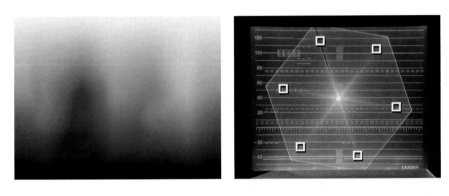

5.33 The color spectrum on the left, as viewed on a scope, right, goes beyond the scopes "legal" range (the six white-outlined squares) and must be optimized/fixed before being broadcast.

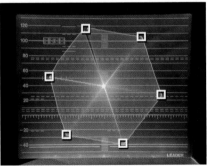

5.34 This figure shows how the "illegal" colors, left, have been brought into the "legal" range by reducing the saturation of the image and are now "safe" for broadcast.

5.5.1.2 INTERLACED FIELDS

Unlike computer monitors, which use progressive scanning (lines are refreshed one after the other), television sets create their images by the use of horizontal interlaced fields. As they are refreshed alternately, however, both fields are never seen on screen at the same time.

5.35 Left, vertical lines don't pose much of a problem on TV. However an animation of these lines rotating, right, shows substantial staircasing or tearing.

These fields and the way they refresh, however, cause certain textures to crawl, buzz, or tear. On TV, certain fabric patterns can create what is similar to a moire pattern produced in printed images.

As texture painters, we must watch for fine lines and intricate patterns, which cause stair-casing or tearing when they move across the screen (see Figure 5.35). This not only applies to the color texture but also for slightly angled horizontal lines such as venetian blinds, and bumps or specular maps as well. Large blocks of color and pattern are not as noticeably affected.

PAL and SECAM, two other formats widely used, are similar to NTSC but have better resolution and color quality.

5.5.1.3 TELEVISION AND TEXTURE RESOLUTION

Regardless of how big your television screen is, you will probably render images between 640×480 pixels to 720×540 pixels. Because of this relatively small display, you can usually paint textures with much smaller file resolutions and not notice any degradation. If the camera gets too close to a texture, however, you may need to increase the resolution to double (1024×1024 or 1K) or quadruple (2048×2048 or 2K) or higher. To see an example similar to this effect, check out Figures 5.7, 5.8, 5.40 and 5.41.

5.5.1.4 CONSIDERING THE PROJECT

You now know the limitations inherent in working for TV; how do they affect creating textures for The Project?

ON THE CD

On the CD there is an example of how certain textures can buzz. It is called "buzzing.avi" or "buzzing.mov." Look for this in the textures on the road and sidewalk. (Buzzing usually occurs when the camera or the object is moving, but not always.)

- **Be sure the colors are NTSC legal.** We want this animation to be colorful. The car body is red so you need to do some color-safe checks.

- **Beware of fine lines and intricate patterns.** The graphics on the hot rod should not be too linear and the dirt ground should not be peppered with intricate specks.

- **The texture resolutions will tend to be small in size.** I anticipate 1K will be plenty big. Still, you must consider the few close-ups established in the pre-vis animation.

5.5.1.5 DIGITAL TELEVISION

The Digital TV or DTV, is now on the market and will probably replace all other television sets eventually. DTVs use digital signals, which increases both picture and sound quality substantially. Two basic formats of digital TV are delivered: Standard Definition (SDTV) and High Definition (HDTV). Some key aspects that affect your final textures and rendered output are

- SDTV comes in 480×640 and 480×704 resolutions.

- SDTV has both interlaced and progressive scanning.

- SDTV offers 4:3 or 16:9 ratios.

- HDTV has resolutions of 720×1080 and 1080×1920.

- HDTV uses interlaced and progressive scan lines.

- HDTV's aspect ratio (16:9) is much larger than present-day analog television's (4:3).

Basically all this information sums up to the fact that DTVs produce film-comparable quality and our textures must reflect this enhanced quality shift. This means more work for us, and more RAM and extra hard disk space to handle these larger texture canvases, as well as the larger rendered final frames.

Another factor we may not need to consider in the future is the problem caused by interlaced fields. With progressive scanning (just like your computer screen), we may be able to get away with more finicky details and finer lines.

> **NOTE**
>
> Today, an average rendered frame size for TV is around 1MB. The file size for the largest HDTV resolution is just under 6MB. That's an increase of 600%. Ouch! It's a good thing hard drives are getting cheaper.

5.5.2 FILM

Film, unlike television, has no problems with things like illegal colors or interlaced fields, yet it has some rendering limitations.

5.5.2.1 FILM COLOR SPACE

The most important thing to watch out for is the presence of pure blacks or pure whites in the final rendered stills. The pure blacks can appear in the shadowed areas and when printed to film stock cause details to fall off. For example, a very dark shadow under a person's nose will still show subtle detail when viewed on your computer monitor. On film, though, it will have no detail and will look like a big black blob instead of evoking shadow. Pure whites need to be carefully addressed as well. This is actually quite a basic premise in photography: Your blackest blacks and whitest whites should contain detail.

Because of this rendering limitation in film work, you can decide to make the blacks 90% and also add some color into them such as red or blue. For whites, make them 10% black and add a warm or cool tint to them. Of course, lighting will further influence these colors once rendered.

5.5.2.2 FILM AND TEXTURE RESOLUTION

The typical resolutions that are rendered for film are 914×666 or 1K, which is then enlarged 200% when printed to film, or 1828×1332 or 2K, which is not enlarged. The smaller size when blown up creates a softer CG look than the crisper look of the larger rendered resolution. To render a film for IMAX requires that the rendered output be 3K square which is then blown up to 4K.

Film is big and beautiful and your textures must be absolutely flawless. That's a tall order, and I say it to encourage you. Your texturing takes cues from what the camera is doing, so if the camera is moving quickly, you need not worry too much. If it is focused on an object or character you painted, then be sure the texture's final resolution holds up to the view without pixelating and breaking down.

5.5.2.3 OTHER FILM DETAILS

Printing rendered frames to film stock is a very intricate process. You will have to convert your rendered frames before they are printed. Before you begin, contact professionals at facilities like Technicolor, Cineon, or Arriflex to find out what is involved for your particular project.

5.5.3 WEB

It's obvious that the Web is here to stay and is the newest successful avenue for advertising and content. This has created a huge market for artists.

Even though users of the Internet may have access to cable modems or DSLs in their homes that allow for speedy delivery, there are a few concerns that you as a texture artist will have to keep in mind when creating for the Web. Three major concerns of image optimization for the Web that affect the images you create are: color palette, file format compression, and file size.

5.5.3.1 WEB COLOR SPACE

Images that you create on the computer or scan into the computer most likely contain thousands of colors (16 bit) or millions of colors (24 bit). Web browsers, however, only display 216 colors known as *Web-safe colors*. This means that if your image has only Web-safe colors in it, it will look the same on any computer platform out there today. Changing technology and computer price decline are allowing more users to have 16- or 24-bit graphics cards, which may soon make the Web-safe color issue obsolete.

If Web-safe colors are a priority, then think about:

■ Creating your image/texture using colors from the Web-safe palette in your image-editing program (see Figure 5.36) and "colorSpectrum_web.tif" on the CD. Adobe Photoshop 6.0 provides many different settings in its color palette that are Web sensitive and make it easy to stay "safe."

ON THE CD

Open "colorSpectrum_web.tif" on the CD. The color spectrum on left shows the colors in 24 bit while the right spectrum shows the same colors in Web-safe spectrum.

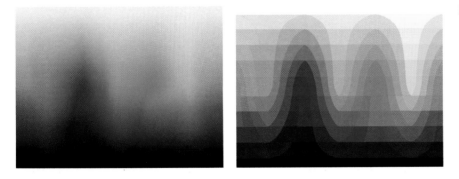

5.36 Take a look at the colors on the left and compare them to the Web-safe spectrum on the right.

■ Converting and saving your image to a GIF or a PNG8 file format. See the next section, "File Formats and Compression Schemes," for details.

Many Web designers, however, still try to keep their graphics and textures limited to an 8-bit palette for purposes of faster downloading. The more color information you have in a file, the larger it will be and the slower the file will download to someone's machine. Many Web programs, such as Macromedia's Fireworks (see Figure 5.37) or Adobe's ImageReady, can take your 24-bit images and convert them to Web-safe images, as well as saving them in a Web-savvy file format.

5.37 Programs such as Macromedia's Fireworks allow you to preview four different compression types of your choice at one time.

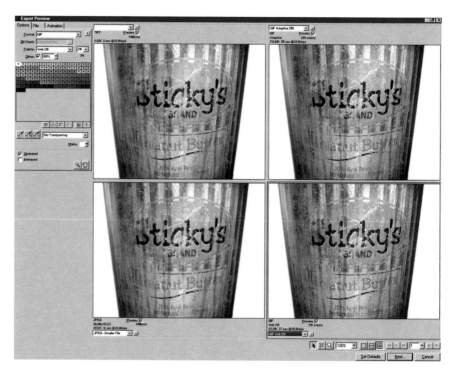

5.5.3.2 FILE FORMATS AND COMPRESSION SCHEMES

Another consideration for your Web imagery is the file format in which you save your image. Each format has its own way of handling color depth and the compression (making the file size smaller) of your image. The popular graphic formats for the Web are GIF (Graphics Interchange Format), JPEG (Joint Photographic Experts Group), and PNG-8 or PNG-24 (Portable Network Graphics; 8-bit or 24-bit color). Each of these file formats has its strengths and weaknesses and is used for different reasons. Let's look at a quick list of these.

GIF supports 8-bit color only and works well for:

- Sharp details associated with line art, graphics, and logos
- Images containing areas of flat or solid color
- Certain small continuous tonal and photographic imagery
- Small graphic animations
- Transparency

It also has dithering capabilities and is browser safe across platforms. See Figure 5.38.

GIF does not work well for:

- Large continuous tonal and photographic imagery
- Imagery of many colors

In addition, converting from a 24-bit image to an 8-bit GIF results in lost image quality.

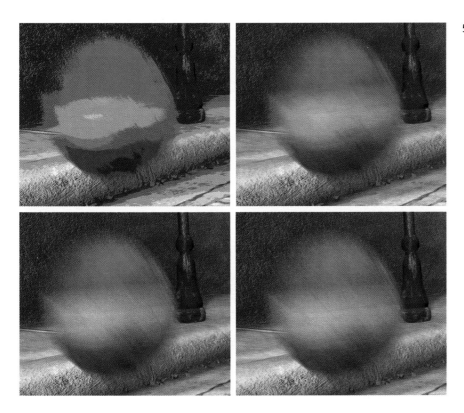

5.38 Four different GIF compression settings and their effect on 24-bit imagery.

5.39 The top image is the original uncompressed file, while the bottom image has been severely compressed by the JPEG codec. Note: You can get much better results than this. This is an example of what JPEG compression can do to an image when it is saved successively in the JPEG format.

JPEG **supports 24-bit color and works well for:**

- Large and small continuous tonal and photographic imagery
- File size compression

JPEG **does not work well for:**

- Small text
- Transparency
- Relief from visible artifacts, such as blocks and banding, when saving with low-quality settings.

JPEG is supported by most browsers.

Keep in mind too, that successive saving of a JPEG file continuously degrades the image. Always save a JPEG from the original format. See Figure 5.39.

PNG-8 **and supporting 8-bit color only. Works well for:**

- Sharp details associated with line art, graphics, and logos
- Images containing areas of flat or solid color
- Dithering (diffusion, noise, and pattern)
- Certain continuous tonal and photographic imagery
- Transparency
- Small file size compression

PNG-8 **does not work well for:**

- Large continuous tonal and photographic imagery
- Imagery of many colors
- Conversion from a 24-bit image (image quality is lost)

PNG-8 is not supported by all Web browsers.

PNG-24 **supports 24-bit color and works well for:**

- Sharp details associated with line art, graphics, and logos
- Images containing areas of flat or solid color
- Continuous tonal and photographic imagery
- Multilevel transparency

PNG-24 is not supported by all Web browsers.

Experiment with these file formats and their many settings to achieve the best results. What may work great for one image, may not work as well for the next.

Be aware that the 24-bit images that you are saving as JPEG or PNG-24 may look totally different on a machine that only displays 8-bit color. To get an idea of what an image will look like you need to change your monitor color depth to 256, or turn on browser dither in programs, such as ImageReady, and it will emulate an 8-bit depth browser for you. If you are a serious image creator for the Web, then it is best to view your Web work on a variety of machines, in different bit depths, on different browsers and connections.

5.5.3.3 FILE SIZE

The dimension of your images for the Web should be kept small. If this is not possible, say in the case of a background painting, then images can be broken up into chunks called *slices*. These sliced squares download quicker than one large one. This gives viewers the sense that something is taking shape in their browsers, and they may be more likely to wait to see the whole image.

If you need to cover a large area, say a background, on a Web page with an image, then another possibility is to create a smaller and tileable image that repeats. Browsers will tile an image that fits any size.

5.5.3.4 PAGE SIZE

Some companies are quite strict about the size of each HTML page. Savvy Web designers will keep their page and image sizes down and may have a restriction of, let's say, 56K modems for their low-end users, because of slow downloads. One company I talked to has an 80K total main page size limit and 40–50K total successive page size for all elements. If you are working freelance for a Web company creating images, then you will need to ask if it has a size limit per page.

5.5.3.5 MOVIES AND THE WEB

Just as there are compression algorithms for still images, there are also compression/decompression algorithms (codecs) for moving images. If you are creating an animation/movie for the Web, you need to be concerned with what format that movie should be saved in. There are several codecs out on the market, such as Animation, CinePak, and, most recently, Sorenson. These codecs usually ship within a movie editing or compositing package such as Adobe's AfterEffects or Adobe's Premiere.

ON THE CD

Open the movies "Blur_8bit.avi" or "Blur_8bit.mov." These are obvious examples of what may happen to a movie when it is converted from 24-bit to 8-bit color depth. They also show compression artifacts resulting from the conversion. Note that much better results can be obtained with a little (or a lot of) finessing.

These codecs, as for still images, can affect the quality of your final output, so beware that certain details are going to be compromised when this final step is applied to your textured animation.

5.5.3.6 OTHER ISSUES

Macintosh and Windows machines have different monitor gamma settings. This means that an image that you create on a Windows platform will be lighter in tone when viewed on a Macintosh. The gamma on a Windows machine is darker. If you're concerned that your artwork look relatively the same on both Mac and Windows machines, then you should save your artwork with these different gammas in mind and offer your viewers the opportunity to view an image especially for their platform.

5.5.4 PRINT

If you are not aware of the challenges in creating textures for printed matter and you don't deal with them, flaws in your work will be detected because the image is no longer moving. Let's go through the list of considerations you must address for print.

5.5.4.1 PRINT COLOR SPACE

Not all the 16.7 million colors on your computer are printable on paper. As you may remember from the color theory discussion, computer and television screens use an *Additive* color process, and printing processes use *Subtractive*. In print, because light no longer projects behind the image, you cannot easily create the same range of colors on paper as you can on a computer screen.

5.5.4.2 RGB TO CMYK

When you render an image on your computer for print purposes, you do so in RGB space. When you print the same image, you use CMYK inks: Cyan, Magenta, Yellow, and Black. To more accurately understand how the RGB image will print, open it in a paint program and convert it to CMYK.

Sometimes, even if you start with printable colors, they can still become illegal colors for print due to the lights you use in your scenes (lights increase the chroma of the hues). Because the lighting in DuneBugs will mimic the harsh sun of the desert, for example, you must consider how some of the reds on the car, the golden yellow sand, and some of the greens will render due to the lighting effect. If you are doing a lot of print work, keep the CMYK palette from the accompanying CD close at hand and pick your colors from it when you begin painting. Also, watch out for the "!" warning in the Photoshop color picker when choosing colors. It lets you know when a color is out of the gamut range for printable colors.

Another important thing to consider is to get a test print on paper of a computer rendering. Study the print, then calibrate your monitor by changing its brightness and contrast settings or use Adobe's calibration kit that comes with Photoshop.

5.5.4.3 PRINT RESOLUTION

Often, the idea of having images printed from an animation comes at the end of the project. This is not the best time to request a high-quality image, because it means you will have to rework many of your textures.

Because I wanted images from DuneBugs printed for this book, I needed to render them at a much higher resolution than what I rendered for TV. Most printed images are 300 dots per inch (dpi), and some are as high as 600 dpi—four times TV's 72 dpi. When you re-render images at four times their resolution you begin to see the actual pixels that describe some of the textures in the piece. Take a look at Figure 5.40 and see the pixelated characteristics that would not be noticed on TV. In most cases, you will not get the desired image for print if you just enlarge the textures to a higher resolution in your paint package. Figure 5.41 shows the same rendering with a larger file texture for the road and how this larger file texture fixes the pixelation.

When you are faced with the task of rendering images for print, you need to know two important ingredients: printed size and print resolution (dpi).

When you render the image, simply multiply the print size by the dpi to get your render size. For example, if the printed image size is 5"×7" at 300 dpi:

$$5 \times 300 \text{ DPI} = 1500$$

$$7 \times 300 \text{ DPI} = 2100$$

Therefore, the rendered size should be 1500×2100 pixels.

Increasing the rendered size, of course, increases rendering time and file sizes. The example 5"×7" image consumes 9.2MB at 300 dpi compared to the 532K at 72 dpi.

ON THE CD

From the CD, open "rgb_computer.tif" and "rgb_to_cmyk.tif" and compare the images. Notice how the lime greens are desaturated in the CMYK version as well as hot red, glowing pink, and the more luminous blue hues. To correct this CMYK version, you could add more saturation to it, even change some of the brightness and contrast to make it more like the rendered version that you desire.

5.40 Notice the obvious pixelation on the road in this hi-res image due to the fact that the texture resolution itself is too small for print purposes.

5.41 This image has been re-rendered with a larger file texture (4096×7088 pixels) for print purposes. Notice the difference in clarity against Figure 5.40.

5.5.5 CD-ROM GAMES

Pre-rendered games allow for a lot of detail. Your approach to texturing and painting for games depends largely on the type of game on which you're working. For example, games such as *Myst* or *Riven* (see Figure 5.42), play back pre-rendered images or movies one after the other, similar to a slide show. In action games, such as *Quake* and *Diablo*, what you see is being rendered on-the-fly as you move through the rooms or worlds. Each type of games has its own standards (if I can call them that for there are few absolutes in the world of games).

All games, whether pre-rendered or on-the-fly, have an underlying "engine" that makes the game run, manages memory, and keeps track of the player's location and activity. Developers choose the engine that is suited best to a game's needs. *Myst's* engine, for example, is Hypercard, and *Quake's* engine is Quake, a proprietary engine created for the game. Each engine type has its own limitations. A game's engine determines how you handle the texturing.

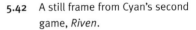

5.42 A still frame from Cyan's second game, *Riven*.

5.5.5.1 PRE-RENDERED GAMES

The main idea behind pre-rendered games usually has to do with intellectual puzzle solving. They provide a slower paced experience. They are also designed to be more detailed to look at, so you are drawn into the environments at the same leisurely pace as you would be into a film.

The worlds in pre-rendered games are based on rendered stills. This means that the stills and movies that make up these games go through much of the same process of creation as animations for TV and film would. You can use any size for texture maps, and any special effects and lighting that your 3D software will allow. Pre-rendered games have no effect on this part of the process.

POSSIBLE LIMITATIONS

Some pre-rendered games, however, can limit you when you want to prepare the images and movies for the type of engine you are using.

Back in '96 my partner and I were creating and developing a game similar in structure to *Myst*. We were using Macromedia's Director as our underlying engine. Some of our limitations were

- Less than full-screen imagery
- 8-bit color palette
- Software standard click and dissolve to next image, position
- Compression of movies for faster loading and playback
- Slow loading times and playback of imagery

Still, these limitations may still be there even if you get the best programmers because of hardware limitations. For example, when I was working on my game, the speed at which images can be retrieved from a CD and thrown onto the screen ready for the user's next click was quite slow. To get around this you have to consider dropping your 24-bit 700–900K images say, down to 8-bit custom palette 200–300K images in a program called DeBabelizer. The smaller size enables faster loading. The size of the screen has to be smaller.

Today, things are better but not perfect. There are no CD-ROMs out there yet that can play back full-screen, navigable images and movies right off the CD. Game companies now more than ever have ventured into the land of developing their own engines. They employ several programmers who write code that takes advantage of today's graphics cards and address their own unique needs for the game that they are developing.

This then lets you know that if you are creating your own game or working for a company that is, you will have to find out about the limitations that are ahead of you and do lots of testing on different target platforms and CD-ROM speeds.

Still, there are many creative ways to hide some of these limitations:

■ The small QuickTime movies that you create can be blown up 200% or more with no playback speed hindrance.

■ Smaller animations can be played in the distance to make a still image look more realistic. For example, add blowing drapes in a window or fly birds across your sky.

■ Have the player read something while you are loading in the next set of images and movies to be played.

5.5.5.2 RENDERED ON-THE-FLY

Games that are rendered on-the-fly are everywhere by the thousands. You'll find them on CD-ROMs, as well as Sony's Playstations 1 and 2 and Sega's Dreamcast platforms. And they all have one thing in common: They all use polygonal models textured with maps at a minimum size resolution.

What does this mean? Unlike pre-rendered games filled with minute details, these games have more simplified details and an increased ease of movement. There is less need for beauty because of the fast-paced action. When you are shooting demons, the last thing you are going to do is stop and look at the scenery. "Twitch games," as they are sometimes called, give players just enough visual information to convince them of being inside the game. There is little need for anything else.

POSSIBLE LIMITATIONS

Although companies work differently for different game titles, there are some similarities in designing for these types of games. The basic rule in designing for these games is realizing that you must create within a pre-defined memory limit per screen. This means that if you keep your geometry and texture information within these limitations, your game will play in real-time. Similar to that of the pre-rendered genre, the main idea is getting the information to the screen as fast as possible.

How is this done?

■ Streamlined polygonal geometry is used instead of NURBs because engines have a limit as to how much geometry can be on screen at one time. This means that models are created as minimally as possible, leaving the texture artists to fill in the visual blanks that are not there to begin with.

■ Keep texture maps small. It used to be that the largest texture map file size was 256×256 pixels. Just recently game developers have been able to use 512×512 maps for their final textures (some even 1024×1024). Texture artists will paint their maps at a higher resolution so as to add more detail and then scale or "rez" them down to the suitable size for the game engine.

■ Shadow and bump detail may be painted right into the color texture if real-time shadows and renderings of bumps are not available by the engine. Today, some engines are capable of this real-time bumpmapping, but even if the engine can do it, you may want to include it in your textures anyway to avoid taxing the engine.

■ Use repeated textures more. It is faster to load one texture that is tileable and repeat it in the engine than to load one large map and lug it around for the whole scene.

With all of this troubleshooting, you still cannot get away from the visible pixelation/deterioration of textures when viewed close-up due to the lack of resolution of the texture maps in these types of games.

Basically, the engine and your graphics card determine how much imagery and geometry can be on screen at any one given moment.

If you are interested in painting textures for these types of games, then you will have to know what type of platform you are creating your game for, what the memory cap that you have to consider is, and you must have a good knowledge of texturing and painting for polygons. See Chapter 10, "Axle's Face: Texturing Polygons" for an example of polygonal texturing.

5.6 DO YOU HAVE ALL THE INFORMATION YOU NEED?

With the information you have gathered thus far, you are now ready to begin your project in the computer. In fact, you have probably been ready for awhile! So, let's move on to the next section, and start painting!

6

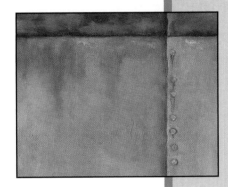

THE PROJECT: TECHNICAL PREPARATION

THE EXERCISES IN THE DuneBugs Project provide you with an opportunity to investigate different texturing techniques. These techniques involve:

- Scanning in real materials

- Making tileable textures

- Using handmade grunge maps

- Procedural textures

- Bump maps

- Displacement maps

- Other uses for maps, such as specularity, transparency, reflectivity and diffusion.

- Painting in 3D programs

NOTE

This chapter introduces the DuneBugs Project. The exercises that make up the Project are included in Chapters 7 through 14.

Further, these maps will be connected to "shaders," which will be rendered in your 3D program. Figure 6.1 shows a few of these shaders.

The exercises and techniques in The Project won't show you step by step how to paint, necessarily, but instead will tell you a story of the process of thought, procedure, and execution which brought me to the final textures.

Once you have a project in mind, it is good to start playing around with a number of different techniques—slowly eliminating the ones you don't need. Once you become acquainted with your own process, the elimination part will happen quickly.

Remember to:

- Ask the right questions before you start.

- Take advantage of pre-production materials, such as storyboards.

- Know your media, audience, and style.

- Consider factors while texturing the project, such as special effects, mood of the piece, and so on.

Taking a little time upfront to plan your work will save you time and headaches once you're deep in your project.

6.1 Here are a few examples of shaders and how they look when they are rendered.

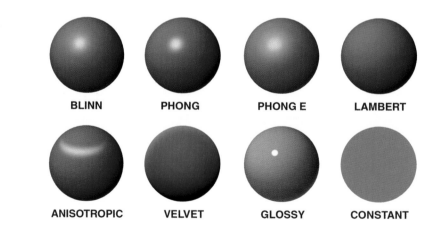

BLINN　　PHONG　　PHONG E　　LAMBERT

ANISOTROPIC　　VELVET　　GLOSSY　　CONSTANT

6.1 TEXTURE MAPPING CONCEPTS

Before you get into the exercises, it is important to know a few things about your texture maps and how they can be used for maps other than color information. In most cases, the color map is created first. From this color map, you can create derivatives that can be used for the many attributes that various shaders contain. These attributes are explained in the following sections.

6.1.1 COLOR

The texture maps that you create to describe the color information can be connected to the *color* (or in some programs, *diffuse*) channel. This is not to say that all your color maps need to contain color. Grayscale images can also be used. Even if your surface is 100% bright red, it can be a good idea to create a solid red texture in your paint program and add subtle nuances in *value* and *hue*. Pure pigment from a 3D program can look unnatural at times. In Figure 6.2, the valve cover on the left has been assigned a blue paint color from within the 3D program. On the right is a simple color map (painted in Photoshop) using the Noise filter to create hue variation.

6.2 The valve cover on the right had noise added to the color map in Photoshop, breaking up the unnatural solid blue valve cover on the left.

6.1.2 TRANSPARENCY

You can create maps to describe the transparent aspects of a model. White is 100% transparent, and black shows no transparency. All the values in-between give you varying degrees of transparency (see Figure 6.3). On the left is the transparency map created in Photoshop; on the right is how that map is interpreted by the renderer you are using. Notice how I used color in my transparency map and how it affects the color of the hose. (See Chapter 1 for more information on transparent characteristics.)

6.3 The colored transparency map created in Photoshop (left), and how it lets certain areas in the hose (right) become transparent with a pink hue.

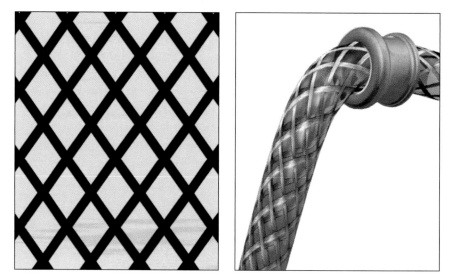

6.1.3 SPECULARITY

Highlight *value* and *color* on a surface can be described with a texture map. Here we can use either color or grayscale information to add convincing detail to a material. Lighter values and hues provide brighter highlights whereas darker values and hues provide more dimmed and subtle ones. Black provides no highlight information. In Figure 6.4, the image on the left has no specular map to define specularity, the middle image is the specular map painted in Photoshop, and on the right, its effect when connected to the specularity channel of a Phong shader and rendered. Lights and their direction reveal these highlights in your scene.

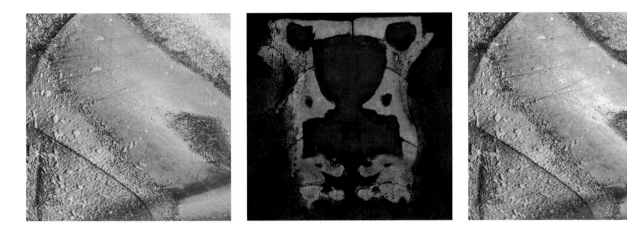

6.4 The specular map (middle) has been applied to the image on the right. Notice the difference between its specular information and the image on the far left, which has no map.

6.1.4 LUMINANCE

Luminance is also known as incandescence, ambience, or constant. Mapping a texture to the *luminosity* channel describes the self-illuminating parts of an object, such as the end of a cigarette or an open flame. (See Chapter 1 for more information on luminous characteristics.) The flame geometry on the left in Figure 6.5 is rendered without a luminosity map. Connecting a flame-colored ramp to the incandescence channel of a shader renders a more convincing flame on the right.

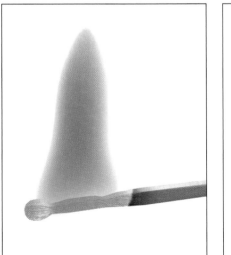

6.5 From "lame" on the left to "flame" on the right using luminance maps.

In some programs, you can use a luminance map, or create another dedicated map, to describe glow, which can add to the luminous effect.

6.1.5 REFLECTIVITY

If a surface is reflective, chances are it is not perfectly reflective in all areas. This is when you can use a texture map to describe *reflectivity*. White is 100% reflective and black is 0%—values in-between are varying levels of reflectivity. On the left in Figure 6.6 is the pool ball with no reflection map, in the middle (inset) is the circular ramp created for the reflectivity and it's positioning, and on the right, how it looks when rendered. (See Chapter 1 for more information on reflective characteristics.)

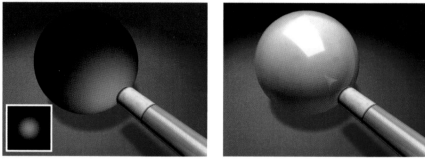

6.6 Notice the difference that the reflection map, middle, has made to the image on the right. It provides a more realistic portrayal of a pool ball's reflective quality than the image on the left.

6.1.6 BUMP

To simulate a bumpy characteristic on a surface in 3D programs, use what is known as *bump maps*. Renderers use the grayscale information from a texture file to calculate the nooks and crannies that may be on a surface. These show up on the final rendered image. The geometry does not change physically; rather it is an effect created at render time that fools the eye.

Bumps can either be positive, such as in indentations to a surface, or negative, mounds on the surface. Let's say that 50% black is the starting base tone. Anything above that tone in value, say 20%, would be higher than the base, and anything lower than that, say 80%, would be lower than the surface. This is shown in Figure 6.7. On the left is the bump map made in Photoshop and on the right, how it looks when rendered as a bump in 3D. A bump also does not affect the shape of a cast shadow at all. (See Chapter 1 for more information on bumpy characteristics.)

Bumps are most convincing from a viewpoint that doesn't reveal the object's profile, or the surface's edges. For that, you need displacements.

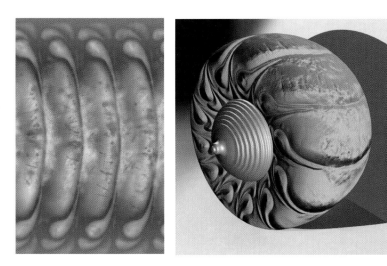

6.7 The map on the left is used to create a bump effect. The image on the right shows how the renderer calculates this information to give the illusion of a rough surface.

6.1.7 DISPLACEMENT

Displacements, like bumps, use maps to perform calculations on a piece of geometry, but with one big difference. Unlike bumps, displacements actually change the shape or silhouette of the geometry. This can be seen in Figure 6.8. Displacements react the same way to changes in tone (variations of gray) as bumps. Here you can plainly see that the shape of the displaced tire has been pushed out and it has also affected the tire's cast shadow.

NOTE

Displacements can be expensive in terms of memory usage and rendering times, so use them wisely and sparingly.

6.8 The image on the left is the texture map that has created the tire displacement on the right. Notice that this displacement map is more simplified than the bump map in Figure 6.7. Both the bump and displacement maps are used together to create the final effect. See the Tire exercise in Chapter 9.

6.1.8 THAT'S NOT ALL FOLKS

You can connect texture maps to other attributes, besides the ones just described. The list is limited only by the shader you choose for your object. For instance, a Lambert shader doesn't have a channel for specularity or reflectivity, to name two. Its mathematics do not take those characteristics into consideration. Some shaders allow you to attach textures to glossiness or refraction or metalness. The list is long.

6.2 GENERAL CONCEPTS

The exercises in the following chapters are meant to show you how to work—not to show you how to paint every brushstroke or create selections and use filters. For each exercise, you'll find a copy of the final Photoshop file—complete with layers—on the accompanying CD. You can use these files to check out how layers can be used to add detail upon detail to create amazing texture paintings.

Here are some basic methods that I use to create my paintings:

1. Before starting a project, I step away from the computer and create hand-painted grunge maps. In the case of this project, dirt, oil, and grease grunge maps are needed. See Figure 6.9.

6.9 Using oil paints on paper (left), or acrylics on card stock (right), I get my hands dirty and create grunge maps that I can use over and over again.

2. As shown in Figure 6.10, I like to paint as many details for objects as I can outside the computer using traditional mediums such as oil paints, felt pens, acrylics, or even sculpting materials such as Sculpey™. (See Chapter 14, "Axle's Chest: Sculpting, Painting, and Projections.")

6.10 These two texture maps were created outside the computer with oil paints (left), and Sculpey™, tinted with acrylics and oils (right).

3. After my work with traditional media is finished, I move to Photoshop, where I layer these paintings overtop each other using different *blendings* and *opacities*, as you will see from my Photoshop documents on the accompanying CD. An example of this is illustrated in Figure 6.11.

6.11 The six images shown here are some of the layers that went into creating the final color map on the lower right. These are taken from the Fin Exercise in Chapter 13.

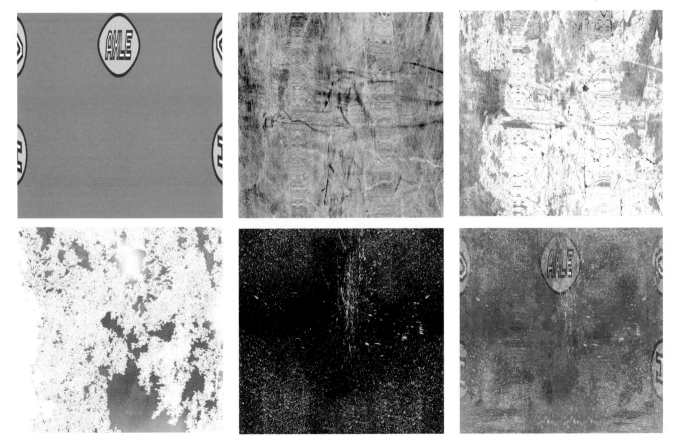

4. I create many of my grungy and rusty shapes using the Magic Wand selection tool in Photoshop on certain areas and deleting these selections or changing their color *balance*, *levels*, or *sharpness*. Take a look at Figure 6.12.

 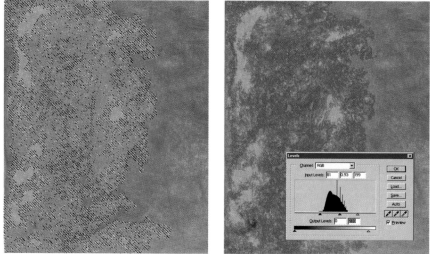

6.12 The grunge painting on the left is the starting image that, when using the Magic Wand selection tool, middle, allows for image manipulation to create things like rust or peeling paint, right.

6.13 This close-up of the bump map for the tire shows painted cracks and airbrushed mounds and indentations painted using a tablet and stylus in Painter and Photoshop.

5. In other cases, see Figure 6.13, I use Painter 6 and Photoshop's Airbrush or Brushes on overlying layers to add detail such as dirt in cracks and intersections. I also create my own brushes in these programs for things like dust or speckles. See Chapter 9, "The Tire: Adding Detail with Displacement Maps" and Chapter 12, "The Car Body: Complexity of Texture."

6. I use certain filters from Photoshop such as Gaussian Blur, Motion Blur, Add Noise, and a couple of others, but I don't rely on many of them to create most of my textures.

7. For some of my grunge map work, I use Painter 6 and its many excellent brushes; watercolor, oil, and FX brushes, combining these with the Define Pattern option turned on for the canvas. This allows you to paint over one edge of the canvas while it continues to paint onto the opposite edge allowing you to create a seamless tile. These along with some of Painter's effects can create some interesting texture maps. See Figure 6.14.

6.14 The image on the left has been painted in Painter with various brushes. On the right is the same image with the "Apply Surface Texture" Effect added. This filter adds highlight and shadow as if it has been rendered in 3D bringing out extra details.

8. I use Illustrator to create some interesting graphics as well as the Hatch Effects filter that can turn any filled shape into a series of lines, crosshatched or otherwise, see Figure 6.15. These later get used as scratch maps in layered Photoshop files. (See Chapter 13, "The Fin: Texturing Uneven Surfaces.")

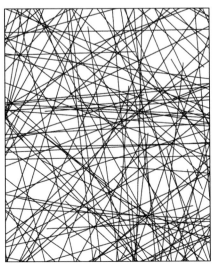
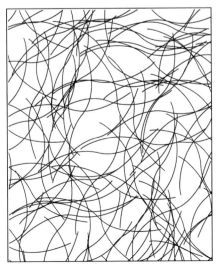

6.15 Here are a couple examples of Illustator's Hatch Effects filter used to create scratches for grunge map use.

My intent is that the concepts of the exercises will build one on top of the other as you work through them. They have been set up in order of difficulty, starting with the easier concepts and gradually increasing in complexity.

Chapters 7 through 14 will take you through the creation of most of the DuneBugs Project. All of the exercises and techniques have a lot to teach you about technique and decision making. Have fun and be inspired.

7

THE BANDANA: A SIMPLE TILE AND SCANNED TEXTURE

THE BANDANA SHOWS YOU the simplest way to acquire a texture: scanning real textures in Photoshop and making a tile with no seam. The tileable texture is wrapped around a NURB model. I wanted the bandana to be made from real cloth (rag) that was already soiled, so I scanned some of my own paint rags that I had lying around. I later manipulated the texture of the paint rag to make it part of Axle's environment.

1. From my pile of paint rags, I chose this one.

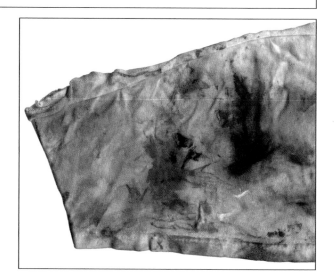

2. I didn't worry about wrinkles when I scanned in the rag; the wrinkles add to the detail. I scanned both sides of the rag at 300 dpi and merged them into one by:

   ■ Increasing canvas size at 200% to the right.

   ■ Copying and pasting scan #2 into scan #1.

   ■ Butting them right up against one another.

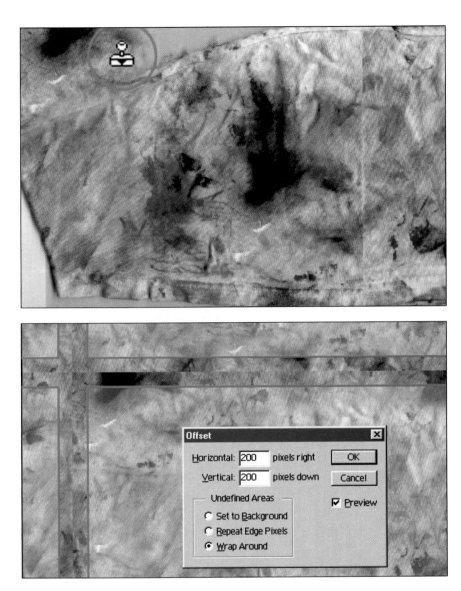

3. I needed to fill in the empty spaces with the texture, and fix the seam. I used the Rubber Stamp tool and used a 300-pixel brush at 0% hardness.

   To see the results of steps 1–3, open **RagCombo_Maker.psd** from the CD.

4. Once all the areas are filled in, you need to make the image tileable, hiding any evidence of seams. To find these seams, flatten the file and then use the Offset filter as shown.

> **NOTE**
>
> You may want to make a copy of your file before flattening it to retain the layers in case you need to go back to them.

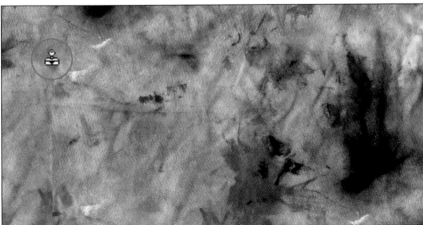

5. Continue with the Rubber Stamp tool to hide seams. If you go past the edges of the canvas while touching up, you'll need to apply the Offset filter again and use the Rubber Stamp tool until you get a completely seamless texture.

6. Here is the final tileable texture map in Photoshop. For the purposes of the bandana, the visible repeats are fine (the red spots). In some circumstances, you may want to avoid a pattern that is too repetitious.

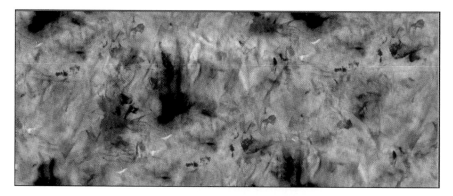

APPLYING THE TEXTURE TO THE GEOMETRY

7. The bandana texture rendered on the geometry looked pretty good, but for my own aesthetic reasons, I felt that there were too many dark, black blotches.

> **NOTE**
>
> If your original position of the texture is important (i.e., the centering of a logo), then you must offset the image back as many times as you went forward. In other words, you must move as many times to the left (×200 pixels) as you went to the right (×200 pixels).

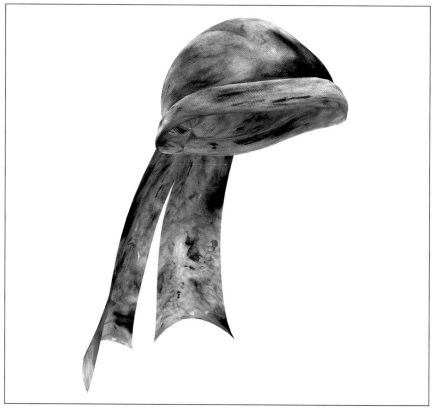

8. I used the same Rubber Stamp tool to cover up the dark blotches.

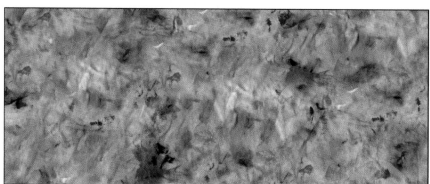

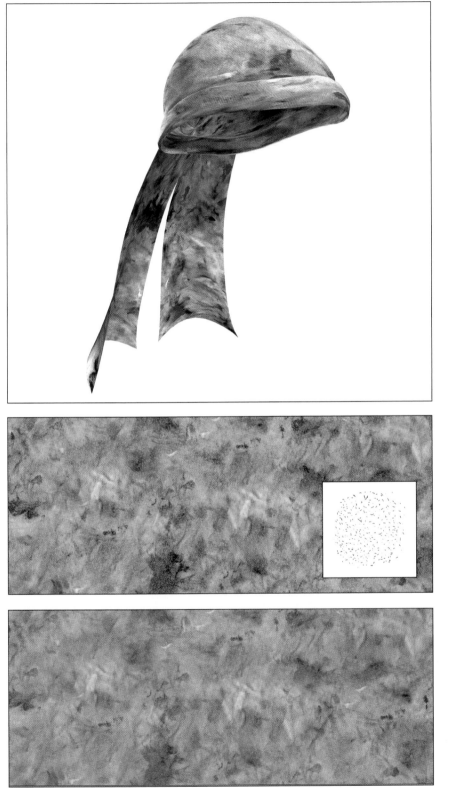

9. Here's the rendered image without the dark blotches.

10. Decreased saturation of the rag made it look sun-bleached and old. For the dusty quality, I created a brush like the one in the inset figure.

11. I painted the dust layers one by one, four in all. I blurred two of the layers and slightly changed the color of the other two for variation.

12. The end result is a dust-peppered, sun-bleached cloth texture. Compare this to the images in steps 7 and 9. For myself, I like both versions in steps 9 and 12. Which one do you like best?

You can use **RagCombo_ MakerV2.psd** from on the CD to see the results of steps 10 and 11.

RENDERING AND SHADING

This bandana surface is quite simple. It has no specular highlights to speak of so I used a Lambert shader. Describing any bumpiness at this point isn't necessary either. If the camera were to get really close to the bandana, however, then I would probably add some sort of bump detailing.

As simple as this exercise may seem, it is important to realize that a scanned texture may require you to do "your thing" to it; make it sit well in your scene. Don't be afraid to manipulate your scanned-in imagery to make it "behave." Just because it's "real" doesn't mean it's "perfect."

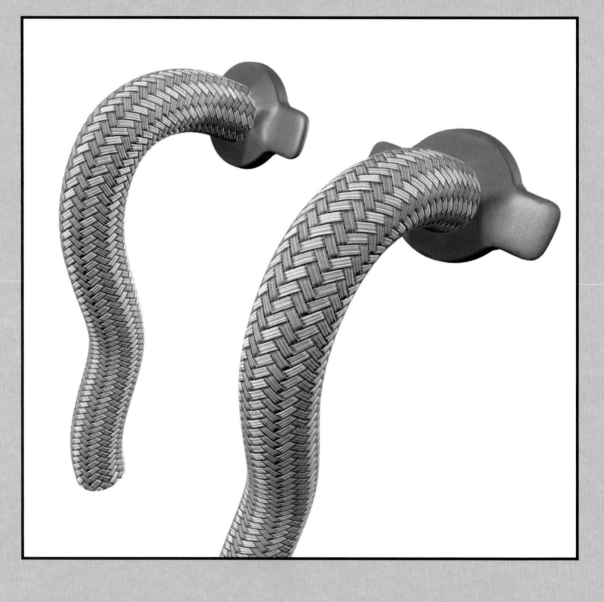

8

STEEL BRAIDED HOSES: A SMALL TILEABLE TEXTURE

THE FIRST PART OF THIS EXERCISE will show you how to create and use small patterned textures that can be repeated on a piece of geometry. In the second half I will show you how to use a manipulated version of the tileable color pattern to describe the bumpy quality of the model.

If you can break down a pattern into something that is tileable, it can be very helpful when rendering. A tileable map at 128 pixels×128 pixels (a 48KB file size) can be loaded by your renderer much more easily than a larger file at 2048 pixels×2048 pixels (a 12MB file size). This minimizes rendering times and RAM usage.

The braided hoses are made from woven steel that can be broken down into a small repeatable unit. This makes it a perfect candidate for the tileable texture approach.

1. This is my main photo for reference. Looking at the pattern, I determined that it was made up of threading, which wove over and under in an "over-two-under-two" rhythm. I like this photo also because it gives me great textural information of the metal housing the hoses fit into.

2. Here is a scan of a similar weave. It is smaller in scale, but this weave texture gives me more information than the one above.

3. This reference photo gave me some ideas for other hoses and metals on the dune buggy car body.

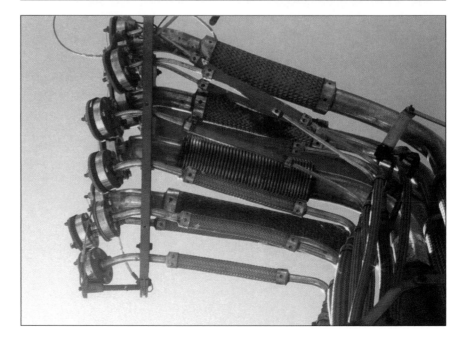

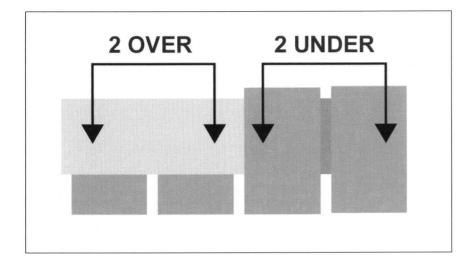

MAKING THE PATTERN

4. In Illustrator, I created my modular woven steel unit. I used a dark tone for the vertical threads and a light tone for the horizontal ones. Darker versions of these two tones were used to show the thread that runs underneath. This made it easier to see the pattern, and to isolate the horizontal from the vertical elements.

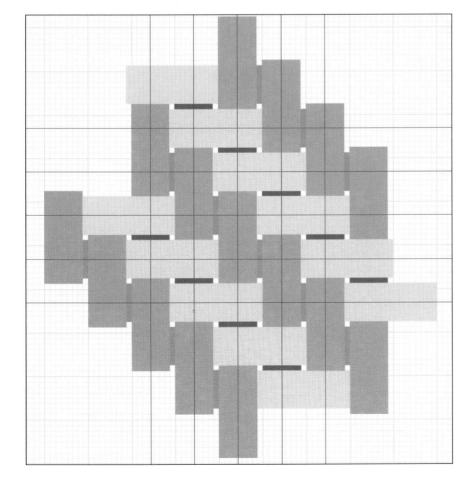

5. I repeated enough of this steel unit to capture a tile.

    You can use the file **hose_ weavePattern_Maker.ai** from the accompanying CD to see the result of step 4.

6. I drew a square around the pattern and selected all the elements. I used the Trim function to get rid of the excess. The trick to finding a tile is to understand your whole pattern. In this case, the tile has to contain the modular unit both horizontally and vertically.

You can use the **hose_ weavePattern_Tile.ai** on the CD to see the results.

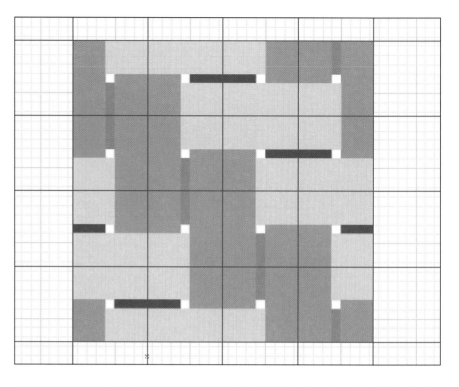

7. Always test your tile. Here is an easy way to do that in Illustrator: Create a square white box the same size as your tile and Object > Arrange > Send To Back. Select all elements and choose Define Pattern as shown. Name the file Cable Pattern.

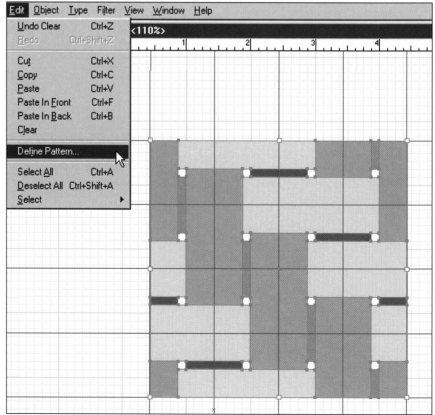

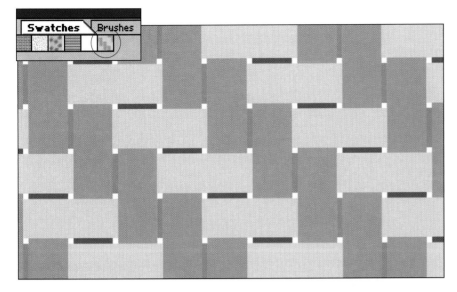

8. This pattern now shows up in your Swatches palette. Create a large rectangle and fill it by clicking on the Cable Pattern swatch. If it is successful, you won't notice the individual tile, just one large pattern.

Open the document **hose_steelWeave.psd** on the CD.

TEXTURING THE TILE

9. To add color map details, open **hose_steelWeave.psd** in Photoshop. Create a new layer above the color layer and name it Horizontal Weave. Using the customized brush shown, make brush lines to suggest threads. Duplicate this layer and rotate it 90 degrees to create the vertical threads.

You can use the **hose_steelWeave_Maker.psd** on the CD to see the results of steps 9–12.

10. In the **color** layer, using the Magic Wand and Shift, select all the horizontal blocks of color. Select the **horizontal weave** layer and create a layer mask as shown. Do the same for the vertical weave layer.

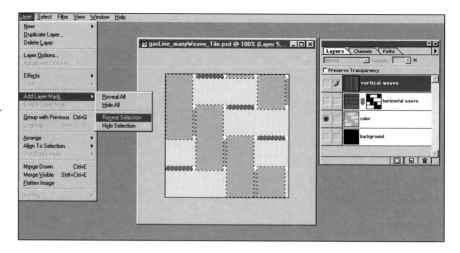

11. Create a new layer and load the **vertical weave** layer mask and airbrush dirt and shadow into the creases.

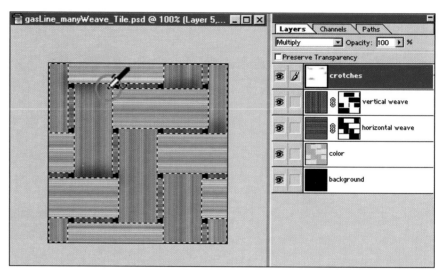

12. When you do the same for the **horizontal weave** layer and set its Blending Option to Multiply, it looks like this. Duplicate the file and flatten it.

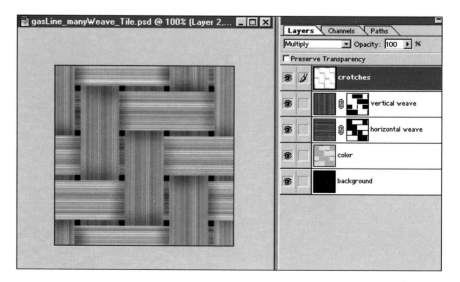

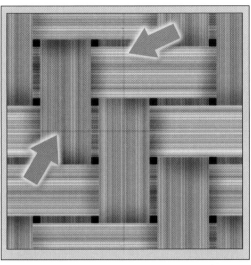

13. Offset this duplicated file by 128 pixels × 128 pixels to see if there are any visible breaks in the pattern (see the previous exercise). As you can see, there are flaws in the file, both in the vertical and horizontal elements.

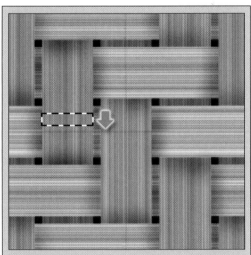

14. I eliminated the flaws with the Marquee tool. Define a region just above the flaw, switch to the Move tool, hold down the Option key, and Shift-drag over top the blemish. When the flaw is covered, deselect the region.

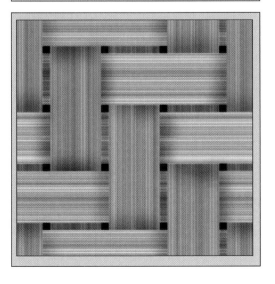

15. Repeat step 14 for the remaining flaws. Your result should resemble the figure.

16. Here is the render of our pattern on the geometry. It has been rotated by 45 degrees, and repeated a number of times. Compare this to the reference pictures. To me, it looks very close, but it still needs a bit more detail. Let's add a bump map to it.

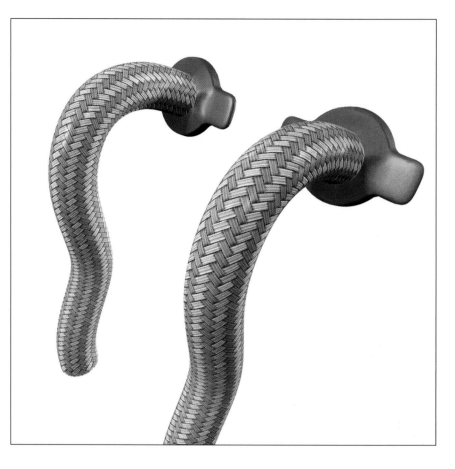

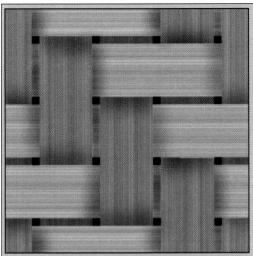

CREATING THE BUMP

In some cases, you can use the color map directly for the bump map, but in this case we'll need to manipulate it a bit.

17. Open the file **hose_steelWeave_BumpMaker.psd** from the accompanying CD. This is the color map converted to a grayscale image. I need to decrease the two-tone quality of the pattern. The vertical weave is darker in tone than the horizontal weave. There should be no tonal distinction between the two; as it is, the darker-toned weave would be deeper set than the lighter-toned weave and wouldn't have been true to the material.

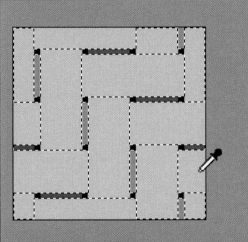

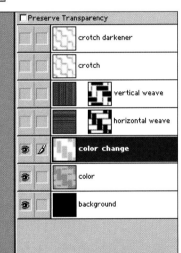

18. Here I decrease the two-tone quality by loading the **vertical weave** mask layer as my selection, and then create a new layer called **color change**. With the Eyedropper tool, I click on the light gray tone from the **color** layer and fill the selection on the **color change** layer with that tone.

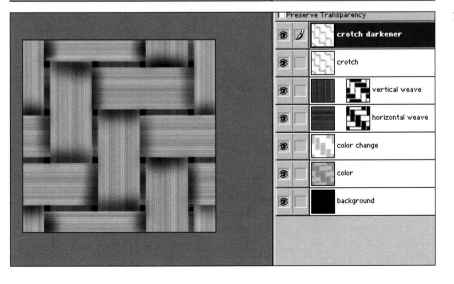

19. I duplicate the **crotch** layer to further deepen the places where the threads go under one another. This is the final bump map.

All this color and bump map work has been created at 256× 256 pixels. I make a copy of both of these and flatten them. Then I scale down the color map 50%, which decreases the tile size to 128×128 pixels. Once scaled down, the map looks a little soft and unfocused, so I use the Unsharp Mask filter in Photoshop to bring out more of its detail.

SHADER AND FINAL TEXTURE MAPS

I chose a Phong shader to describe this steel braided hose. It, like most metals, has some specular information, so I connected the color map to the specular port. I also connected a map, created from the color map, to the Reflectivity channel of the Phong shader, to describe its reflectivity.

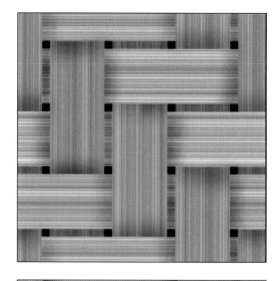

20. This is the final color map, which is also used for the specular color.

21. The final bump map.

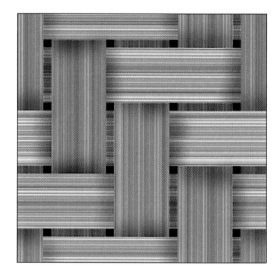

22. The reflectivity map, made from the color map, has had its contrast intensified slightly so that there are definite reflective and non-reflective areas.

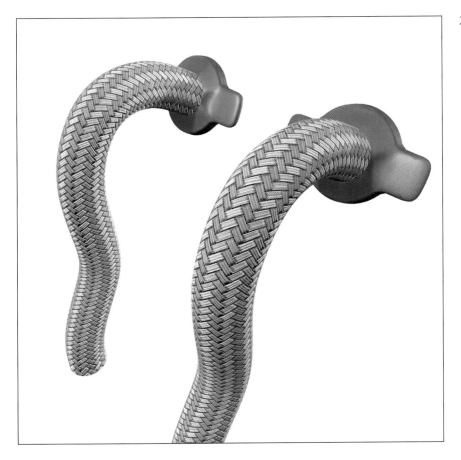

23. This is the final render of the braided cable with all the final maps connected. Compare this to the render with the color map only. Do the extra maps add any useful textural information to the hose or is it overkill?

You have to be the judge when it comes to deciding how far to take the creation of a texture. I believe that if I am creating a metal, as in this exercise, I include the attributes that describe metals; reflectivity, specularity, and so on. It adds to the depth of the texture, and I use it in the animation under different conditions—lighting or even weather—hoping that this extra work will pay off in the end.

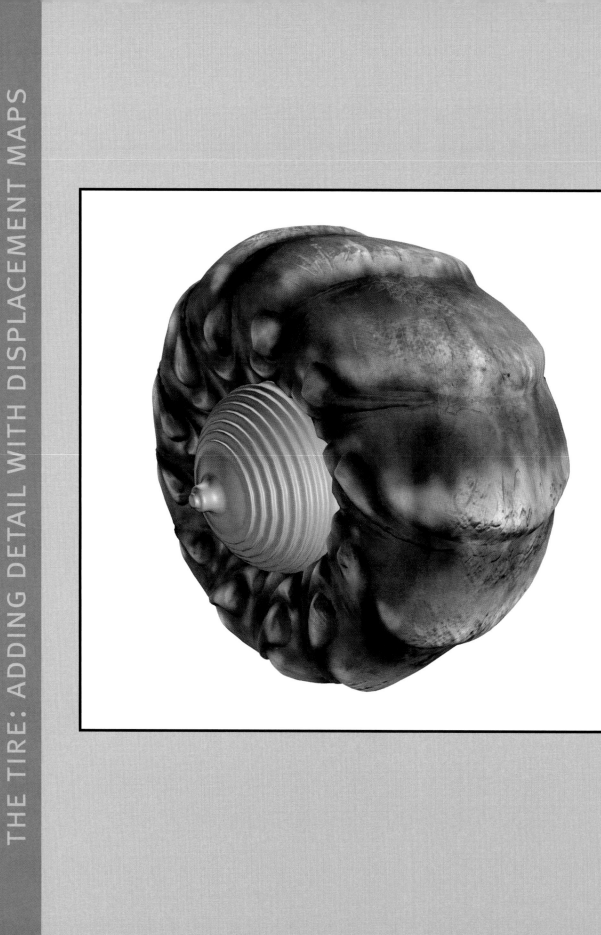

9

THE TIRE: ADDING DETAIL WITH DISPLACEMENT MAPS

WHEN WORKING ON A PROJECT, sometimes an object or segment of an object, might call for details too complex for the modeler to model in the time allotted. Or you may want to add details to a model long after the modeler has finished. You can use displacement maps instead of adding geometry for this extra detail.

With this tire exercise, you will concentrate on creating a grayscale texture map that displaces the modeled tire in Figure 9.1 to create the tire's treads on the opening left page.

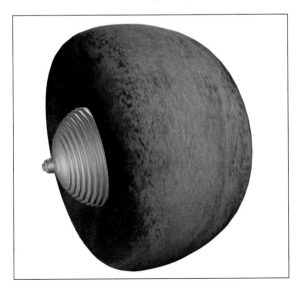

9.1 This is the original modeled tire with no tread detail at all.

PRE-PRODUCTION

Don't limit yourself to the expected when looking for textures.

1. I cross-referenced larvae- or armadillo-like retractable bodies of shelled insects, with the latest in tire tread design for sand and off-road vehicles to create my design of the tire.

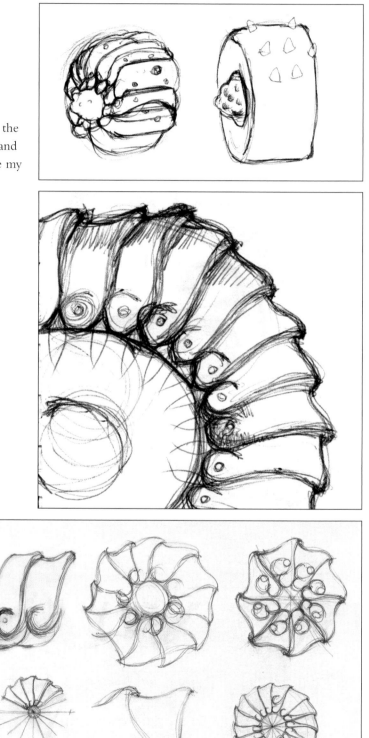

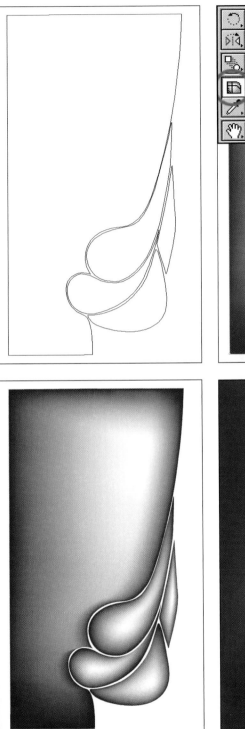

2. In Illustrator I drew my shapes as per my drawings (left) and filled them with black. Notice that I only drew the bottom half of the design. I will later duplicate it to make it a whole tile.

Using the Gradient Mesh tool (right), I changed the foreground color to white and clicked in the areas I wanted the lighter blends to be.

You can open the file **tireDisp_Curves.ai** from the accompanying CD to follow along with the first part of this exercise.

3. The figure on the left is the result of four clicks with the Gradient Mesh tool. This is much easier than using an Airbrush tool, and the points are all editable so you can move them or change their colors on-the-fly.

The figure on the right, after a bit of tweaking and creating a black rectangle to sit in the background, is the final half of the displacement map. Check out the final file, **tireDisp_Final.ai**, on the accompanying CD.

4. Now we need to get this Illustrator file into Photoshop to continue. After naming the layers, export the Illustrator file as a Photoshop document. Set the resolution for 300dpi and turn on Anti-Aliasing and Write Layers. I named this export **tireDisp_TileMaker_pt1.psd**.

Open the exported **tireDisp_TileMaker_pt1.psd** file in Photoshop. Notice that it has kept the layers and their respective names. Follow along to see how I made the part 1 of the tile and the changes I made to each layer as I talk about the steps.

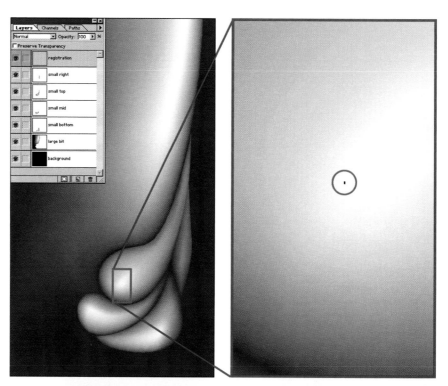

5. With the Move tool, I dragged the new, flattened duplicate layer while holding down the Shift key and dropped it back into the **tireDisp_TileMaker_pt1.psd** document. In the Layers palette, I positioned it above the **background** layer and named it **duplicate flattened**. On this layer, I did a Shift-drag to the right, butting up the "small middle" mound to the "small bottom" mound. Notice the layer settings for this new addition in the Photoshop file.

As you can see in the document, I changed the Blending Options on each layer to Lighten and set their opacities at different values. This allowed the amount of displacement to get larger gradually from the bottom (or the areas closest to the rim) to the center of the tire.

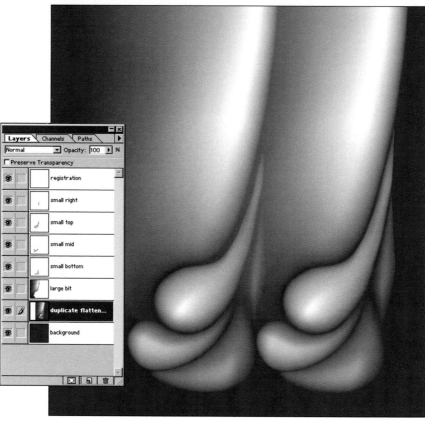

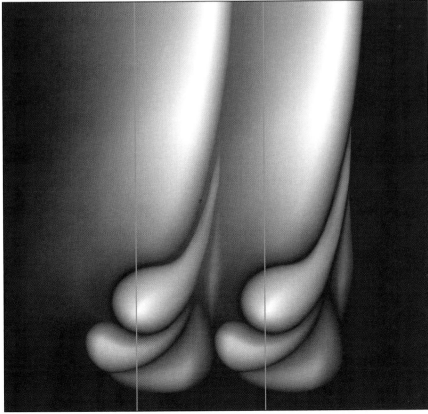

CREATING THE TILE

6. I created a new layer named **registration** at the very top of the Layers palette. I took a one-pixel square brush and made a mark on this layer overtop of the small top mound. This will serve as a place-mark to define the tile later. I then duplicated the whole image (Image > Duplicate > Merged Layers Only).

Now it's time to make the tile. Zoom in to the one-pixel mark that you made in step 4, making sure that Snap to Pixel is on, and drag a guide next to it as shown. Do the same for the second tread.

7. Zoom out. The area between the guides is the tile. Want to test it to make sure?

8. Drag a Marquee selection from guide to guide and top to bottom. (Be sure Snap-To-Guide is on.) Go to Edit > Define Pattern.

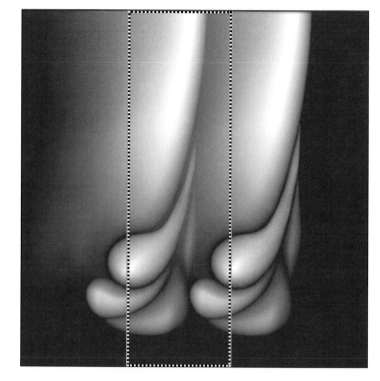

9. Create a new document at 2500×2957 pixels, 300 dpi for the tile test. Grab the Paint Bucket tool and change its fill option to Pattern. Click in the new doc, and you should be able to tell if it is indeed a tile. This one is! Close and don't save the test tile document.

Go back to the **tireDisp_ TileMaker_pt1.psd** document. Duplicate and flatten it. This leaves the layered original as is in case you want to go back into it and make further changes later.

Remarquee the duplicated file at the guides and crop the image. Get rid of the one-pixel registration mark on your artwork with a small white brush.

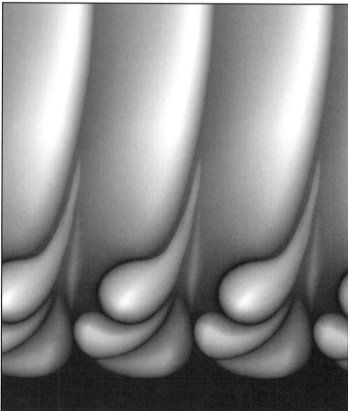

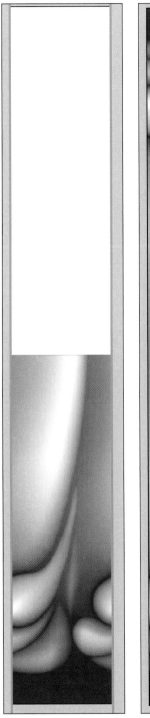
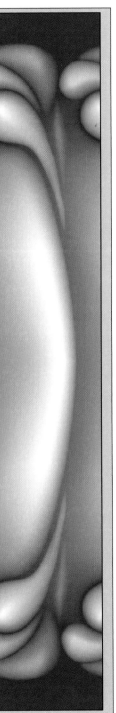

10. We still need to make the full tile, so select Canvas Size and trim three pixels just from the top of the artwork to get rid of the aliasing on that edge due to the conversion process from Illustrator to Photoshop. Now there will be a seamless butting up of the two pieces.

Open the file **tireDisp_ TileMaker_pt2.psd** on the CD to follow along.

Select all, and copy the image into the clipboard. Go to Canvas Size again, and increase it 200% vertically.

11. Paste the artwork that you copied to the clipboard on top of this document, vertically flip the new layer, and move it into place, far right. This tile (862×5569 pixels) is ready to be used in a 3D program and repeated as many times as needed.

12. The displacement map applied to the tire with a repeat of 12 in one direction and rendered.

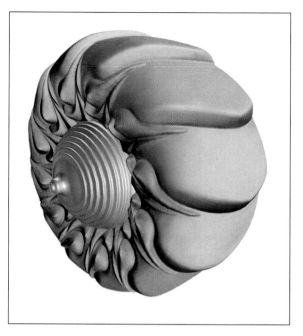

COLOR MAP

13. This final color map for the tire was made in Photoshop by repeating the displacement map on a canvas four times. This allowed me to describe each of these four treads a little differently from the others to avoid obvious tiling.

    You can open the **tireColorMap_Maker.psd** from the accompanying CD to follow along.

> **NOTE**
>
> I made the color map and the bump map much smaller in size (1268× 2048) than the displacement map, but they are large enough for the information that I needed in the final rendering.

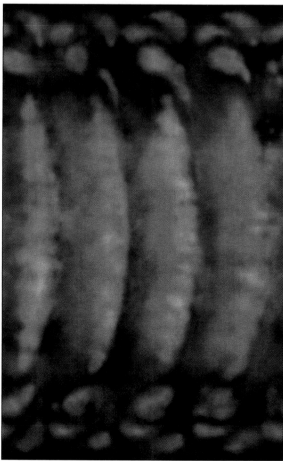

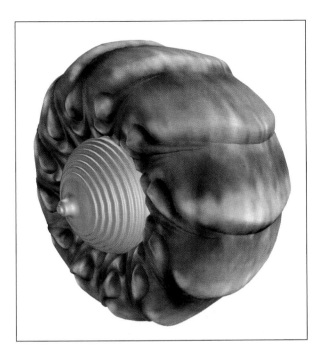

14. In my 3D program, I repeated this color map three times around to make the 12 treads. This is the rendering of the tire with the displacement and color map.

BUMP MAP

15. I painted the bump map from the color map as well. It can be found on the CD as **tireBumpMap_ Maker.psd**.

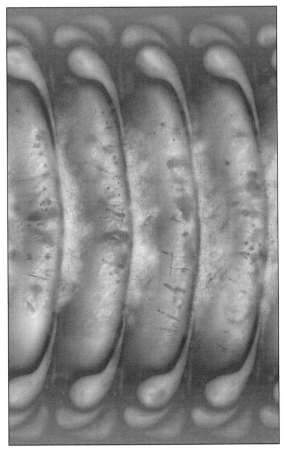

16. This is how the final tire looks. Look at the difference the bump map makes to the detail of the displacement as well as the color information of this tire.

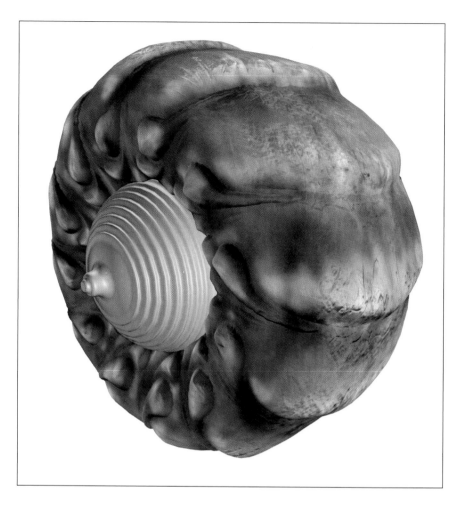

SHADER STUFF

I chose a Lambert shader to describe the surface quality of the tire. Because of the amount of dust and sand in Axle's environment I wanted no specular highlights at all. You, on the other hand, may want to add some sort of highlight detail. To do so, you would need to use a shading model that was equipped with specular information, such as a Blinn or a Phong. You would also need to create a specular map for that channel. It is hard to believe that this new tire design has been created solely with a texture map. The differences between this and the very first tire I textured are night and day. (Take another look at the **DuneBugs2.mov** or **DuneBugs2.avi** on the CD.) Not only does this add model detailing, but it also enhances the character design of the Bug/Dune-Bug hybrid.

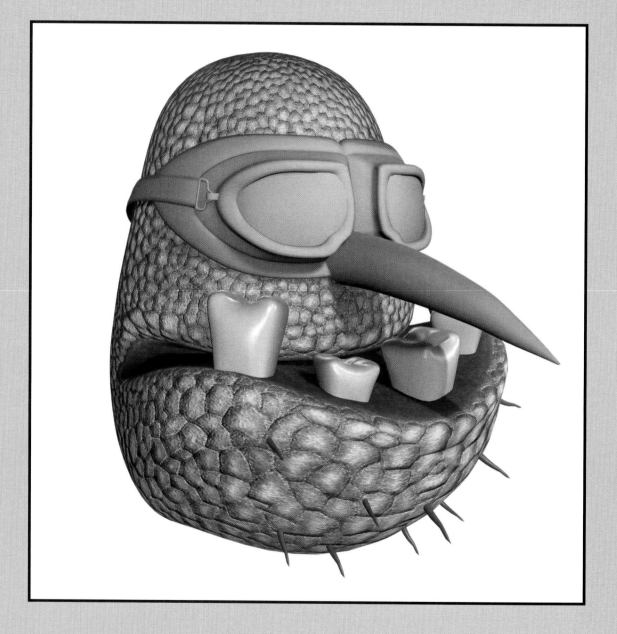

CHAPTER 10

AXLE'S FACE: TEXTURING POLYGONS

THIS EXERCISE IS DESIGNED to show you, first, how to set up polygons for texturing, and second, how to paint bump detail in your 3D paint program. I used Maya to prepare the polygonal mesh, but most 3D programs have their own tools to do much the same operations. I used Right Hemisphere's Deep Paint to paint the bump map, although most 3D paint programs can handle this exercise.

PREPARING POLYGONS FOR TEXTURING IN 3D

Texture maps attach themselves to geometry by texture coordinates called UVs. The NURBs surfaces you create come complete with UVs. In most 3D applications, NURBs' UV coordinates are always locked; you cannot adjust their position without adjusting the geometry as well. Polygonal geometry you create, on the other hand, needs UV coordinates assigned to them by using *projections* (Planar, Cylindrical, Spherical, and so on). You can edit their position without affecting the geometry.

PRE-PRODUCTION

I want Axle's face to look dry and scaly like a lizard's skin with dirt in the cracks. Here are some of the pre-production images I created.

1. This very quick style study of coloration approximates the look and feel of the character. This is one way I immerse myself into a project.

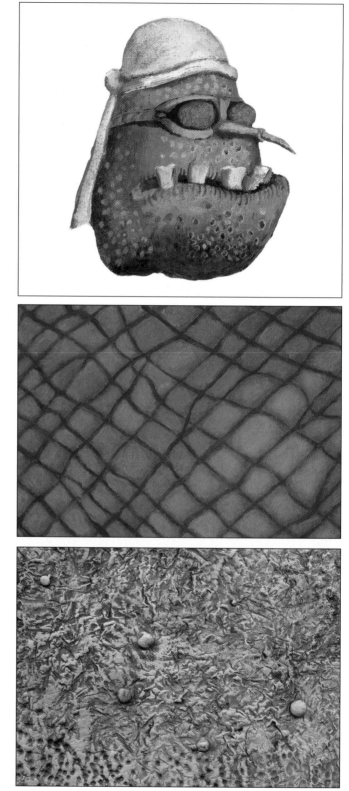

2. I tried some "scale" tests of patterns and color with oil paint on paper. I liked this one, but the scales were too square.

3. I like to use sculpting materials to investigate what look I want, and to experiment with texture. I use modeling wax, clay, and in this case, Sculpey™. It is easy to apply color to this material once it is cured. I used green and brown acrylic paint for this study. I never used this example in the final project, but by experimenting in this way, I got some ideas for other parts of Axle, such as his chest.

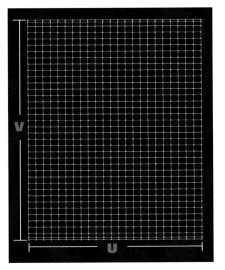

4. The yellow squares in the left figure describe NURBs' UV coordinates in a simple, uniform grid pattern. The right figure shows how this translates in 3D software.

When a checkered pattern is applied, you can see that even though the UVs on the left look even, there is still a lot of distortion on parts of the model, such as his mouth, and the top of his head.

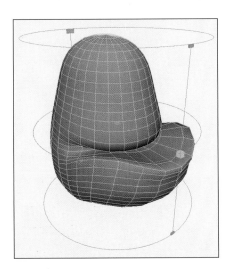

5. This image shows the application of a cylindrical projection to the selected polygonal faces of Axle's face.

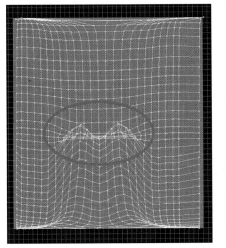

6. The left figure shows how this projection arranges the pattern of the UVs. As you can see, there are some problems with the mouth overlapping (circled in red), and this would cause distortion of the texture.

The figure on the right shows how this projection makes the checkered pattern look. Notice the checks are quite stretched in the mouth and are pinching and spiraling on the top of his head.

7. To get a more uniform checkered pattern, the UVs need to be adjusted. Adjust the pinching at the top and the bottom of the head by applying *Planar projections* to these parts. Select the polygonal faces that you want to apply a projection to (left).

Apply projection to just those faces (right).

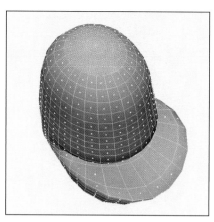 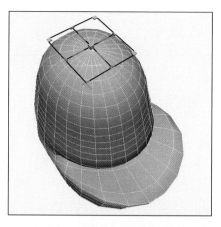

8. This is how the UVs look in Maya's Texture Window after the projection is applied to the top of the head.

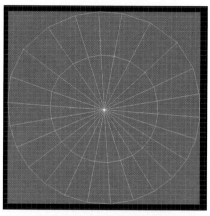

9. Now, one map has the main, top, and bottom head pieces separated. The mouth area and other parts on the main body of the face need to have the UVs cleaned up.

As I stated before, you can manipulate these UVs. I maneuvered them so that there were no overlapping polygonal faces.

NOTE

You can view UVs in most 3D animation packages and 3D paint programs. For instance, in 3ds max you can view and edit UVs in the Edit UVWs Window.

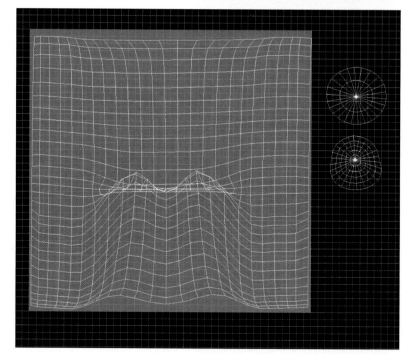

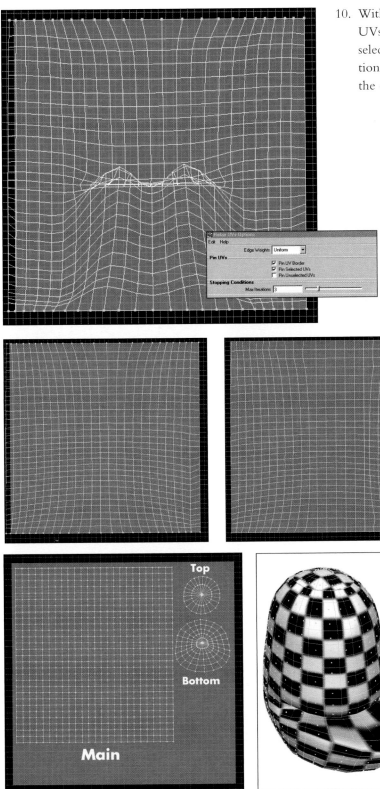

10. With the top and bottom rows of UVs in the figure on the left selected, Maya's Relax UVs function is applied repeatedly with the options shown.

11. The results look like the left figure.

    The rightmost figure shows that I continued manipulating UVs. Selecting each row one by one, I moved them with Snap to Grid turned on.

12. The result of the final adjustments to the UV layout (left).

    This is how the checkered pattern now looks with the adjusted UVs (right). Notice that the top of the head is completely even. The mouth still has a little stretching, which I can fix up some more, but the teeth in his mouth will hide this stretching.

CREATING THE BUMP PATTERN

13. For the next phase, I imported the geometry into Right Hemisphere's Deep Paint and assigned a 4K color map to it. I painted the scaly pattern on the "model" with a simple brush. I started around the eyes and worked my way around the face (left). Because the face is symmetrical, I drew on only half the face. The red line indicates the halfway mark on the full face.

14. In Photoshop, I duplicated and mirrored it, and then applied it to the other half (left). We are now finished with Deep Paint. On the right is a close-up of the final drawing.

    You can open the **AceFace_ Bump_Fix3.jpg** file from the CD to follow along.

15. The quality of the line is not a concern at this point because I know I am going to work with filters in Photoshop that will hide inconsistencies.

    I applied a Gaussian Blur at 9 (left).

    Then I applied a Maximum filter of 5 applied (right). It gives you a soft, pillowed effect for the bump.

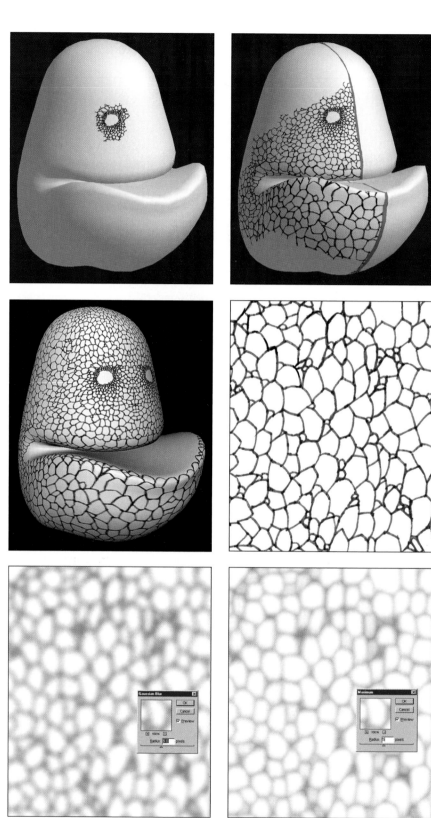

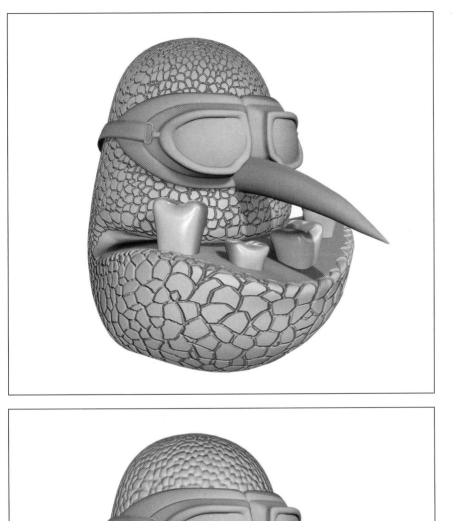

16. The cracks in Axle's face are not gouges with sharp shadows, shown in this render of the bump before I applied the Photoshop filters.

17. Instead, they are expressed such that the bump looks softly contoured and rounded, as in this figure on the left.

CREATING THE COLOR MAP

18. The color map is half the size of the bump map at 2K. (You don't need as much information as you do for the bump map in this case.)

    I used the inverse of this version of the bump map as an Alpha Channel to make a unique color map that suits and fits the bump and Axle's face. This is important because, instead of using a straight color and relying on the bump for definition, the color map can add some of the flare.

    You can use the CD file **AxleFace_Color_Maker.psd** to follow along.

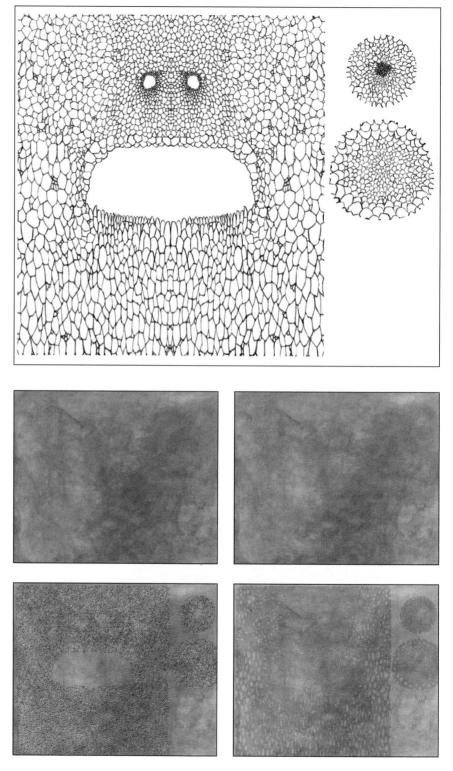

19. I started with a very simple grunge map (left) that I used for the car body as well. I colored it green, duplicated this layer, and changed the new layer's hue to brown. Using a Layer Mask, I painted away most of this brown layer, leaving just enough to create color variation (right).

20. I then found a way to impress the pattern onto the color map.

    Load Alpha Channel 1 as a selection, invert it, contract it two pixels, and feather it two pixels. Control+J (Windows) or Command+J (Mac OS) puts that into a new layer (left). I named this layer **Lighter Cells**. I then played with color balance and color levels to make a lighter tint (right).

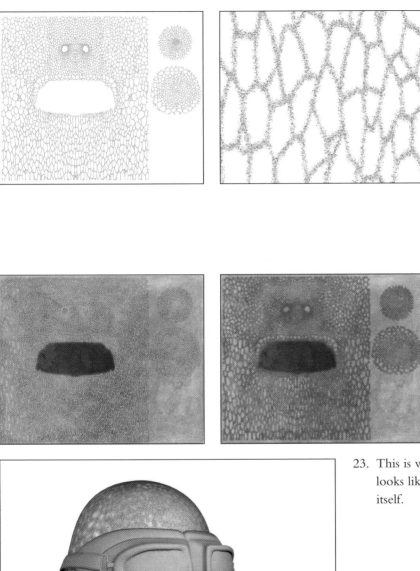

21. Load Alpha Channel 1 again, create a new layer named **Brown Cracks**, and using the Paint Bucket tool, fill it with a lighter warm brown (left). Deselect this selection. Next, apply the Stylized > Diffuse (Normal Mode) filter twice to this layer to break up the hard perfect edge. Now apply the Add Noise filter with Uniform and Monochromatic for settings to express the peppered, powdery dust in the cracks. See the close-up of the result on the right.

22. I darkened the interior of the mouth (left), duplicated the bump drawing layer, and put it at the very top of the Layers palette. I applied a Gaussian blur to it, and in a layer mask that I created for it, I reduced its coverage. Setting this layer to Multiply at 61% adds darkness to certain areas of the cracks (right).

23. This is what the final color map looks like on Axle's face all by itself.

FINAL MAPS

As in the other exercises, it's a rewarding experience to look at all the maps created for one piece of geometry next to each other. It is a lesson in how much work you may need to do per model. Next time you watch a 3D animated film, try to guess how many texture maps were painted in total for the piece.

24. The final color map. Notice how the color map resembles the bump map pattern, adding that much more personality to Axle's face.

25. For the final bump effect, I ended up using two bump maps, one on top of the other, as well as the color map. This one is the bump that I created with both Photoshop filters applied.

26. I saved another version with just the Maximum filter applied to be used to deepen the cracks.

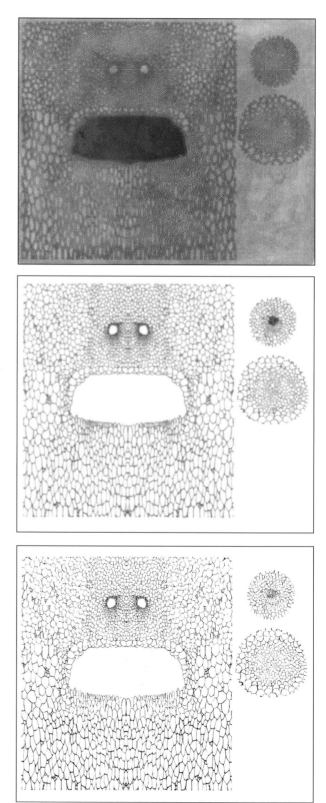

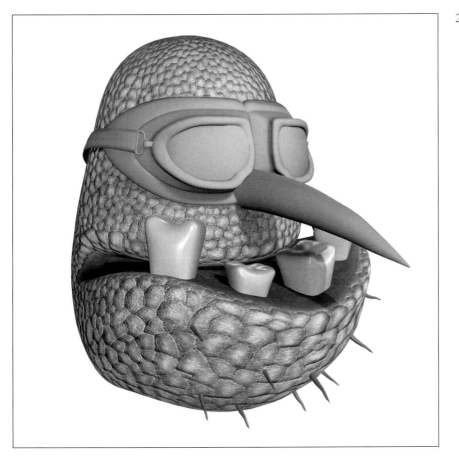

27. This is the final rendered result
    with all the painted texture maps
    connected to the Blinn shader.

SHADER STUFF

I chose a Blinn shader because I wanted his face to have highlights in certain areas. At this point, I didn't create a specular map. To control the level of bumpiness on Axle's face, I used three separate files to describe it. In this way, I could effect just the cracks and accentuate them without changing the bump map settings, which give me the pillowed quality of the skin. Most 3D programs allow you to layer one bump on top of another. If your package does not, then you will have to merge all this bump information into one map.

There are many ways to get to the final texture. Sometimes, as in this exercise, it is necessary to start creating a texture from a bump map instead of the color map. Can you think of any other starting points for creating a texture—for example, creating a color map based on the incandescent part of an object?

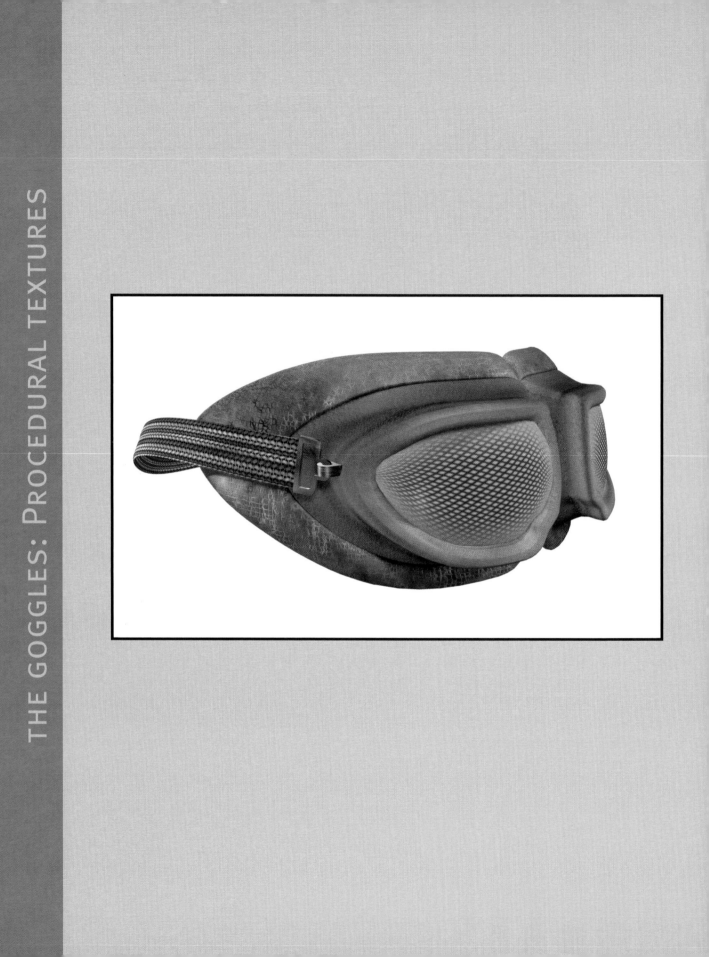

11

THE GOGGLES: PROCEDURAL TEXTURES

THIS SERIES OF FOUR EXERCISES is designed to show you how to use procedural textures. Procedural textures are created through mathematical calculations and have no limitations in size (resolution). Useful for a number of reasons that you will learn in these exercises, they can make texturing in 3D programs seem easier and faster. Using them verbatim, however, can result in an incomplete or unnatural textural expression. In combination with one another though, they can create some very realistic results.

There are two types of procedurals: 2D and 3D. Most, if not all, 3D packages on the market ship with their own flavors of these procedural textures.

A 2D procedural acts much the same way as a 2D painted file. For example, it is defined by the object geometry's textural coordinates (UVs). 2D procedurals create textures such as cloth, fractals, and checkered patterns.

3D procedurals are a bit more complicated. Think of them as a "world" filled with a particular texture. They ignore the UVs of the object. They are textures such as granite, wood, leather, or cloud. These 3D procedurals have the unique capability to ignore what the UV information is on Polygonal or NURBS surfaces, as shown in Figure 11.1.

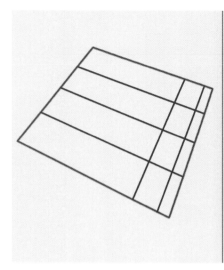

11.1 The unique ability for 3D procedurals to evenly texture non-uniform
geometry as seen on the far right.

If you like to use 3D procedural
textures and you have textured
an object that is moving, then you
must parent or group the 3D texture
to the object so that it moves
along with it. Compare the
movie Swimming3D.mov
(or Swimming3D.avi) with
non_Swimming3D.mov (or
non_Swimming3D.avi) on
the CD. 3D procedurals, as
you can see, need to be grouped
or parented to the geometry that
they describe if that geometry is
moving or animated.

On the left side of the figure is a simple NURBs plane that is unevenly
parameterized. In the middle is a render of a 2D procedural checkered pattern
applied. Notice the stretching of the texture. On the right is a 3D procedural
Leather texture applied and rendered. There is no stretching of the leather pattern at all. This is one great reason to use these 3D textures.

I used four procedural textures for the goggles to describe four
materials:

- **Leather:** Describes the Leather mask.

- **Rock:** Describes the Rubber lens casing.

- **Cloth:** Describes the Cloth strap.

- **Bulge:** Describes the iridescent bug-eye lenses.

In this exercise, I used Maya. This is not to say that this is an exercise only for
those of you who use Maya. Any software out there can give you similar results,
and I point out similar procedurals that can be used in other packages below.

I selected the following procedurals as a starting point:

Cloth

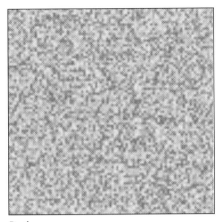

Rock

2D cloth texture for the cloth of the strap.
Softimage/XSI = Fabric,
Renderman = Cloth Shader,
3dsmax = Water

Combination **3D rock and 2D fractal** for the casing of the lenses to make it look like rubber.
Softimage/XSI = Rock and Fractal
Renderman = Fractal
3dsmax = Noise

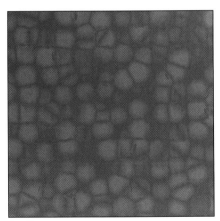

Leather

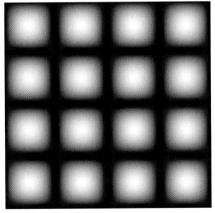

Bulge

3D leather texture to represent the leather mask of the goggles.
Softimage/XSI = Cell
Renderman = Gray Cells or Worley
3dsmax = Cellular

2D bulge texture for the bug eyes.
Softimage/XSI = Grid
Renderman = Shapes
3dsmax = Checker

> **NOTE**
>
> Some other Maya items I will be mentioning have counterparts in other packages, as well. For example:
>
> - Ramp = Color Ramp in Renderman; Gradient in most other packages.
> - Snow = Snow in Softimage/XSI, and Falloff in 3dsmax.
> - Brownian = Fractal or Cell in Softimage/XSI, Brownian in Renderman, and Noise in 3dsmax.

The procedural textures need some messing or dirtying up in order to make them look like they are a part of Axle's environment. I'll start with the strap.

THE STRAP

1. This is what the 2D cloth texture looks like without any of my changes. The strap for the goggles is made from a cloth-covered rubber material. Using Maya's 2D cloth and a ramp texture, I will show you how I created it.

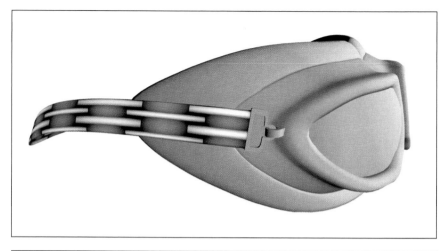

2. At left is the cloth texture straight out of the box. In the middle are the changes I made. I wanted the threads to show some wear and tear so I played around with the Widths and Waves settings and changed the colors from black and white to subtle grays. At right are the changes to the repetition of the thread of the cloth texture on the strap to create the correct scale of the cloth band.

3. Notice how the changes shown in step 2 look on the strap. To give the strap a more recognizable personality—like a striped strap from 1920s car goggles—I will use a Ramp texture.

> **NOTE**
>
> If you own Maya, you can open the goggles.mb file located on the CD and follow along with the exercise.

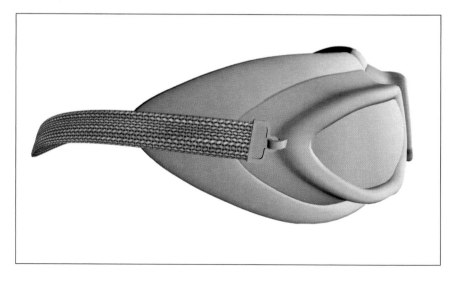

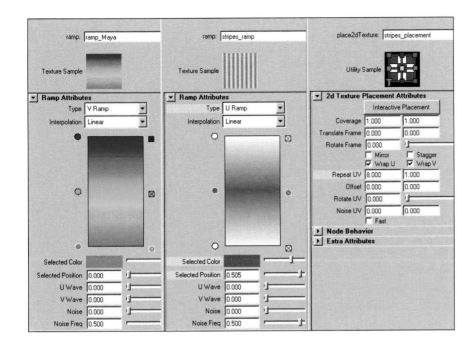

4. Compare the changes I made to the ramp's color and repeat (middle and right) to the typical Maya ramp/gradient on the left. I kept changing values until I was satisfied with the placement and number of the stripes.

5. Check how these changes look on the rendered version.

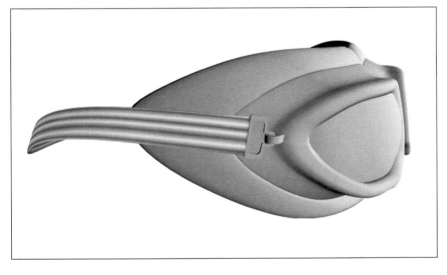

6. I connected this ramp to the diffuse channel which affects the brightness of the Lambert shader's color. This ramp acts as a multiplier on top of the cloth color to add light and dark stripes to the cloth-weave.

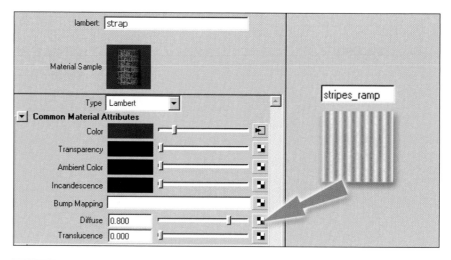

7. As you can see, the stripes ramp and the cloth texture combine well when rendered.

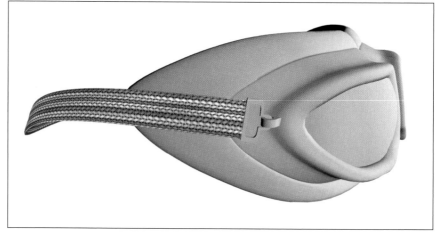

SHADER STUFF

You could have made this in a more complicated way, using layered shaders or layered textures, or even hiring a programmer, but I think this simple way works best for this project's purposes.

The shader I choose for this is a Lambert. The strap has no specular/highlight information. I didn't want to add any bump information because it may have created buzzing when rendered, and I think it would be over doing it. Bumps on most fabrics are very slight and, in this case, not necessary. If there was a bug crawling on the strap near his ear and the camera focused in on that, however, I would have accentuated the fabric with a bump to make it hyperreal.

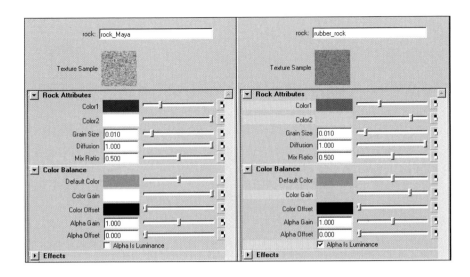

THE CASING FOR THE LENSES

1. The lens casings are the next to get the aging treatment. On the left is the Maya 3D rock texture straight out of the package. On the right are the adjustments I made to it. I want the rubber of the casing to look old and deteriorated.

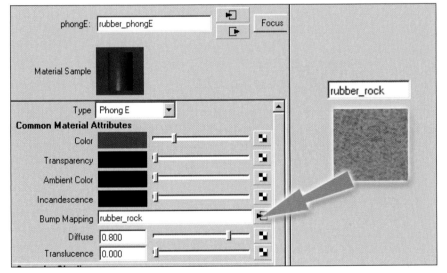

2. I used a PhongE shader, changed the color to a dark gray, and connected the 3D Rock texture to the Bump channel. You can experiment with other procedurals offered in your package. I found that the 3D Rock procedural worked best for the bumpy quality I was looking for.

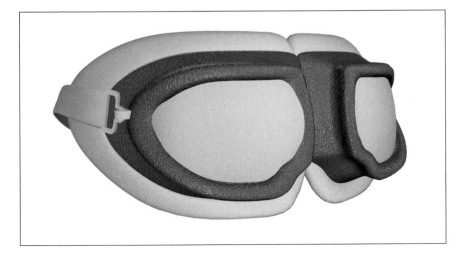

3. Here is how the adapted 3D Rock texture looks as a bump on the rubber.

4. I needed to create a dirt overlay, and decided to use a 2D Fractal texture to describe the dusty, sandy texture. The middle and right images show the changes that I made to the standard 2D Fractal to reflect the dustiness I was looking for.

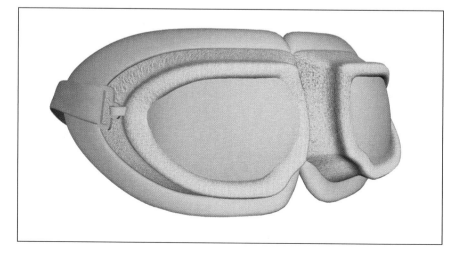

5. I then connected this Fractal to the Color and Bump channel of a Lambert shader.

6. Here's how the dust shader looks by itself rendered.

ADDING A DIRT LAYER USING A LAYERED SHADER

Next, I layed a dust/dirt Lambert shader overtop of the PhongE rubber base shader. This is very simple to do using a Layered shader, which enables you to layer many shaders of different types on top of one another. For the lens casings, I wanted to use a Layered shader to place a specular highlight material (PhongE) under a non-specular one (Lambert). Layered shaders need to have transparency or transparency maps connected to them to allow the underlying layers to show through.

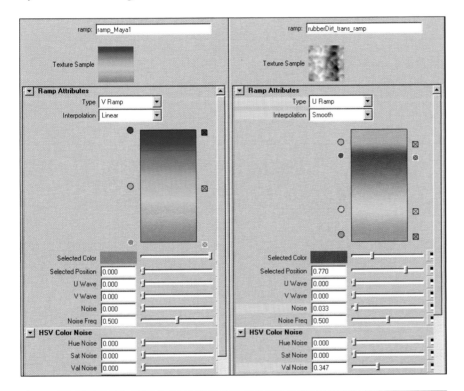

7. For the dirt shader, I created a ramp for the transparency of this new DIRT shader overlay. The left side of the figure shows a typical Maya Ramp, while the right shows changes to the ramp. The Noise settings break up this uniform Ramp adding a more random look to the transparency texture.

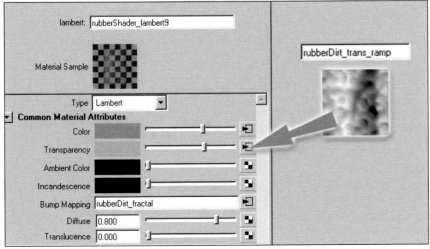

8. The transparency Ramp is then connected to the transparency channel on the Lambert.

9. The transparency and color layer alone on the Lambert shader looks like this.

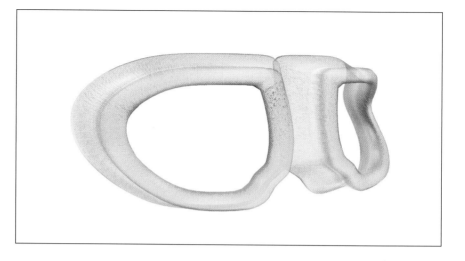

10. Here again, the rubber base texture on the PhongE shader.

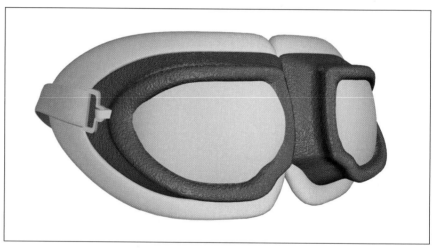

11. Dropping these two shaders onto the Layered shader and assigning this Layered shader to the goggle casing produces this render.

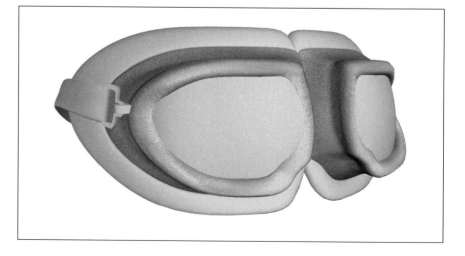

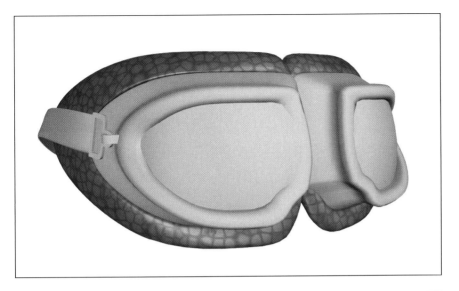

THE MASK

1. The mask part of the goggles is made out of worn, soft, and old leather. To start, I chose a 3D Leather procedural texture straight from the package and applied it to the mask of the goggles.

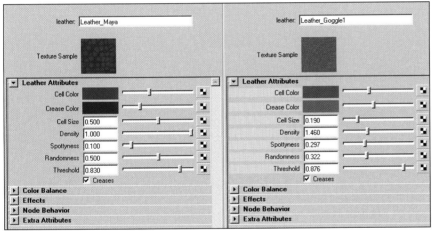

2. Obviously this is not very worn-looking, so it needs some work. The right side shows the changes made to the "pre-packaged" leather texture. I decreased the cell size to create a more fine leather pattern. This with the other changes make it look less CG perfect.

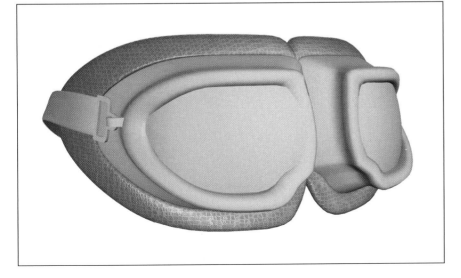

3. I applied this Leather to the goggles and rendered it. The result looks a bit more interesting. Notice the crease color is lighter, showing dust has gathered there. Still, the color is too uniform for me so I don't want to stop yet.

CREATING COLOR VARIATION

A 3D Brownian texture added to the colors of the Leather texture creates more color variation.

4. I created two 3D Brownian textures. The first was used for the cell color of the Leather texture and the second was used for the crease color of the Leather. Compare a standard 3D Brownian texture (left), how I altered the first Brownian's attributes (middle), and the changes made to the second Brownian (right).

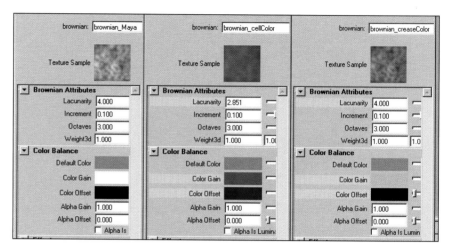

NOTE

It isn't necessary to know what "Lacunarity" or any other of these attributes do mathematically. All you need to do is notice the changes that occur when you change their values.

5. Connect the "Brownians" to Leather as shown: cell Brownian to cell color and crease Brownian to crease color.

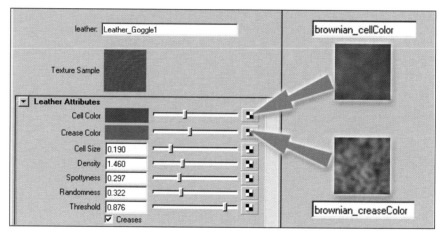

6. The result. Compare this with the previous goggle render. As you can see, there is more color variation as well as the Leather pattern is broken up a bit more. Now the mask texture is becoming a lot more interesting, but it's not done yet.

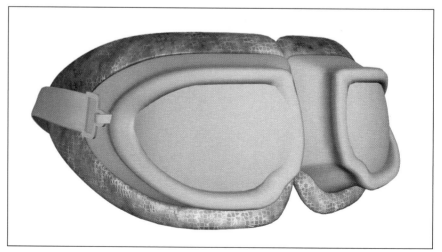

CREATING DUST USING SNOW

I want to show you another great way to add a dirt layer to this part of the goggles. Maya has a 3D Snow texture that understands and calculates how snow, or dirt in this case, sits on a surface.

7. To show you an example of this, I applied the Snow texture to a sphere. The white part represents the snow color and the red shows the base color. As you can see, the snow is thick and opaque at the top. As it nears the center of the sphere, it starts to dissipate, and at the bottom it has completely disappeared. I don't need snow on the goggles, but with a simple color change to light brown it becomes dust!

8. Compare the pre-packaged snow (left) with the two Snow textures I created: one for the dust color (middle) and the other (right) for a transparency map. We need a transparency map created because we are going to use a Layered shader again for the final look.

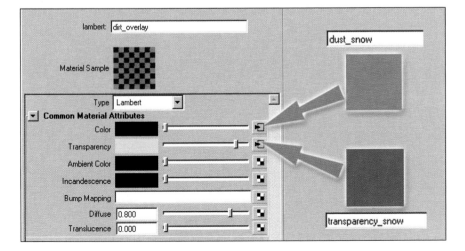

9. Choosing a Lambert shader for the non-specular dust material, I connected the Snow textures as shown.

10. This is how the Lambert dust color and transparency layer look on the rendered goggles by themselves.

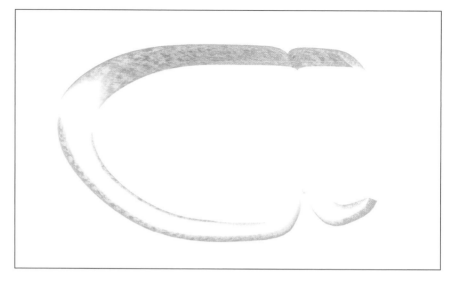

11. Again, using a Layered shader, I attached the Lambert dust overlay on top of the Phong Leather base. The final leather texture on the goggles looks like this.

As you can see, with a few simple steps, we have put personal touches to the leather goggles that definitely were needed to make this material more real.

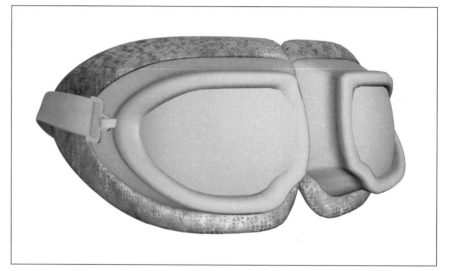

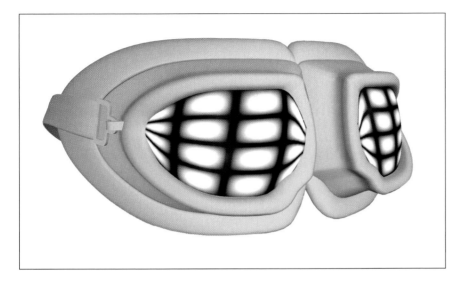

THE LENSES

1. I wanted Axle's eyeballs to be the lenses of the goggles; therefore, the lenses need to look like bug eyes. I decided to use a Maya 2D Bulge texture to achieve this. This is how the "pre-packaged" texture looks applied to the goggles.

2. Consider how the typical 2D Bulge (left) can change. For the middle image, I adjusted the color and UV width. In the right, I altered the rotation and repeat of the texture to resemble a more accurate representation of bug eyes.

3. This is how those changes to the new Bulge look on the lens geometry when connected to the color channel of a shader.

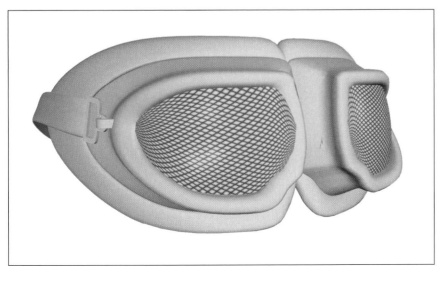

ADDING A DIRT LAYER USING A LAYERED TEXTURE

Of course, I need to add a Dirt layer. I will use a Layered texture to accomplish this. A Layered texture is similar to a Layered shader. It allows you to combine as many textures as you want on top of one another and then it is, in most cases, connected to the Color channel of one shader. A Layered texture renders faster and is more economical RAM-wise than a Layered shader.

In Maya, each file texture you add to the Layered texture has a channel for Alpha. This is the place where you connect a transparency map or define its transparency with a simple color value. The other great thing about layered textures is their ability to change the blending modes of each layer, just like to Photoshop's blending operations between layers.

4. As in the Rubber exercise, I used a 2D Fractal for the color of the dirt shown here with changes to the color and repeats of the Fractal.

5. I created a circular 2D Ramp for the transparency of this dirt overlay.

   Because Layered textures use an Alpha to determine the transparency of a layer and not the RGB values, the white areas are 100% solid letting the dirt layer be revealed, and the gray to black areas allow the bug eyes to show through. This is the same concept as a Layer Mask in Photoshop.

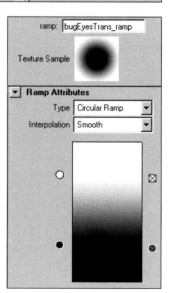

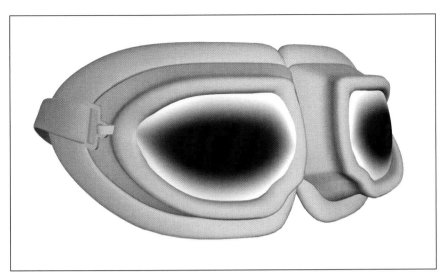

6. I attached the ramp to a shader, applied that shader to the lenses and played with the position of the Ramp colors until I liked what I saw.

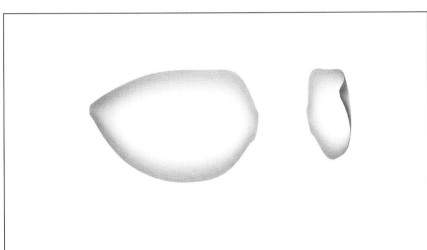

7. Notice how the 2D fractal dirt layer, along with its 2D ramp transparency, looks on the lenses by themselves.

8. This is what the lens Layered texture looks like on the lens geometry. Little touches, like dust in these creases, add a lot to any "realistic" surface.

ADDING IRIDESCENCE

To make the lenses look more like bug eyes, I added an iridescent quality. Sometimes it is necessary to go beyond painting textures and using procedurals by having a programmer write a unique texture or shader. For instance, many studios will write their own proprietary shaders for things like skin, which is too difficult for the base shaders that come with 3D packages to describe due to its beautiful translucency. These custom textures or shaders can be very complicated shader networks. Maya, along with other packages, allows you to create your own shader networks complete with mathematical inputs and outputs. One utility of great help is the "Sampler Info" node that can produce some interesting results when attached to attributes like color, specularity, and so on.

9. Clicking on the checkerbox button next to the Specular Color slider of a PhongE shader allows me to choose a Sampler Info node from the Utilities section of the Create Render Node window. This brings up the Connection Editor window.

10. This is where I then connected the RayDirectionX to the Specular Color R (red), and the Facing Ratio to Specular Color G (green), as shown.

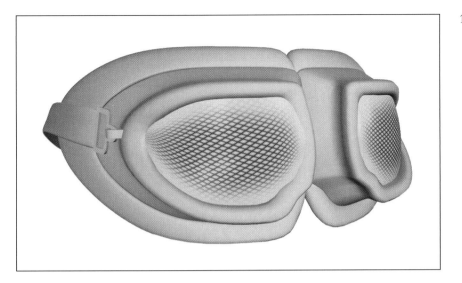

11. Notice the green tinge these connections from the Sampler Info node give to the final render of the lenses. (I could go into a discussion on why this looks the way it does but I really don't know exactly what the math behind it is.) As mentioned above, what is important is that you *look* at the effects of these connections. If your 3D package has these types of utilities, I urge you to experiment with them as they can be very useful.

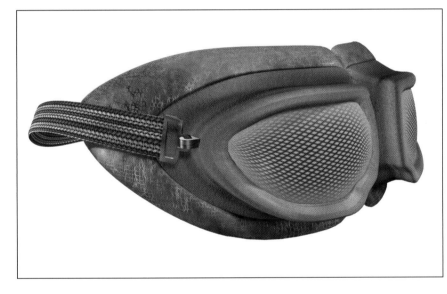

12. Here is the final render of the goggles with all the pieces together—all done without even lifting a paintbrush.

SHADER STUFF

Just to recap, here are the shaders that I used for the goggle pieces:

The Strap: Uses a Lambert shader; no specular highlight or reflection information is needed.

The Rubber Casing: Uses a Layered shader with a Lambert "dirt" shader overtop of a PhongE "rubber" shader.

The Leather Mask: Another Layered shader using a Lambert "dirt" shader overlaying a PhongE "leather" shader. I wanted the leather to have a slight specularity to it, which the Lambert shader provides.

The Bug Eyes: Uses a Layered texture to get the job done. A 2D Fractal "dirt" texture is "over" (the Blend Mode) a 2D Bulge "bug-eye" texture. This Layered texture is connected to the color port of a PhongE shader.

If you really enjoyed this exercise, then maybe you prefer this texture creation method over painting. Just remember that you still need to study surfaces and their materials and textures for either method of texture creation. If I had not looked at reference materials, or thought about the "dirt" aspect on these materials, my final imagery would be quite weak whether working in paints or procedurals.

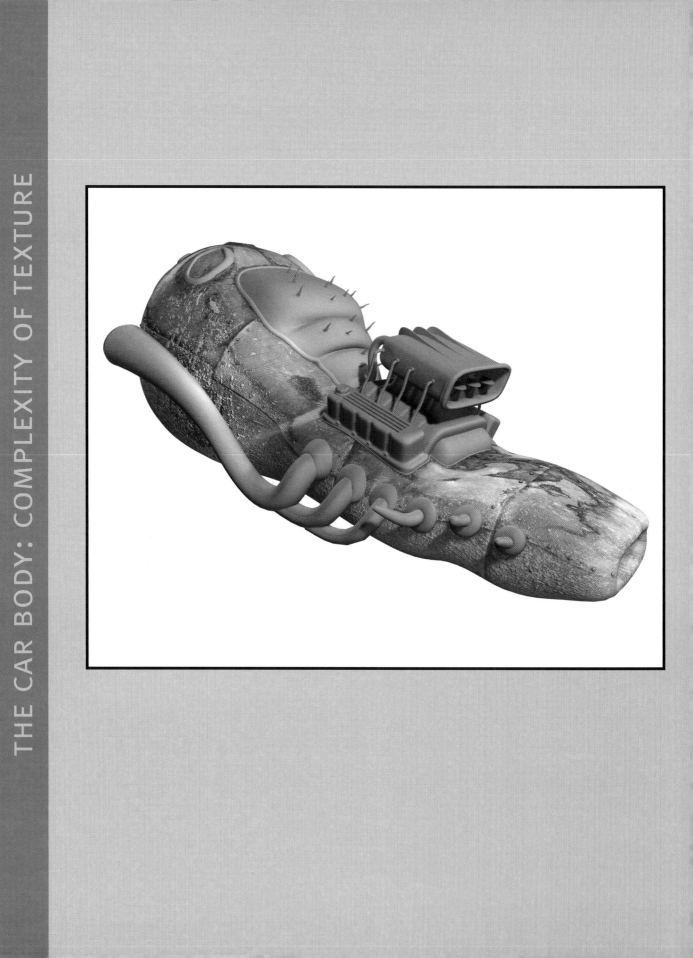

CHAPTER 12

THE CAR BODY: COMPLEXITY OF TEXTURE

T HE CAR BODY IS AN EXAMPLE of how I create 90% of my textures. I like the mix of creating maps outside the computer (on paper, or acetate, with paint or ink), combined with digital painting in Painter 6 or Photoshop. I rarely use photographic textures in my work. This is a personal choice: I love to paint. Whatever way you choose to get *there*, just remember to manipulate them so that they live in harmony with each other in the scene.

The car body is a combination of a bug and a dune buggy. I picked up elements of both and combined them. For the various characteristics of the car, I looked at lots of reference for insects. As I searched, I noticed small designs in the shells of their bodies and thought that this would be a fun element to express. I decided that the "flame decal" of the car would mimic this. The rust and wear and tear of the metal in desert conditions would mimic my reference of the design on the bug's body.

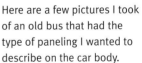

Here are a few pictures I took of an old bus that had the type of paneling I wanted to describe on the car body.

I also wanted to add paneling, which wasn't implicit in the model. I decided that this paneling would express the armoring found on some bugs, and would look like the paneling on some vehicles.

I looked at all the *Motocross*, *Offroad*, and *Dragster* magazines I could find, as well as my own photographs and Internet references of dune buggies and other cars. All of this gave me ideas for paneling, rivets, paint, rust, and mud splatters. See sidebar figures.

PRE-PRODUCTION

I started with some oil painting, and hoped it might reveal some interesting possibilities. So with my reference at my side, I did some rough color paintings to explore how several elements could look:

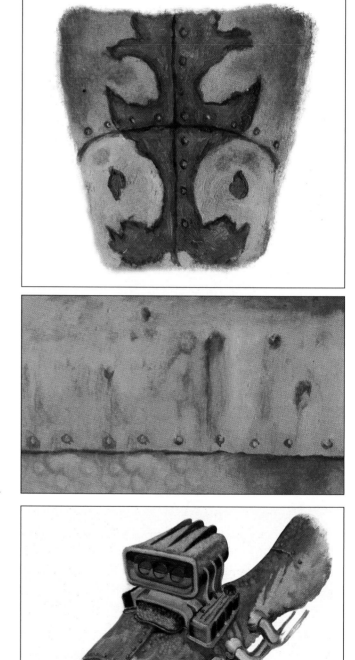

1. Bug marking.

2. Paneling.

3. Overall look and feel of the vehicle.

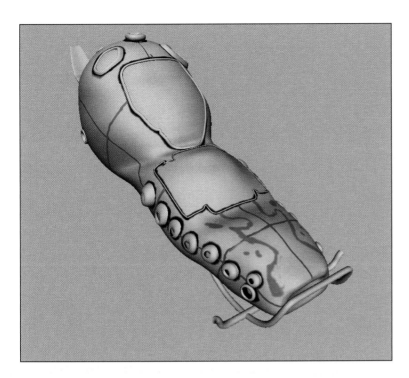

4. After I established what kind of pattern I wanted for the car shell's texture, I used a 3D paint program to mark different colors right on the body. I marked not only the flame and the paneling, but also anything that intersected the body that could tell me where mud splatters should be and where rust would occur.

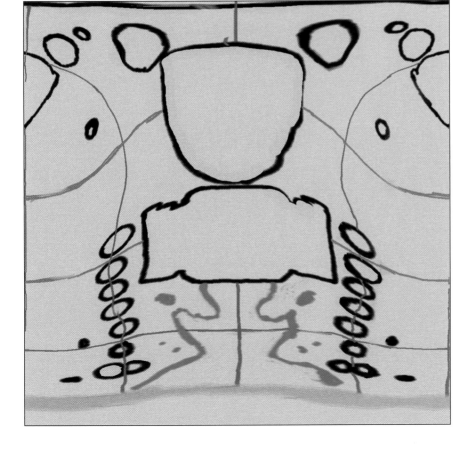

5. Opened in Photoshop, this is the unwrapped pattern that resulted.

6. This grunge map was made by a light scrumbling of oil paints on card stock. You can open **stoneBase.tif** and **carBodyColor_Maker_pt1.psd** from the CD to follow along.

COLOR MAP

Now it is time to use this pattern in Photoshop to lay in the basic colors and textures on different layers.

7. I put the stone base grunge map on top of the pattern, and using a layer mask, painted out where I wanted the red to remain and where I thought mud would be. Using Hue/Saturation and Levels, I changed the color of the grunge map to a sandy dirt color.

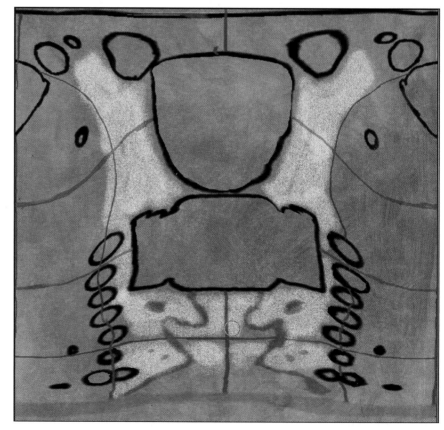

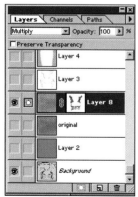

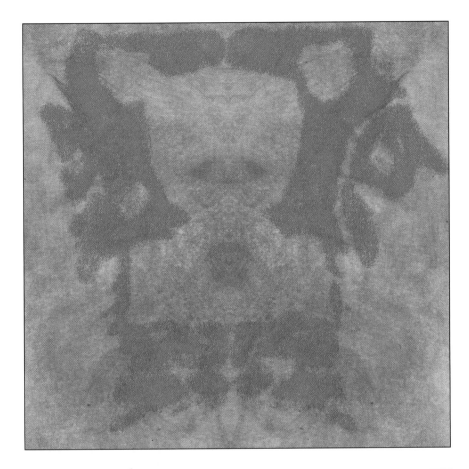

8. This is my starting point with the red paint layer showing through.

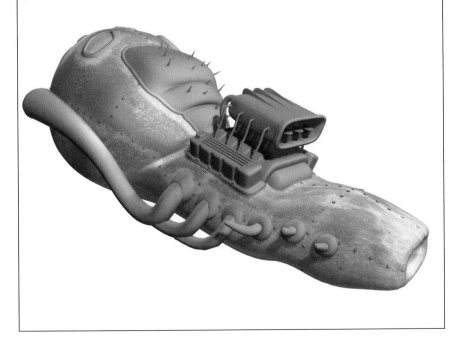

9. Looking at the car, I decided the mud needed to be defined and designed better.

10. For the next stage of development, I went into my 3D paint program and made a new map that stylized the mud splatter. This is the beginning stages of that stylization.

11. Clearly the mud has become more stylized. I used this brush to add different tones of brown. I kept adding to the layer, in the same way as I did in the Bandana exercise, to get a layering effect.

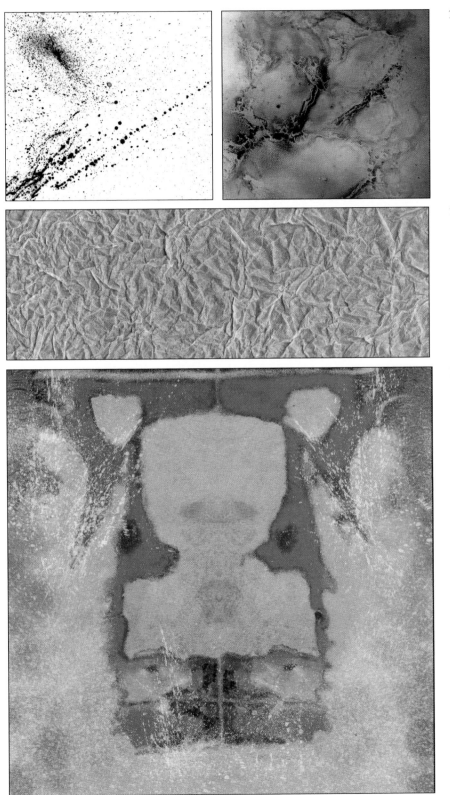

12. I made these splatters by taking some diluted black acrylic paint on the end of a brush, splattering it on a piece of paper (left). I also experimented with some washes and drippings of oil paint on top of acetate film (right). It gives a nice oil stain pattern. I eventually used an inverted version of this beside the bug flame decal to look like salt stains.

13. Crinkled tissue paper effectively simulates the crackle of the dried mud. I used this scan very subtly in the upper corners of the pattern.

14. The results of these grunge maps are added to the base painting of Step 11. Slowly this painting is coming to life.

    The grunge maps above (**splats1.tif**, **splats2.tif**, **oilonAcetate.tif**, and **tissue_crumpleFine.tif**) are on the CD if you want to use them on this or any of your projects.

MAKING THE DECAL

As discussed previously, I want a bug marking/flame graphic on the front of the car. What follows is how I made it, continuing in Photoshop. You can open the **carDecalColor_Maker.psd** file from the CD to follow along.

15. To create the bug marking, I used the color map up to this point as a positioning guide for the decal. I liked my pre-production painting of the decal so I pasted that on top of this color map, created a new layer and with a black brush…

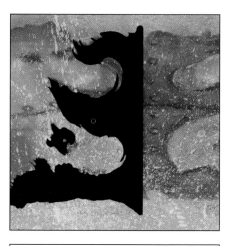

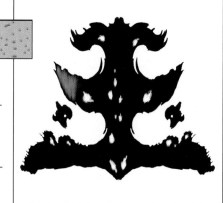

16. …I painted half the design, duplicated and flipped it to make the other half.

    I used the brush (inset) and painted the textural quality of the marking…

17. …and continued to fill the pattern in this way (left).

    I filled in the white dots with the same red color as the car (right).

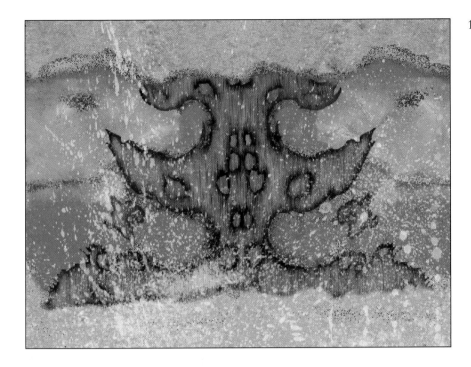

18. At this point I hid the color map layer and in the layer palette chose Merge Visible. This flattens only the bug marking layers into one, leaving the white areas transparent. Holding down the Shift key, I dragged and dropped this merged layer into the **carBodyColor_Maker_pt1.psd** document. This is the result of the decal in position with some of the other interacting grunge layers.

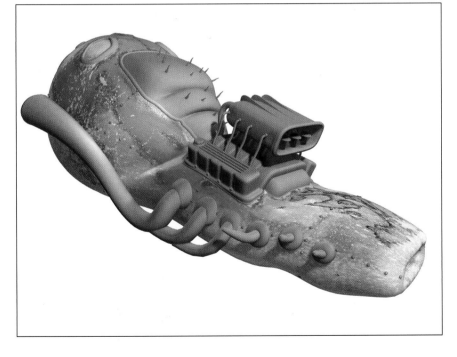

19. This is what the car body map looks like rendered up to this point.

MAKING THE PANELS

It is time to create the panel design for the bump as this will also affect the color map details where dirt, rust, and chipped paint will occur.

20. Open the **carPanelBump_ Maker.psd** from the CD. Using the original pattern in Photoshop, I used the Pen tool and drew shapes that defined each panel. I filled them with different values of gray to make the Panel bump map.

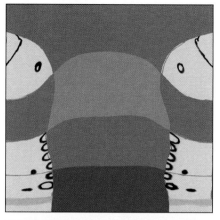

21. Here is the final Panel bump map with a few added little details. Remember that the different values of gray define how deep the bump will be when rendered.

You can open the **carBodyColor_Maker_ pt1.psd** on the CD to follow along.

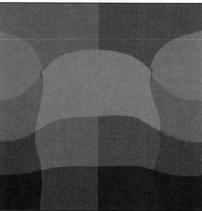

22. Using the Panel bump map as a guide, and the Magic Wand to select each panel, I added dirt, grease, and dust in the creases using the Airbrush and Smudge tools on a new layer (left). I set this dirt and grease layer to Multiply at 90%, and moved it above the **splatter1** layer. This adds more definition to the color map, as well as helps accentuate the bump map's effect in describing the panels even more (right).

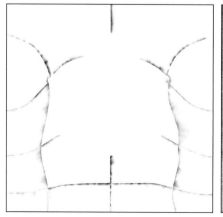

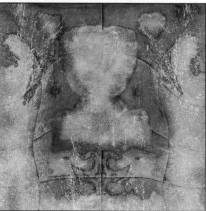

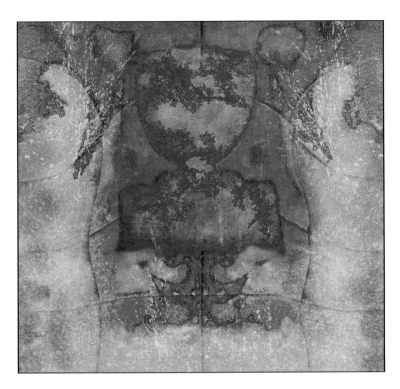

23. The final color map. Take a close look at this image and the one on the right in step 22. I have made even more changes to the color map. First, I thought that the bug marking decal was too clean and bright, so I made it a bit more dingy. Second, I added paint chips on the front edge of the first panels. Third, I darkened the dirt/rust on the interior shapes and fourth, I lessened some of the rust that outlined the dirt on the sides of the car.

You can open the **carBodyColor_Maker_pt2.psd** on the CD to see the layers that make these changes.

24. The Car Body render with the final color map only; no bump or specular maps.

FINAL MAPS

Now that I have the color map finished, it is time to create the remaining maps that will be applied to the final shader. Using the layered Photoshop files that created the color map, I will save an alternate version and convert it to grayscale, without flattening it. I go through each of the layers and decide how it needs to affect the bump, or specularity; whichever map I am creating at the time. I want to show you the final maps and talk about some of the changes I made to them.

25. The color map, from which most of the other maps were created, was converted to grayscale and manipulated to create one of the bump maps needed for the car.

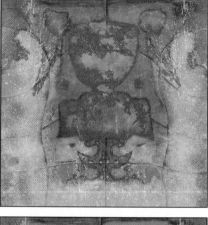

26. I painted a uniform gray tone over the red paint part of the car body because I didn't want the scratches and grease marks to be shown in the bump. I darkened the bug decal and paint chip areas as well. Other changes that were made can be seen in the **carBodyBump_Maker.psd** file on the CD.

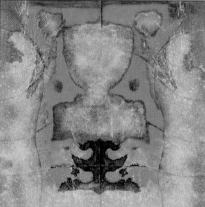

27. Two more bump maps were used for the buggy. The left map is the panel pattern with added imperfections to the edges of some of the panels. It supplies the bump for the panel depths. The right map, which was taken from the **carDecalColor_Maker.psd** file, accentuates the bug marking/decal on the surface of the car.

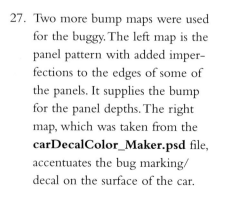
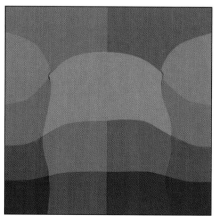

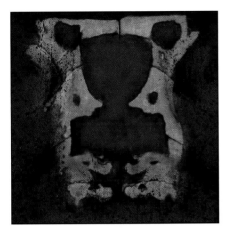

28. The map used for specularity and reflectivity. This is where it gets a bit tricky. As you can see from comparing this map to the bump map on the right of step 23, it looks as if it is inverted. *Most* of it is. Dark areas are less specular, or reflective, so things like mud, rust and the corroded bug decal need to be darkened. I did this by performing the same procedure I did in the beginning of this section, but this time going layer by layer, inverting the necessary layers and changing their Blending options and opacities. Open the **carBodySpec_Maker.psd** on the CD to see the changes that I made to create this final map.

SHADER STUFF

29. Knowing that the buggy body is made of painted metal, I chose a PhongE as the shader. Because of the reflective quality in certain areas, as well as the specular highlights, this shader describes these attributes well. You could just as easily use a Blinn or even a Glossy shader and get similar results.

   All the maps and the PhongE shader combine to produce the final Car Body.

You might find it tough at times to "mess up" your precious perfect textures. For me, it became a difficult decision when I needed to dirty up things like the bug decal and the car paint. To take away some of the pain of decision-making during the actual creation, you can save different versions of your maps and render them in your 3D package, selecting your favorite later. This, of course, creates a new problem—which version do you like best? The opinions of others can be a big help, because sometimes our vision becomes clouded by looking at something for too long, and it becomes difficult to be partial. Step away from your work often, or work on another part of the project to gain clearer vision on creatively stagnant areas.

13

THE FIN: TEXTURING UNEVEN SURFACES

IN MOST INSTANCES, if a model has an uneven UV mesh, or parameterization, you can rebuild it to be even, but sometimes it isn't feasible. We, as texture artists, need to learn a few tricks to get around these problems.

This exercise is going to show you how to texture a piece of unevenly parameterized geometry without the aid of a 3D paint program, or projections (next exercise). This can be executed by using Photoshop along with a checkered texture grid and your 3D software. The Photoshop creation documents on the CD also show how the clean graphics created in Illustrator are made grungy in Photoshop later.

PRE-PRODUCTION AND DESIGN

I did most of my design work right on the computer in Illustrator for this exercise. I knew that I wanted Axle's name on the top of the fin and his initials on the sides. The only thing left to do was decide what typeface to use and how to make it look like graphics that you see on race cars, dune buggies, or motocross bikes. I experimented with:

1. Several different fonts.

2. Assorted designs for the fin top (left) and fin side graphics (right).

3. Decal designs. The oval background proved to be a more authentic decal/sticker design (left) than the other shapes above. I also made changes to the letters A and E to suit my design criteria (right).

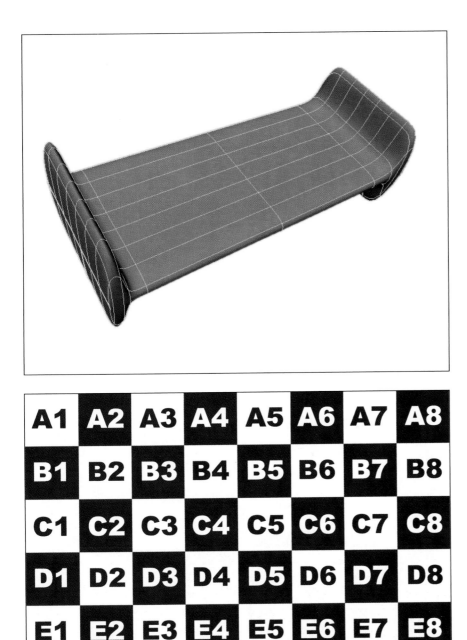

4. The first graphic to position is Axle's logo. The light green lines on the fin geometry are the curves/isoparms that make up the model. As you can see, they are not evenly spaced.

5. You can use this checkered pattern with letters and numbers as a systematic guide to help you locate where your textures should go in your paint program.

You can use the *texture placement grid* (**textureGrid1k.tif**) found on the CD for this exercise or any of your projects. (An Illustrator version of the file, **textureGrid.ai**, is also on the CD.)

6. I assigned the checkered pattern on the geometry and took four snapshots of it: left, right, top, and front. I saved these and then opened them in Photoshop. The top view verifies the stretching caused by the uneven mesh.

On the CD, the file **Fin_Color _Maker_1k_pt2.psd** has all the finished steps that follow, as well as all the color map layers.

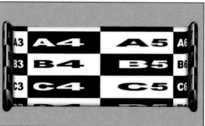 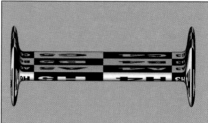

7. In Photoshop, create an oval roughly the shape and size of where Axle's logo will be positioned and apply a red stroke around it for reference.

8. Open Axle's logo (**axle_logo_sm.tif** on the CD) and paste it on top of the texture grid pattern (left). With this on its own layer, scale and move it into position (right) based on the coordinates shown in step 7. Save a copy of this file flattened (no layers) and apply it to the fin's geometry in your 3D software package.

9. This is how the texture map looks on the fin. As you can see, it is in the correct position vertically but still very stretched horizontally. This horizontal stretching poses another kind of problem, that of non-uniform stretching. This is easily fixed in Photoshop.

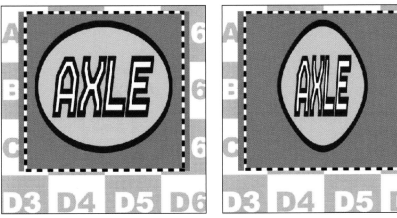

10. Using the rectangular Marquee selection tool, make a selection as shown on the far left. Now select Filters > Distort > Spherize. For this filter, choose Horizontal Only. Apply the filter at −100 and then again at −45.

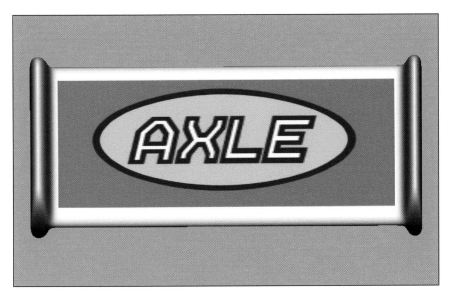

11. This Spherize filter squeezes the graphic more radically near the center and gradually lessens as it nears the marquee selection border, thus performing a non-uniform horizontal scaling. There is a real difference to the selected graphic on the model. I like how this looks better than the original graphic. Now, you're ready to place the graphic on the sides.

PLACEMENT OF SIDE GRAPHIC

12. The graphic on the left is the one I chose to place on the fin's side. Creating a stroked circular selection on top of the *fin right* snapshot gives us our placement coordinates, right.

13. I dimmed the background checkered pattern so I could easily see the red oval halves that I created as guides (based on the coordinates from the snapshot above), and pasted the graphic (called **axle_graphic_sm.tif** on the CD) on a layer over top of this.

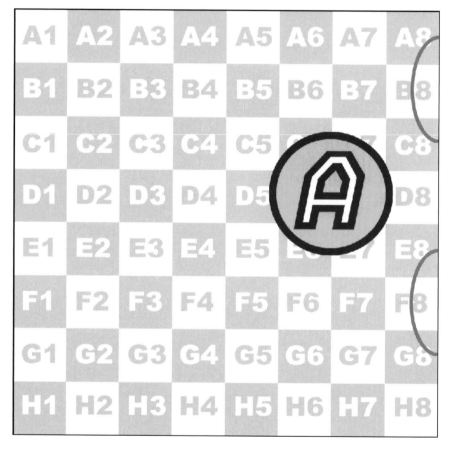

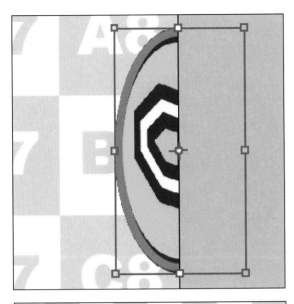

14. Using Photoshop's Transform selection (Ctrl+T on the PC, Cmd+T on the Mac), I rotated the graphic 90 degrees counter-clockwise and moved it into position. The Transform tool allows us to see the center pivot point of the graphic, which is important in this manipulation because we need to line it up with the edge of the canvas. From here I scaled it from the center by holding down the Alt key (Option key on the Mac). I copied this layer and moved the graphic onto the canvas to see the whole shape.

15. I then flipped it horizontally and vertically and placed it into position for the bottom half of the graphic.

NOTE

The same procedure above has to be executed for the left side of the Fin.

16. Viewed in a 3D program, the two halves of the model (left) do not match. Moving down the top half 5 or 6 pixels before rendering again fixes it (right).

17. Back in Photoshop, I applied a numerical scaling of 120% on the height to both the top and the bottom graphic to make it more circular when rendered.

NOTE

This is just one of many ways to fix textures in Photoshop for uneven meshes. Explore other filters or scaling methods to see if there are better ways than this.

You could have also used a planar projection to apply the texture to the fin, but I wanted to show you an alternate way of solving the uneven mesh problem. For example, a typical instance on NURBs that could not use a projection would be lips on a talking model. A projection would not follow the lip movement because the texture is not attached to the UVs. (Remember: Projections are like a slide show on a screen. If the screen moves, the projection does not.) Even if you parent or group the projection to the geometry, it is still not UV specific. In this case, the texture must be painted on a map that corresponds to the UVs of a NURBs surface.

Of course, having said all that, there are tricks and software-specific ways to deal with the above texture projection limitation. Know your software and read the manuals.

FINAL MAPS

The maps that follow were created in the same manner as the Car Body exercise. Because the fin is the same material as the car, it has the same amount of dirt, grease bumpiness, specularity and reflectivity. You can find the final maps on the CD.

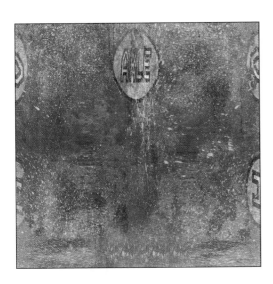

18. The final color map for the fin. The layered Photoshop file is called **Fin_Color_Maker_ 1k.psd**.

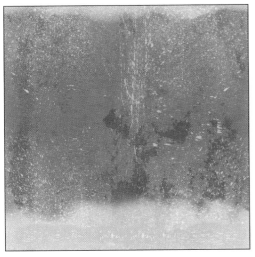

19. The bump map generated from the color map with a few alterations to color values. The procedure to derive the bump map for the Fin is the same as in the Car Body exercise. It is called **Fin_Bump_Maker_1k.psd** on the CD.

20. The map used for both the specular and the reflective attributes of the shader. The file on the CD is called **Fin_Spec_Maker_ 1k.psd**. Notice the differences made to it in regards to the bump map. The procedure to derive the specular map for the Fin is the same as in the Car Body exercise.

FINAL RENDER

21. The final rendered top fin.

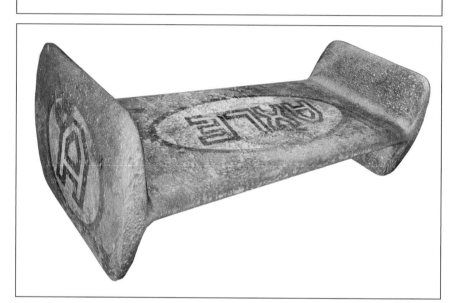

22. Left three-quarter render.

23. Right three-quarter view. Notice that the sides are unique in wear-and-tear, adding to the realism of this material.

SHADER STUFF

I used a Phong shader for the fin. As mentioned above, it is made out of a similar red-painted metal as the car body so it needs some specular highlights and reflection where there isn't any dirt or other obstructive elements such as scratches or grease.

GENERAL NOTES ON THE COLOR MAP

Most of the layers that make up the color map also had to have the same scaling applied to them as the logo and graphics did. It is a good idea, then, to write down all the steps or settings on filters in order to reapply them if needed.

There was a lot of pinching to the texture on the front edges of the fin. These were fixed in much the same way as the other parts of the fin using proportional scaling with a Feathered selection. See if you can spot them on the final color map. The Photoshop files that fixed these problem areas, called **Fin_Color_Maker_1k_pt2.psd** and **Fin_Spec_Maker_1k_pt2.psd**, are on the CD.

Also, on the CD are the Illustrator pre-production design documents for you to play around with. Try this exercise with a different graphic for Axle's logo. These files are located on the accompanying CD.

[CHAPTER] # 14

AXLE'S CHEST: SCULPTING, PAINTING, AND PROJECTIONS

IN THIS NEXT EXERCISE, I will present to you two techniques. One will show you how to use a sculpting material, Sculpey™, to get an imprint from a real material, and later, tint it with paints to create an interesting texture that will be scanned and manipulated digitally.

The second technique will show you another way to texture an unevenly isoparameterized surface using a projection. You already used a projection for the polygonal texturing on Axle's face, but you can also use them on NURBs surfaces. There are several different types of projections for NURBs: planar, cubic, spherical, cylindrical, and tri-planar. I like to think of these projections as slide projectors that will project an image or texture onto one or any number of surfaces regardless of UV structure. I will also show you how to use a projection to texture several pieces of geometry.

PRE-PRODUCTION

Axle's chest texture is similar in design to his face but a little more gnarly. It has a harder, more worn look to it. The scales are much larger and pronounced. I continued to look toward insect references as well as crocodiles, alligators, and turtles for ideas on how to texture the chest.

CREATING THE SCULPEY TEXTURE

I love to experiment with different ways of creating textures, especially outside the computer. One of these ways is to take imprints of existing textural surfaces using clay, plasticine, or Sculpey. I prefer to use Sculpey because you bake it to harden it, and then you can paint, sand, or manipulate it any way you want.

1. The first thing I did was look around my apartment for something that had the kind of texture I was searching for. I found the texture under my kitchen sink in a sponge. This proved to be perfect because it was the "inverse" of the texture; therefore, the Sculpey, when pressed into it, would make a "positive" imprint.

2. I needed to consider the scale of this texture on Axle's chest, and since the area was small, the size of the imprint didn't need to be that large. Taking a small bit of Sculpey, approximately 1 strand, I kneaded and flattened it out in my hand, making it more malleable for filling into the sponge texture.

3. Pressing the softened Sculpey into the dry sponge and peeling it off produced this beautiful imprint. Next, I cured it before painting it.

   To cure the Sculpey, I baked it at 275° for 15 minutes for every quarter of an inch in thickness.

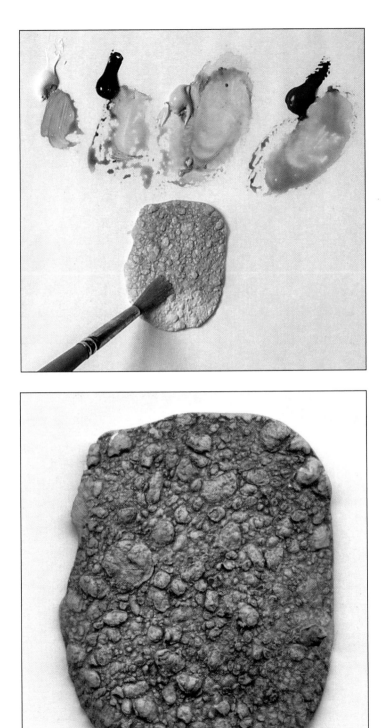

PAINTING THE SCULPEY IMPRINT

4. After the Sculpey has cured and cooled down, I started painting it. The first wash that I lay down was an acrylic base color—in this case, a fairly vibrant green. I diluted the paint quite a bit so that it filled into all the nooks and crannies of the imprint.

   I also tried to avoid creating an even coloration. In this example, I added Ultramarine blue, a bit of Phthalo Blue, Titanium White, and Cadmium Yellow Medium together to get the green hue.

5. Each time I applied more pigment, I re-mixed another tiny batch on the end of my brush so that there were slight variations in tone that sunk in and blended together on the Sculpey surface. Here is a scan of the first wash.

TIP

It is a good idea to take more than one impression of a texture while you are at it. In this case, I took three, each from a different sponge. This gave me the opportunity to digitally combine different parts of each of them into one.

6. After the first acrylic wash has dried, I take out my oil paints. In my experience, I have found that using oil paint works best for the second pass as it dilutes into a thinner wash that sinks more easily into the cracks. It also stays wet longer so that you can rub off pigment from any areas you need. Mixing Alizarin Crimson and Ultramarine Blue in the same fashion as step 4, I paint over the dried acrylic green wash.

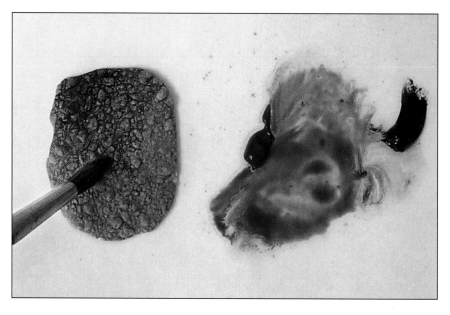

7. I didn't do anything else to this imprint. There was no need to rub off any of the oil paint or add any highlighting to the mounds. I just let the paint dry, and this is the result.

8. I scanned the painted imprints into Photoshop, and used the Rubber Stamp tool to clone areas from two imprints to make a larger pattern. You can find this scan, called **sculpeyChest_Maker2.psd**, on the accompanying CD. This is the result of the first cloning layer overtop of the scan.

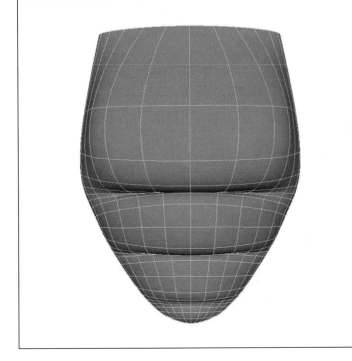

9. Now let's move into our 3D program to see how this looks on Axle's chest. This is a snapshot of the chest's geometry. As you can see by the yellow highlighted lines (isoparms), this geometry has an uneven mesh.

10. This is what the texture grid file looks like on the geometry. Notice it is deformed in several places; the edges and the folds are squished and the top chest is stretched out compared to the middle and lower chest.

11. Using a planar projection remedies these deformations. This is how the texture grid now looks using this projection.

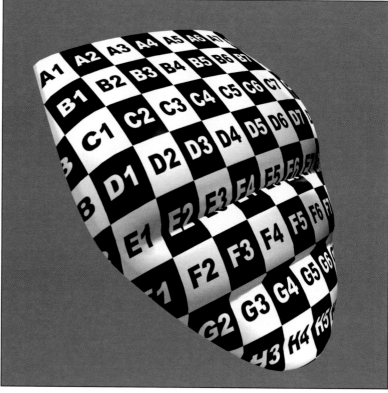

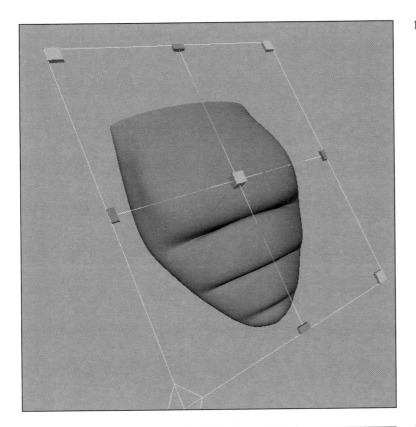

12. I created a Phong Shader, attached a texture using a planar projection (yellow highlighted plane), and positioned it over the chest area.

13. I am fairly happy with the rendered design, but it still needs some work. The large scales in the center of the chest drop off too quickly, and there are too few. Massaging the texture in Photoshop can help.

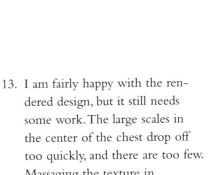

NOTE

I included the rubber gasket around the chest in my renderings so I could see where the visibility of the chest is cut off.

14. Back in Photoshop, I used the Rubber Stamp tool to add more scales to the top part of the chest texture and gradually lessen their presence as they near the edges and bottom of the chest. Here is what those efforts look like on the texture now. This can be seen in the **sculpeyChest_Maker2.psd** file with the addition of the **crack lightener** and **second cloning** layers added on top.

15. Bringing this new texture into the 3D software and rendering it gave me this. Notice that there is slight stretching on the sides of the chest.

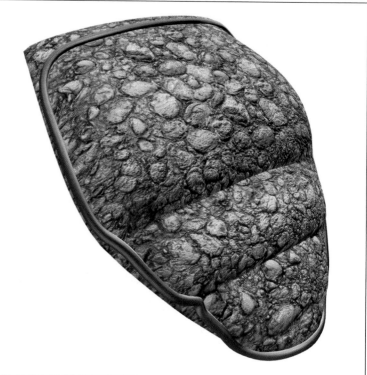

> **NOTE**
>
> The Sculpey impression part of this exercise is one of a thousand different ways to create handmade textures outside the computer. You could also take a rubbing of some material on a piece of paper, or better yet, take Sculpey outside and take impressions of items not found in your studio or house. It is fun to experiment in this way, and can be a refreshing change to your creative workflow.

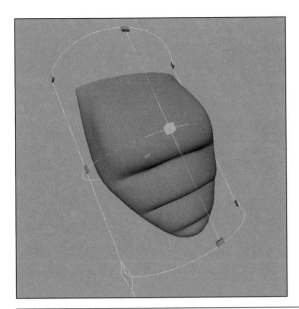

16. The stretching can be easily remedied by changing the type of projection from a planar to a cylindrical one. I reduced the amount of revolve on the cylindrical projection so that it just wraps around to the edge of the chest sides.

17. Here is the final chest.

    For the time being, I am only using the one color map for both the Color and the Bump. When you are using a Projection as a bump, remember to connect the Projection part and not just the texture file to the Bump attribute. This is one instance where I wouldn't create a separate bump map unless I had to, such as an extreme close up. As it is, I don't want it to take focus away from Axle's Face, so I need not accentuate the chest anymore.

SHADER STUFF

As stated earlier, I used a Phong shader for the chest material. The specular highlights are not extremely visible, but it helped with accentuating the mounds a bit better.

PROJECTIONS ACROSS MANY SURFACES

Projections can also cast an image or texture across several surfaces. The example that follows is taken from a job I worked on at Curious Pictures for Lugz Shoes. It takes place on a rooftop where the hero activates a power station. I used a Planar Projection to apply one oil painting to the power station's many pieces.

LUGZ COMMERCIAL POWER STATION: PROJECTION ON MULTIPLE SURFACES

In the Lugz Shoes folder on the accompanying CD, you can see the final movie (**Lugz3.mov** or **Lugz3.avi**).

PREPARING THE TEXTURE

1. Here is the model of the power station. It has a front panel, bolts, dials, and brackets included. I decided to do most of the front with one painting instead of texturing each bolt and bracket separately.

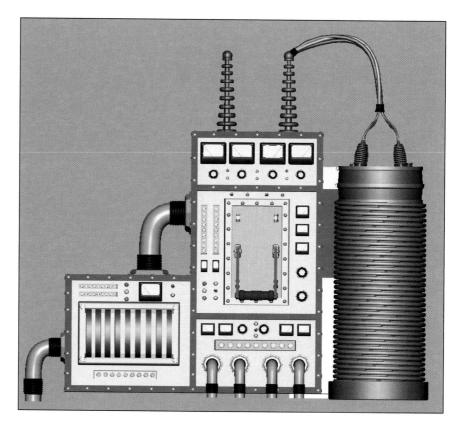

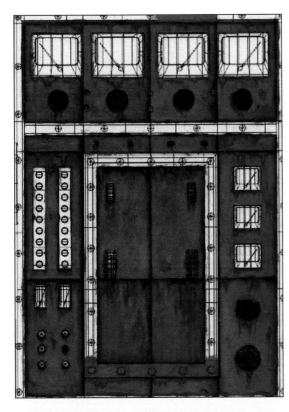

2. I took snapshots of the front of this model and printed it out onto an 8.5×11-inch card stock. Using oil paints on card stock, I defined and added paneling, grease drips and rust. Painting in this way helped me create more color variation in the paint of the object. I started painting the power supply in red.

3. I scanned this into Photoshop and added more bolts and brackets to the painting by cutting and pasting from the one bar I had already painted. By using the Magic Wand tool for selections and changing their levels, I created even more variance in the painting.

4. The color needed to be changed to something less vivid, so the director and I decided on a cooler gray instead. I changed this by using Hue/Saturation in Photoshop. I then accentuated more rust grunge under some of the dials, painted dirt on top, and developed the final color map in this way.

> **NOTE**
>
> One thing that I didn't do, and should have, was to cover up all instances of white paper and snapshot lines in the final painting with the same color as the power station. Not doing this led to the chore of having to line up my painting perfectly so as not to see any of these artifacts when rendered.

APPLYING THE PROJECTION TO ALL THE SURFACES

5. The procedure for this is very simple. You just select all the geometry that you want to share with this texture map and apply the shader that uses a Planar Projection to assign the color map to those bits of geometry. The only real tweaking you must do is to line up the projection properly so that it matches your geometry. The Planar Projection is shown by the yellow highlighted plane.

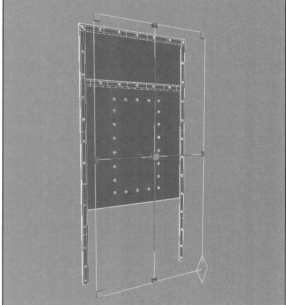

6. I used this painting and projection technique for all the sides of the power station. Here is how it looks in the final render.

Art is an exploration, and for me, to do the same thing over and over again leads to stagnation. There are many things to learn from mixing things up a bit. So to reiterate, I recommend trying to paint outside the computer for some of your texture creations. It is a freeing experience not to sit in front of a monitor and push pixels around all day.

NOTE

In the Lugz Shoes folder on the accompanying CD, you will also find two other movies that Curious Pictures did for Lugz Shoes. The files are called "Lugz1.mov" and "Lugz1.avi" and "Lugz2.mov" and "Lugz2.avi."

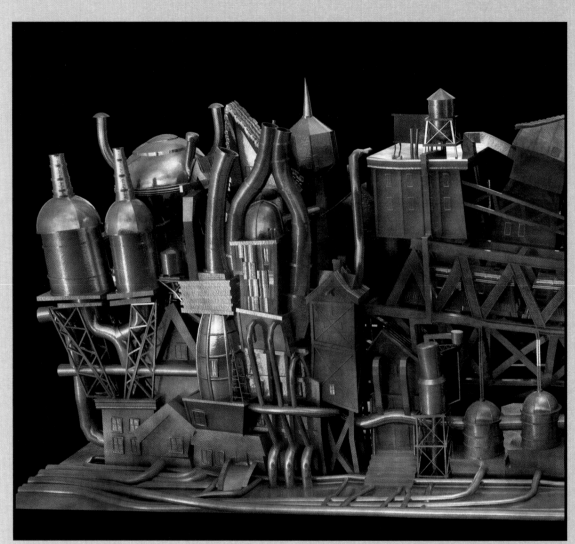

City Metal by Brian Drucker

CHAPTER 15

WRAP-UP: SOME THINGS TO THINK ABOUT

I THOUGHT THIS WOULD be a good place for a critique of the work that I have done on Axle the DuneBug and his DuneBuggy.

15.1 NOW THAT THE PROJECT IS DONE

It is a good exercise, as artists, to admit, not only to your shortcomings, but also to your successes. This industry is filled with criticism, and some of it can be deflating. This is not to say that it is intended to be, but we artists can become very attached to our work. This, coupled with sleep deprivation and stressfully tight deadlines, can be somewhat disheartening. In cases where we don't agree with the criticism given us, especially if it comes from the director and you have little or no chance to change her/his mind, it is comforting to know that everyone on the planet has an opinion, including you. If you like something you've done and it can't be used on a particular project, remember it, and use it on one of your own. Everyone I know in this industry is "…working on their own project."

It is important to remember that everything has a deadline, and there are very few projects that you create that work out exactly as you planned. It is healthy to realize that some things are "good enough," and you must move on. If there is time to fix it later, then do so. A project needs to be completed, and you must keep this in mind.

The DuneBugs Project is an example of this. The following list is predicated upon the fact of not having enough time. So I took the liberty of critiquing my own work—to no one's standard but my own—and admitting to myself, and you, my own shortcomings as well as my successes.

Anyway, on with my critique...

- I wanted to have more caked-on dirt all over everything. In particular, the chest, where the goggles meet the face and the headlights.

- The panels on the car body did not get to the point that I had envisioned. I was hoping for a more realistic look for the paneling, such as the photographic reference that I provided at the beginning of the exercise. The rivets also needed more texturing where they meet the car body.

- I wanted to add more textural detail to his teeth to show poor dental hygiene.

- No grease! This time I thought for sure that I would be able to have globs of grease on the manifold and where the cables and hoses meet the car body. (Maybe next time?)

- Next time it would be great to work on achieving a more convincing weld on the exhaust pipes as seen on motocross bikes.

- I wanted more convincing corrosion in general.

- I liked how the chest turned out and would like to pursue this kind of texturing for his face and arms.

- The fin turned out quite well, and I had a lot of fun creating the graphics for it.

- The tires also worked out very well and definitely added to the custom design of Axle and his "bug-ness."

- I am very pleased by the look of the goggles. They feel and look the way I had envisioned them.

Well, that's some of it. Nothing is ever perfect. In fact, there are bits of geometry that I never even got to texture. I invite you to paint and texture them to your heart's content. See the Read-me file on the CD that tells you where to find them.

15.2 YOUR PLACE IN THE PIPELINE

For a texture artist, it is important to be involved in many aspects/ departments of a project. CG production houses have coined the term "pipeline" to describe the assembly line of artists involved in a project. It refers to the various talents that need to be involved in a production for its successful completion. The typical pipeline components are:

- Modeling

- Texturing

- Rigging and animation

- Dynamics (particle systems, and so on)

- Lighting

- Rendering

- Compositing

Each of these departments can affect the others so it is good to be pro- active and know that your presence may be needed and vice versa. CG productions are a group endeavor, so be willing to help others. What fol- lows is a brief list of what you need to know in regards to each of these pipeline parts.

15.3 MODELING

Make sure that the models you receive to texture are as evenly parame- terized as possible. As you have seen through the exercises in Chapters 7 through 14, uneven meshed geometry can greatly affect the way you do your job. Some modelers are not savvy to your needs, and you may need to educate them in this area. Don't be afraid to ask the modeler if some- thing can be rebuilt if it is unsatisfactory to you.

It is also a good thing to let the modeler know that less dense geometry is preferable than heavy. If you are also the rendering part of the pipeline, you need to make sure, in some programs, that the tesselation value is not too high. Tesselation is the process of the renderer breaking down geometry into tiny triangles based on a number of variables. Be aware of how dense a model is, and assess whether you need to change the tesselation parameters by increasing or decreasing the amount of those tesselated triangles.

> **TIP**
>
> It is a great idea to familiarize your- self with basic modeling techniques as you may need to solve some para- meterization issues yourself. In cer- tain cases, the modelers may have finished their job a month before you start on the project.

- You can add details to geometry by using bumps and displacements instead of them being modeled, as in Axle's tire treads, for example.

- You can use transparency maps to create holes in geometry without the modeler having to cut pieces out with expensive trims.

- You can paint in details that don't need to be modeled. For instance, a building in the distance may be created strictly through a texture painting applied to a plane, so windows and doors need not be modeled. Take this one step further. If the camera never gets close to the city in the background, it's entirety can be one full matte painting. No modeling necessary at all.

If you are an active participant in the modeling discussion you can save them quite a bit of time. Let them know about the texture artist's bag of tricks for "faking" geometry.

ON THE CD

Take a look at "dustFX.mov" or "dustFX.avi" on the CD as an example of these effects.

15.4 EFFECTS

You may need to texture particle systems, such as dust, smoke, lightning, or explosions, with a painted map or procedural texture, or you may have to create the effect yourself through the use of textures and shaders on simple models.

15.5 ANIMATION

You may need to generate a series of texture files for animation purposes. For example, you could provide animators with several paintings of mud dripping off a character's face instead of using modeled mud.

15.6 LIGHTING

Be aware that your textures can change drastically due to the amount of light that illuminates them. Sometimes textures may have to be reverse-engineered if they do not look like you intended.

- You may need to create texture files or patterns for gobos (also known as go-betweens) or cookies. These textures may be things like window frames or patterns of leaves from a tree that get attached to the light color port to simulate shapes thrown by items obstructing the light.

- Textures may need to be created for lighting effects, such as light glow or halo.

15.7 RENDERING

At this phase, you can offer:

- Paintings that will be used as reflection maps.

- Softened textures in the distance so that the rendering engine need not employ depth of field.

- Textures for the Glow attribute of a shader.

Make sure your texture resolution sizes are as optimized as possible. The larger the texture file, the more memory and rendering times increase.

15.8 COMPOSITING

Be aware that your textures can change due to the compositors blending options. Make sure that what you painted looks the way you want it to.

You also may need to generate a series of texture files for compositing purposes. For example, if you provide several paintings showing the stages of a tin rusting, the compositor can fade from one to the next.

15.9 FINAL THOUGHTS

No matter how much technical know-how you have and cooperation you give, you can not begin to create these textures without knowing what you are looking for. That is why this book took on the task of teaching you how to look at surfaces, and discern what it is you are looking at. Simply, if I don't know what an oil stain looks like; how it forms on metal, dried or freshly spilt, or stained on a piece of cloth; satin or cotton, I cannot make my own grunge maps to mimic its qualities.

All the tricks in the world can't help you if you haven't trained your eye to distinguish the characteristics of the materials you are wanting to re-create. It may seem like a waste of time, perhaps; everyone knows what wood looks like, right? I will tell you that, after this book, the way your well-trained artistic eye interprets and expresses textures will be leaps and bounds more provocative and engaging, whether you design something in a simplistic or hyper-real style, than even your last work.

I encourage you to get in touch with me to share your thoughts about this book and the artistic journey you have taken throughout this book. I'd love to hear from you (www.tingun.com). And remember to paint!

READING LIST

On Reflection, Jonathan Miller, National Gallery Publications Limited, London, 1998, Esso.

The Power of Color, Dr. Morton Walker, Avery Publishing Group Inc., Garden City Park, New York, 1991.

The Handy Physics Answer Book, P. Erik Gundersen, Visible Ink Press, MI, 1999.

Still Life: A History, Sybille Ebert-Schifferer, trans. Russell Stockman, Harry N Abrams, Inc., New York, 1999.

Surfaces: A Visual Reference for Artists, Architects, and Designers, Judy A. Juracek, W. W. Norton & Company, NY/London, 1996.

Color in Contemporary Painting, Charles Le Clair, Watson-Guptill Publications, NY, 1997.

Exiles, Joseph Koudelka (photographer), Czeslaw Milosz (contributor), Aperture Foundation Inc., 1998.

Shadow Light: A Photographer's Life, Freeman Patterson, HarperCollins Publishers Ltd., 1998.

Tom Thomson: Design for a Canadian Hero, Joan Murray, Dundurn Press, 1998.

Tim Burton's Nightmare Before Christmas: The Film, the Art, the Vision, Frank Thompson, Hyperion Publishing, 1993.

Lucian Freud Paintings, Robert Hughes, Thames and Hudson Inc., 1998.

1000 Tin Toys, Kitahara and Shimizu, Taschen, 1996.
And similar books in the "1000 of…" series published by Taschen.

Eyewitness Books: CAR, Richard Sutton, DK Publishing, 2000.

Eyewitness Science: Electricity, Steve Parker, DK Publishing Inc., 1992.
And similar books in the "Eyewitness Books" series published by DK Publishing.

DK Handbooks: Insects, George C. McGavin, DK Publishing, 2000.
And similar books in the "Handbook" series published by DK Publishing.

Ways of Seeing, John Berger, Viking Press, 1972.

Color Psychology and Color Therapy, Faber Birren, Carol Publishing Group, 1989.

Robert Rauschenberg: A Retrospective, Guggenheim Museum Publications, 1997.

Any CINEFEX publication.

The End of Print: The Graphic Art of David Carson, Lewis Blackwell and David Carson, Chronicle Books, 1995.

Creating 3-D Animation: The Aardman Book of Filmmaking, Peter Lord and Brian Sibley, Harry N Abrams Inc., 1998.

Toy Story: The Art and Making of the Animated Film, John Lasseter, Steve Daly, Hyperion, 1995.

A Primer of Visual Literacy, Donis A. Dondis, MIT Press, 1973.

INDEX

COLOPHON

Digital Texturing & Painting was produced with the help of Microsoft Word, Adobe Photoshop, and QuarkXPress on a variety of systems, including a Macintosh G4. With the exception of the pages that were printed for proofreading, all files—both text and images—were transferred via email or ftp and edited onscreen.

All the body text was set in the Bembo family, and all the headings and figure captions were set in the Meta Plus family. The Zapf Dingbats and Symbol typefaces were used throughout the book for special symbols and bullets.

The interior pages were printed sheetfed on 70# Sterling Ultra Litho Satin paper at Graphic Arts Center (GAC) in Indianapolis, Indiana. Prepress consisted of PostScript computer-to-plate technology (filmless process). The cover was printed on 12 pt. Carolina, coated on one side.

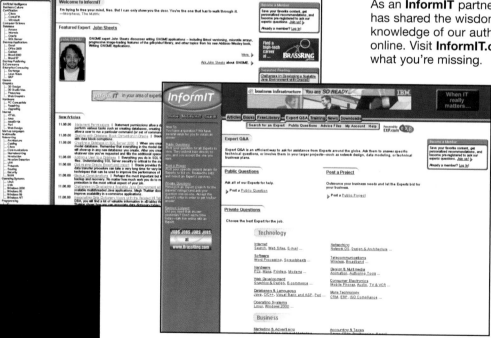

Digital Texturing & Painting

Each New Riders book has been created with you, the computer graphics professional, in mind. Complete effects, adaptable solutions, time-saving techniques, and practical applications. Buy your favorite LightWave, 3ds max, Maya or [digital] series book online today.

3ds max 3D Workstation with Accelerated Graphics

Build and purchase online your own customized 3ds max 3D workstation, and choose from a wide selection of hot 3D OpenGL graphics cards including Nvidia, Intense 3D, ELSA, and IBM FireGL2, plus plug-ins and monitors.

3ds max 4

3ds max™ for Windows® is the world's best-selling professional 3D modeling, animation, and rendering software for creating visual effects, character animation, and games development.
Suggested List Price *** **$3,495**

3ds max Plug-ins & Real-Time Animation Systems

We carry every 3ds max plug-in made, as well as TYPHOON—which is a versatile real-time animation solution fully integrated with 3ds max for "live to air" and "live to tape" productions. Call for special pricing and FREE demo tape.

*** Call us today, mention this ad, and get discount prices on ALL discreet products.

Intellistations.com

The Ultimate Internet Resource for Video, Film, 3D, and Creative Graphics Professionals.

Buy Online via our secure ordering system for VISA, MC, and AMEX

Build your video/3D dream machine with our **Online Configurator**

3D — design your 3D object

process with your favorite software

graphics

video — output to DVD, CD-ROM, Web/Streaming media, or any other tape format

IntelliStations.com is your source for digital content creation tools that will allow your projects to be done on time, every time. The one you really want for video editing, 3D animation, Web design/graphics, and more.

Our knowledgeable technical production engineers will also ASSIST you with INTEGRATION of your IntelliStations.com system with your professional production equipment.

If you have questions while building your dream system, you can call us 24x7x365 at 1-800-501-0184 for assistance from one of our IntelliStations.com DCC specialists. Ask about our no money down and creative financing programs.

 channel.com

Check out CGchannel.com, our content provider for 3D reviews, demos, and more!

IBM Business Partner

discreet™

SONY Authorized Professional Reseller

What's on the CD

The accompanying CD-ROM is packed with all sorts of exercise files and products to help you work with this book. For more information about the use of this CD, please review the ReadMe.txt file in the root directory. This file includes important disclaimer information, as well as information about installation, system requirements, troubleshooting, and technical support.

Technical Support Issues

If you have any difficulties with this CD, you can access our web site at http://www.newriders.com.

System Requirements

This CD-ROM was configured for use on systems running Windows *9x*, Windows 2000, Windows Me, and Macintosh OS 8 or higher.

Loading the CD Files

To load the files from the CD, insert the disc into your CD-ROM drive. If, on the PC, autoplay is enabled on your machine, the CD-ROM setup program starts automatically the first time you insert the disc. You may copy the files to your hard drive, or use them right off the disc.

This CD-ROM uses long and mixed-case filenames, requiring the use of a protected mode CD-ROM driver.

If you are working on a Mac, please activate the MAIN.HTML or view the Readme.txt file to get started.

Exercise Files

This CD contains all the files you'll need to complete the exercises in *Digital Texturing & Painting*. The layered Adobe Photoshop files (.PSD) and Illustrator files (.AI) used within The Project can be found in their respective chapter folders; the .AVI and .MOV movie files can found in the Movies and LugzShoes_Movie folders.

Read This Before Opening the Software

By opening the CD package, you agree to be bound by the following agreement:

NOTE